Cottage Country in Transition
A Social Geography of Change and Contention
in the Rural-Recreational Countryside

The cottage is a powerful image of rural Canada. This image, however, often ignores the rural community that surrounds it, producing a geographically and socially divided landscape and creating friction between cottage owners and rural communities. *Cottage Country in Transition* is a wide-ranging exploration of the interaction and evolution of these two communities.

Using the Rideau Lakes region of eastern Ontario and the Cultus Lake area of southwestern British Columbia as case studies, Greg Halseth examines the ways in which economic, political, and social power affect community change. He focuses on specific issues, such as residential change, land-use planning, property taxation, and social organization. Moving beyond empirical research, Halseth sets the changes occurring in these communities within a broader intellectual context of "community power" and "commodification of the rural idyll." He pays particular attention to how general processes and pressures work themselves out in particular places.

Written in an accessible style, *Cottage Country in Transition* will be of great interest to rural geographers, planners, sociologists, and community researchers as well as to rural residents and cottage owners.

GREG HALSETH is assistant professor of geography, University of Northern British Columbia.

Cottage Country in Transition

A Social Geography of Change and Contention in the Rural-Recreational Countryside

GREG HALSETH

McGill-Queen's University Press
Montreal & Kingston · London · Ithaca

Legal deposit third quarter 1998
Bibliothèque nationale du Québec

Printed in the United States of America
on acid-free paper

This book has been published with the help of a grant
from the Humanities and Social Sciences Federation of
Canada, using funds provided by the Social Sciences
and Humanities Research Council of Canada. Funding
has also been received from the office of the Associate
Vice-President for Research/Dean of Graduate Studies
at the University of Northern British Columbia.

McGill-Queen's University Press acknowledges the
support of the Canada Council for the Arts for its
publishing program.

Canadian Cataloguing in Publication Data

Halseth, Gregory Rae, 1960–
    Cottage country in transition: a social geography of
    change and contention in the rural-recreational
    countryside
    Includes bibliographical references and index.
    ISBN 0-7735-1729-4
    1. Community life – Case studies. 2. Urban-rural
    migration – Case studies. 3. Rural development – Case
    studies. 4. Cultus Lake Region (B.C.) – Rural conditions.
    5. Rideau Lakes Region (Ont.) – Rural conditions.
    I. Title.
    HN110.Z9C6 1998   307.72'0971   C98-900487-2

Typeset in Palatino 10/12
by Caractéra inc., Quebec City

For Regine

Contents

Tables

Figures

Acknowledgments

This book is an adaptation of work carried out for my doctoral dissertation in the Department of Geography at Queen's University. The faculty, staff, and graduate students at Queen's provided not only a stimulating intellectual environment but also saw to it that the department served as something of a "home-away-from-home" for its community members. I would especially like to note the assistance of Eric Moore and Anne Godlewska. Mark Rosenberg served as my supervisor at Queen's, and I cannot thank him enough for the guidance, advice, and assistance he generously and unselfishly offered throughout. I wish to pay a special thank-you to Peter Goheen, Brian Ray, and Heather Nicol, three colleagues who have become good friends. During my term at Queen's I was fortunate to receive financial support from the Social Sciences and Humanities Research Council of Canada, Canada Mortgage and Housing Corporation, the Department of Geography, and the Queen's School of Graduate Studies and Research. I am most grateful for this tremendous support – graduate studies cannot be fruitfully undertaken without this type of strong foundation.

The translation of the dissertation into this book was undertaken during my first year at the new University of Northern British Columbia. I would very much like to recognize the support and encouragement I have received from the fine faculty and staff of the Faculty of Natural Resources and Environmental Studies. I would thank Ellen Petticrew, Gail Fondahl, Josef Ackerman, and especially Kevin Hall for all they have done to assist my transformation from graduate student to faculty member. In this regard I would also like to acknowledge the patient support and advice received from John Pierce and Len Evenden of the Department of Geography at Simon Fraser University. In helping to move this book towards publication, I would like to thank the staff at McGill-Queen's University Press, including Susan Kent Davidson for her wonderful assistance. I would especially like to thank Philip Cercone for his interest and support. I would also like to acknowledge the very helpful comments offered by the anonymous manuscript reviewers. Kevin Driscoll helped tremendously by taking my maps and figures and creating much-improved computerized versions.

McClelland and Stewart Publishers and Graham Pilsworth granted permission to reproduce two cartoons from Charles Gordon's book *At the Cottage: A Fearless Look at Canada's Summer Obsession*. The journals *Professional Geographer* (Blackwell Publishers), *Canadian Geographer*, *Journal of Rural Studies* (Elsevier Science), *Environment and Planning A* (Pion Limited, London), and *Canadian Journal of Regional Science* also kindly gave permission to include materials in a revised form. Some of the data reported here was originally presented in the Canada Mortgage and Housing Corporation publication *Recreational Home Conversion in Canada*.

A great many people also offered support and assistance during my field research. In the Cultus Lake area, I would especially like to thank Peter Cave and Hugh Sloan of the Regional District of Fraser-Cheam, and the Regional District Planning and Building Department staff of Robert Brown, Jack Bakker, and Vaclav Kalyna. The manager and staff of the Cultus Lake Park Board office were also of great assistance. I would like to thank Chief Commodore, as well housing officer Janey Commodore, of the Soowahlie Band for the time they spent with me. Donna Cook deserves a special note for generously offering to introduce me to her "community" at Cultus Lake. Along the Rideau Lakes, I would like to acknowledge the support and assistance of the clerks and staff of South Elmsley, North Elmsley, North Burgess, Bastard and South Burgess, North Crosby, and South Crosby Townships. Again, a special note of thanks must go to local building inspectors Derek Turnbull and Doug Beesley and to Marion Macleod of the VON Seniors' Support Service in Elgin. Additional research on cottaging was carried out in the Shédiac and Cap-Pelé region of New Brunswick. I would like to thank Armand Robichaud of the Commission d'Aménagement Beaubassin, Floyd Dykeman and David Bruce of the Rural and Small Town Research and Studies Programme at Mount Allison University, and the Department of

Geography at Mount Allison for being my hosts during that wonderful summer in the Maritimes.

I would also like to thank all those who took the time to complete and return my questionnaire survey and all those who graciously agreed to be interviewed. I found the process of interviewing local residents and decision-makers to be most rewarding. A great many people opened their homes and made me feel welcome as we sat and discussed the changes they have witnessed in their community. Many times I found that I learned more about how the local community was organized when my interviewees offered lengthy asides (usually including family anecdotes) on topics only suggested in part by my scripted questions. The generosity shown by my hosts in these cases was tremendous.

The most important "thank yous" must go to my family, for they are the solid foundation upon which all I do rests. The love and support offered by my brothers, parents, and grandparents continues to be both valuable and important to me and my wife. Not to be left out is Dorothy Ray, who along with her late husband Lee opened their home to us on many special occasions and became our adoptive "family" in Ottawa. To my three children: yes, I'm nearly done – you can use the computer in a couple of minutes! Finally, to my Regine – you not only bring out the best in me but you give worth to all that I do. My debt to you is deep indeed.

For all the help and support I received, I am grateful. Any errors, failings or faults are, however, mine alone.

Abbreviations

CULTUS LAKE

APC	Advisory Planning Commission for Electoral Area 'E' of the Regional District of Fraser-Cheam
ALR	Agricultural Land Reserve
DND	Department of National Defence
ORP	Official Regional Plan for the Lower Mainland of British Columbia
OSP	Official Settlement Plan for Electoral Area E of the Regional District of Fraser-Cheam
RDFC	Regional District of Fraser-Cheam
RSBC	Revised Statutes of British Columbia
SBC	Statutes of British Columbia

RIDEAU LAKES

BRLA	Big Rideau Lake Association
CORTS	Canada-Ontario Rideau Trent-Severn Agreement
FOCA	Federation of Ontario Cottager's Associations
MAPLE	Mutual Association for the Protection of Lake Environments
OLA	Otty Lake Association
OPOC	Opinicon Property Owner's Community
RVCA	Rideau Valley Conservation Authority
URLA	Upper Rideau Lake Association
WI	Women's Institute

Cottage Country in Transition

1 Introduction

The image of a small, rustic cottage nestled beside a forest-fringed lake has come to form an important part of the Canadian geographic imagination.[1] Ideally, this image is seen in our mind's eye from a slightly elevated point looking over the cottage and across the front porch out across the calm waters of the lake. This image represents a common summer, weekend, or vacation destination for millions of people across North America. But the idyllic calm of that lakeside scene belies a more complex and often somewhat contentious landscape. Missing are the rural communities and the farm and rural residents who surround such cottage areas. Missing are the local debates and controversies over lakeside development and pollution of waterways. Missing as well are the changes happening to the cottaging areas themselves – changes that include the conversion of lakeside summer retreats into year-round permanent residences. This book seeks to explore these issues and to highlight the complexity beneath the image. Focusing upon the issue of cottage conversion – that is, the conversion of seasonal-use cottages into year-round residences – I examine the processes and implications of residential change on the local community.

The pressures of residential development and change within local areas, and the formation of community-based opposition to these pressures, can complicate both local planning debates and our understanding of community change. Geographic research focusing upon rural Canada continues to highlight the complex outcomes arising from rural-urban interactions within particular geographic settings.[2]

This book turns instead to the issue of community change, and contention over that change, in rural areas featuring large numbers of lakeside summer homes and cottages. It is concerned with understanding local residential change as an outcome of broader social and economic pressures, and the consequences of this change for the social and political organization of the community. The specific community context under consideration is a rural and cottage residential area situated near the outer bounds of an urban field, an area undergoing increasing change prompted by a growing demand for cottaging properties by non-local purchasers. The specific mechanism of community change concerns the transformation of the resident population through the dynamic of cottage conversion. While research has recognized important social and economic modifications from the influx of seasonal residents on a host community,[3] detailed attention has not been paid to impacts within the host community when seasonal residents make it their permanent home.

The conversion of cottages into year-round homes is an important issue in many rural communities. Conversion generates changes and demands that a host community often finds difficult to manage.[4] Pressures include demands for new or improved levels of services such as paved or widened roadways, garbage collection, water supply, and the like. Changing social structures resulting from conversion can also generate conflicts over attitudes towards local norms, institutions, and political activity in these rural communities. A separation in social and geographic space of the rural and cottage residential landscapes marks the fulcrum of local change and contention.[5]

Previously, many studies of changing rural geographies have tended to focus upon natural-resource issues. These include the "restructuring" of agricultural landholdings and the agricultural industry, and the conversion of farmland to housing and other urban land uses.[6] As well, a literature on the economic and population structures of northern or single-industry resource-town development has emerged.[7] While these issues are most certainly important, they do not capture all issues in the spectrum of rural or countryside change.

This book seeks to contribute to this broad range of research by introducing a very particular, yet quite common landscape. It moves away from an agricultural or resource-town focus and follows that literature interested in reintroducing a social concern into the rural question.[8] Recognizing the complexity of a category as broad as "rural," the research focuses on one particular cross-section of the rural landscape, the intersection of rural and cottage residential landscapes. In particular it examines the characteristics of residents in these areas and their participation in local debates over residential change.

Three themes underlie the research. The first centres on the physical separation of rural and cottage residential areas and is reinforced by the second, the social separation of these two areas. The third theme concerns the recognition by residents of the differences in collective interests between the rural and cottage areas. In presenting this research, I have three goals. The first is to identify this rural-recreational countryside as a divided landscape, with the fundamental division residing between the cottage and the farming/rural residential areas. The second is to identify the characteristics of *converters* and the cottage-conversion process. The final goal is to discern the changing balance of decision-making power within the rural-recreational countryside as property-owner groups seek a legitimation of the right to participate in local land-use planning debates and to speak for a recognized constituency.

STUDY AREAS

While the urban environment continues to dominate the Canadian landscape as both workplace and home, small towns, villages, and rural areas are increasingly subject to new development pressures and demands.[9] I employ a comparative-research strategy in this examination of residential change and contention over that change in two rural-recreational areas. The use of more than one case-study area reflects an effort to highlight locality-specific differences in the outcomes of generally similar processes, recognizing that pressures of change both act within and in turn have their impacts mitigated by the locale. The two study locations are the Rideau Lakes area of Eastern Ontario and the Cultus Lake area of the lower Fraser Valley of British Columbia.

The selection of study areas for comparative research must recognize those characteristics marking important similarities and differences between the areas, as these form the basis for interpretation and explanation. Both study areas are situated near the outer edge of an urban field, contain a mix of dispersed and clustered residential settings, have a large number of cottages and seasonal-use properties within the local housing stock, and are experiencing cottage-conversion pressures. Important differences that mark a challenge for the research include the structure of local government and the pattern of local representation, the regulatory scheme affecting land use and development activity, the basic geographic form and history of cottage development, and the placement of each study area within the national economy.

TERMINOLOGY

A wide range of terms has been used to describe the seasonally occupied dwelling or retreat commonly located on a small recreational-use property.[10] In this book the term *cottage* is used. This choice is based upon writing economy and upon its widespread use and recognition by residents of both study areas. The term in this case embodies a socially recognized meaning much more than it does any architectural or property-use definition. Building from this, the term *cottaging area* defines that set of small-lot waterfront properties developed for cottage units. The notion of waterfront property is included here because in both study areas the key amenity is the lake. To capture the broader area where cottaging occurs within a surrounding, less densely developed countryside, I use the term *rural-recreational countryside*.[11] These definitions are based upon a physical and social separation of the rural and cottaging areas.

Change in the rural-recreational countryside is pursued through an examination of local residential change. Specifically, I compare the socio-economic profiles and selected activities of residents within the rural areas with those of residents moving to live year-round at a former cottage property. My purpose is to explore the implications of this residential change on the local *community,* conceptualized here as collective responses developing from the actions of individuals in specific places. These collective actions then define complex sets of social communities that develop and may overlap within geographic areas, or localities.

To explore local community change, I have organized local residents into three groups: Converters, Seasonal Occupants, and Rural Residents. These groups are operationally defined on the basis of the physical location of residential properties and the annual duration of occupancy by residents. The category of *Converters* comprises those households in cottaging areas that have recently converted a seasonal-use property into their permanent home. *Seasonal Occupants* share the cottaging landscape with Converters; however, they are distinguished by their seasonal or periodic pattern of occupancy. *Rural Residents* are the local population who live year-round in the area surrounding the cottaging landscape but do not share this cottaging space with the Converters and Seasonal Occupants. This distinction of local residents based upon use and location is a significant departure from the standard farm/non-farm treatment of rural populations used in much of the rural-studies literature.[12]

My principal research methods were a questionnaire survey and interviews with community representatives. The questionnaire survey of local property owners was designed to obtain household-level data that would allow specific comparisons of Converter, Seasonal Occupant, and Rural Resident households. Interviews with selected community leaders were used to obtain information about community groups and their organization, operation, and relations with other groups and governments in the local area. The questionnaire data provide directly comparable information at the individual-household level, while the interviews recognize a need for local interpretation of change within the community and of the patterns suggested by the questionnaire survey. A third important data source was local government records on building permits issued and on land-use planning. Records of public-hearing debates proved especially valuable. These sources are augmented where appropriate with local histories, newspapers, and the records of various community groups or organizations.

ORGANIZATION

Part One of the book, entitled "Cottages in the Countryside," sets out the broad conceptual issues and definitions important to the research. Chapter 2, "Cottages, Cottaging, and Cottage Ownership," explores the role of cottages in the Canadian recreational landscape, beginning with a closer evaluation of the folklore associated with cottaging activity. The legacy of land uses and lifestyles associated with cottage property is fundamental to their continuing social and geographic separation from the surrounding rural community. The chapter goes on to survey property-use and ownership data to report on the relative distribution of property between cottage and rural areas in each study area and on the costs associated with cottage ownership. Both the historical and contemporary contexts are important in the argument that the rural-recreational countryside is a geographically and socially divided landscape.

Chapter 3 develops the argument and research questions to be addressed in the book. It opens with a summary and interpretation of rural–urban-fringe research and argues that the interface between cottage and rural residential areas has not been integrated into existing research. It also explores questions related to the definition of community and the organization of individuals into groups, particularly the need to separate local property-based organizations from other groups. Finally, issues arising from community conflict are explored through three separate bodies of literature, the first emerging from rural sociology in the United States during the 1920s and 1930s and aimed at examining rural change; the second from a debate within sociology and political studies over community power; and the third from the radical critique of "politics of turf" undertaken by urban geographers through the 1970s and 1980s. Following this conceptual framework is a summary of the methods and data sources used in the research.

Part Two, "Communities and Change," provides an introduction to the case-study areas and outlines key information with respect to the scale and pace of residential change. Chapter 4, "Rideau Lakes and Cultus Lake Case Study Areas," develops a historical context for the examination of contemporary community change within the rural-recreational countryside. After detailing the geographic and historical development of both study areas, the chapter uses census data to report on recent population change. It closes with an argument for understanding both study areas as regionally important recreational assets, the context that underlies pressures for increased development of high-amenity recreational properties.

Chapter 5 explores local community change at the level of the individual household. It probes the implications of residential change by comparing the socio-economic profiles of questionnaire respondents from the Rural Resident, Converter, and Seasonal Occupant groups. The analysis is extended by an examination of the local/non-local integration of Rural Residents and Converters, including maintenance of ties to former place of residence and participation in local activities such as shopping and neighbouring. The differing socio-economic profiles and distinct local activity patterns support the argument for a separation of cottage and rural-area residents, but also hint at a diversity of respondents within each group.

Chapter 6, "Housing Change and Conversion Pressures," uses data from the questionnaire survey, Statistics Canada reports, and local government sources to explore local housing change as an element of local residential change. The purpose is to identify the different housing sub-markets within and between the study areas and to connect these differences with the characteristics of the resident groups discussed in chapter 5. Chapter 6 begins by setting a general regional context for interpreting housing production and consumption. Local housing-stock change is then evaluated in terms of the pressures from cottage-conversion activity within each study area. Finally, Rural and Converter respondents are compared in terms of the quality and quantity of housing consumed.

Part Three, "Change and Contention," explores the outcomes of pressures for community change by assessing changes to local social and political organization as well as the debates that have brought these changes to the fore. Chapters 7, 8, 9, and 10 move the analysis from an individual to a collective level by introducing the structural organizations through which contention and conflict over residential change are manifested. Chapter 7 explores the organization of "Community Groups." Two principal types of community groups are examined: first, those whose membership is rooted in property ownership; and second, those whose membership is rooted in some common interest. Examples of *property-based* community groups include resident/ratepayer organizations and cottage-owner associations. Property-based groups are important in local debates over land-use planning issues, as they provide both a framework for obtaining and studying information and a platform for voicing of collective concerns. One difficulty in deciphering local debate derives from the practice of property-based groups of phrasing concerns in terms of property-value issues, an outcome of the wording of legislation governing debate at public hearings. Examples of *interest-based* community organizations include local social groups for older residents. The purpose of including interest-based groups is to explore the degree to which the *separate-spaces* argument raised in earlier chapters is reflected in the organization of individuals into social groups. The focus on social groups for older residents derives from the importance of age as a variable in the cottage-conversion process and from the well-established and easily identifiable status of such groups in both study areas.

Chapter 8, "Local Government Structure," details the organization and operation of local municipal governments in each study area. Local government forms an essential building-block for interpreting residential change and community conflict. Their mandate to manage land-use planning and zoning creates the forum in which public contention and debate over residential change is worked out. The role of local governments in developing or adopting new land-use control regulations also makes them important actors in the process and the public debates.

Chapters 9 and 10 review particular examples of planning issues and development proposals that have been at the centre of local debate and disagreement within the Rideau Lakes and Cultus Lake areas. The course taken by each of these individual debates, including the fate of both the proposals and the arguments, are reviewed against the background developed in the preceding chapters. Local history, recent cottage-development pressure, and local population change through cottage conversion all contribute to the evaluation of the debates. Four issues are important in the interpretation. First is the geographic and social separation of the cottaging areas from the surrounding countryside. Second is the role of local property-based resident organizations in providing a structural reference-point in local debate. Third is the continuing importance of individuals within these local debates. Finally, the chapter considers the local character of these debates, with area residents struggling to reclaim the decision-making agenda for the community's future from senior government organizations or external development interests.

In summary, this book seeks to elaborate issues of community change within a particular geographic setting. Its goal in focusing upon the rural-recreational countryside is to contribute to a growing recognition of the diversity of change and the pressures underlying that change in rural Canada. Further, to recognize that residential change occurs within socially and politically defined frameworks is to challenge much current research. The separation of interests between rural and cottage property owners complicates the evaluation of debates and contention over local change.

PART ONE

Cottages in the Countryside

2 Cottages, Cottaging, and Cottage Ownership

The summer cottage at the lake is an immediately recognizable element of the rural-recreational countryside. The long history of cottages, cottaging, and cottage ownership across Canada has generated a geographic imagination that is now intimately connected with this activity and plays an important role in how cottagers and rural residents alike shape and organize their understanding of the issues and participants in debates over local land use and community change. The geographic imagination associated with "cottage country" can be explored by looking at two critical components. The first is the folklore that has developed with respect to cottages and cottagers, while the second involves delineating the extent of cottage properties within the rural-recreational countryside. An outline of critical facets of the cottage folklore is a necessary element in understanding current debates over cottage-area change. At the same time it must be recognized that cottage ownership is not available to all Canadians. The costs of purchase, mortgage, insurance, maintenance, travel to and from the cottage, and property taxes situate cottage ownership within an economic framework where the selectivity, or limits to ownership, need to be clarified. These issues combine to segment cottage ownership within the population, and cottage-property areas within the rural-recreational countryside. The separation in geographic and social space of rural and cottage-property areas is fundamental to understanding contemporary debates surrounding cottage property use and development.

THE FOLKLORE OF COTTAGING

Popular literature[1] and local-area opinion[2] have long recognized a clear distinction between the Seasonal Occupants of cottage areas and the Rural Residents who live in the surrounding countryside. Despite this recognition, there has been relatively little academic research on the "idea" of cottaging and its importance within the rural-recreational countryside.[3] The folklore so intimately associated with cottaging identifies the cottage landscape as something apart from the rural countryside within which it is set, and as such is a fundamental basis upon which a socially constructed and understood separation of cottaging and rural areas is built. This forms the foundation for the competing geographic imaginations of the rural-recreational countryside. Along complementary lines, Bunce's detailed study of the "countryside ideal" clearly shows how the rural landscape has been defined and redefined over time in the Anglo-American imagination.[4] This social-geographic process has shaped the way both (separately of course) Rural Residents and casual or recreational "users" define, interpret, and develop an attachment to these landscapes. In his study of the historical geography of Canadian rural landscapes, Osborne argues that the countryside has become reified in the imaginations of urban Canadians; it has become part of our society's iconography.[5] To these observations I would add that such images of the countryside are especially refined "at the cottage."

In her book *The Summer House: A Tradition of Leisure* Amy Cross explores the origins of the summer house and the intriguing – and often quirky – aspects of its cultural significance. Thematically, the book's chapters play on words like "nature," "simpler life," "home and family," and "cottage culture." Of particular interest is the way Cross details the creation of cottage landscapes and the way in which social meaning has come to be not only attached to but also an integral part of the summer house.

To give the reader a sense of these wilderness retreats, as well as the personalities of their builders and users, Cross interweaves a wide range of contemporary and historical vignettes. Glimpses of summer houses from the past include aristocratic villas from the Gilded Age, Thomas Jefferson's "Poplar Forest" retreat from Monticello in Virginia, Alexander Graham Bell's sprawling "Beinn Bhreagh" on Cape Breton, and the simplicity of Le Corbusier's "cabanon" on the Côte d'Azur in France. Contemporary, and less grandiose examples include geodesic domes among the pine trees and former railway boxcars now resting marooned on short pieces of track beside a lake.

For Cross, however, the summer house is not really about architecture but, rather, its use as a summer "retreat." She argues that in their isolation and simplicity such places have always been havens for personal renewal. As such, the experience of the summer house is very much a personal experience. Cross presents a wide-ranging collection of personal experiences to paint a portrait of life and lifestyles at summer houses. The summer home is a haven for personal renewal because it is not the real world but an "escape." As such, it stands in some ways as a condemnation of the pressures of urban life on the human spirit. The journey to the summer house becomes, in effect, a ritualized and metaphorical journey along which the distractions of our everyday urban lives are stripped away. This idea of escape has evolved into a form of "cottage culture," a culture, as Cross's subtitle suggests, that is intimately bound up with a tradition of leisure. Being at the summer house grants licence for a different lifestyle, a lifestyle of relaxation, of play, of freedom from routine and schedules. The escape that the summer house embodies starts from an old theme, that of a physical escape from the noise and congestion of the city to the idyll of the rural countryside, and ends with the new theme of a psychological escape from the pressures of contemporary life.[6]

Wyckoff[7] offers a critical historical interpretation of wilderness resorts and retreats as part of an influential mélange of landscapes of private power and wealth. For Wyckoff these landscapes of power are part of a long-standing process whereby the affluent within society work towards the creation of landscapes marked by social and spatial exclusivity. The small cottage in the mountains or by the lake or seashore represents in a somewhat more democratized form the desire to capture and be part of the panache, style, and status of early resorts.

The cottage and the act of cottaging have come to assume a place in Canadian folklore. "Cottage country" assumes the identity of a separate place, a special territory within the rural landscape, while the cottage inspires sentiments that go well beyond structural or architectural definitions to become a representation of a state of mind. As described by Cross, such retreats are fundamentally psychological destinations: the "cottage, cabin, or camp mean the same thing, but ultimately the name is less important than how it's thought about – how it's approached."[8] Adding a geographic orientation to this psychological formulation, Jaakson argues that "presence at the cottage implies absence from somewhere else ... This 'absence from somewhere' (their principal, urban home) juxtaposed by the 'presence here' (at the second home), forms one of the foundation blocks of meaning of being a second-home owner."[9]

One of the most insightful critiques of cottaging folklore is Wolfe's commentary "About Cottages and Cottagers," which appeared in a 1965 edition of *Landscape*. Wolfe argues that the summer cottage, the pre-eminent example in his Ontario-centred research, is at the heart of a paradox. The often-expressed desire of cottagers and the goal of cottaging are to seek a peaceful and relaxing, albeit temporary, escape from the pressures of urban life and "to return to a closer communion with nature."[10] Cross picks up this thread when she suggests that a retreat to the cottage allows for a reconnection with the simplicity of life.[11]

The paradox emerges when cottagers, in rushing to the limited range and number of amenity locations in the countryside, simply recreate many of the same pressures and landscapes they sought to escape. Wolfe characterizes Wasaga Beach in the early 1950s as a community where "the traffic jams are as satisfactory as any in Toronto itself. Cars and people fill all the streets. The tourist cabins are bursting, and cars are parked in all the available space. The noise is tremendous, as [children] shout to each other, car-horns blow at them, motorboats roar on the river, and an aeroplane skims the roof-tops. We are no longer in the country. We are back in the city again – or better, we are in the city away from the city."[12] Such seasonal movements of urban residents to densely developed cottage and resort areas can occur on a scale that resembles the "transporting [of] 'the City' and its inhabitants into the countryside," an annual process "of a wilderness being transformed into a peculiar clone of suburbia by cottage development."[13]

In the Cultus Lake study area, for example, the clustered form of cottage properties evokes the image of an urban place in a rural space. In the main beach area of Cultus Lake Park, lot sizes in the order of 1,600 to 2,400 square feet result in a gross density develop-ment of approximately 11 cottages per acre. The residential density of Cultus Lake Park far exceeds the standard of four properties per acre so common in post-war North American suburbs. At the other end of Cultus Lake, narrow streets and lot sizes ranging from 3,700 to 7,500 square feet generate a gross density of approximately 5 res-idences per acre, something more closely approximating a suburban scale of development. Even in this case, however, local zoning and subdivision regulations for these cottaging areas now require a min-imum lot size of nearly half an acre given the available level of services.[14]

Distances involved in the cottage commute, and the crowding or clustering of recreational properties around amenity settings, act to isolate the resort area from the rural context in which it is set. As

Figure 1
Cultus Lake area photos: Lakeside view of cottage development density (top) and view from "the street" (bottom).

Wolfe has described it, the commute "is always the same and well-known, and the journey, even though it may be through a pleasant countryside, becomes of little more significance than the daily journey to and from work."[15] Once arrived at, the summer city is physically and socially self-contained; it is not located in the country at all. In his humorous look at cottages, Gordon cartoons the cottage as a family sanctuary and the nearby small town as an anonymous supply depot.[16] Interviews in both the Rideau Lakes and Cultus Lake areas overwhelmingly identify a clear demarcation of landscapes between cottage-property areas and the surrounding rural areas. Where mixing of these populations occurs, it is in the service-supply sites of local villages or towns, and then usually confined to the transaction at hand, which does little to reduce the social distance between rural and cottage residents.

Jordan turns these attempts to understand cottaging and cottage impacts around by exploring the reactions of local residents to increasing tourist development. Citing examples from Vermont, Jordan argues that, under pressure from "summer people," local residents find it increasingly difficult to maintain a traditional culture or way of life. He notes a conscious attempt at commodification of selected aspects of the rural culture as a means of coping with the consumptive aspects of cottage culture. This creation of a "phony

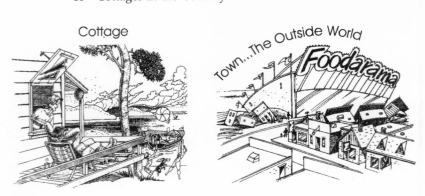

Figure 2
Cottage country cartoons: "Visions" of cottage country and the local small town.
From Charles Gordon's *At the Cottage*.

folk-culture" to be consumed by cottagers includes factory-produced handicrafts, Yankee churches to house summer worshippers, and even the rescheduling of nature to put the maple-sugar season into the tourist season – complete with "a sugar-on-snow party in July for the benefit of the summer people."[17]

The self-contained social milieu of the cottage area is reinforced by the family-centric orientation of cottaging. Many residents interviewed in crowded cottage settings spoke of a tacit understanding among residents to look out from their own properties but politely not to look in from the water, street, or pathway to the property of others. Thus, even in a crowded setting, the cottage can become an enclave for the family. At the cottage, doing without television or telephone, "the family coddled inside this shell closes in on itself, indulging in 'lots of family storytelling at night that you don't have time for at home.'"[18] When held by the same family for a considerable period of time, the cottage may also come to represent the family, to become "the home, the gathering place, to which the far-flung family returns each year, to renew contacts and once again experience the fundamental satisfactions of being part of a family."[19] The cottage "represents a family seat, a place of belonging and identity … a symbol for [the] family."[20]

As on the household or family level, cottage folklore functions within the broader collection of cottage properties, providing the basis for a specific community identity. Beginning with the premise that individuals must see that they together share some form of collective membership characteristics, Wolfe reports that the "form of enjoyment that is universal among owners of summer cottages … is the enjoyment that comes from ownership"[21]. Building upon this, community members identify themselves as having something in common with other community members. The identification for cottagers is that they "have a common interest, that being the use of the lake and surrounding lands for recreation."[22] Combined with the economic sorting processes inherent in the ability to own a seasonal-use property, such basic common interests provide the foundation for a cottage community. At these summer cities there develops a sense of "belonging to a cohesive community. The loss of community spirit in the city is universally deplored; as members of cottage associations, large numbers of city dwellers find it again."[23]

For Cross the cottage is "a carefree sanctuary wholeheartedly dedicated to pleasure ... [because after all] ... it doesn't house 'real' life."[24] Yet it does house a structured life, for cottage culture has "its own traditions and institutions. Like any culture, it has rituals, mythology, codes, traditions, taboos, folklore, totems common to most everyone who holidays at a vacation house."[25] Through a guest column in *Cottage Life* magazine, Canadian comedian Sandra Shamas offers her own unique perspective on such rituals. As an outsider invited to a friend's family cottage, she found that "they had their own rituals; one person opened beer, someone else barbequed; they all got along and made one another laugh. I was about 17 at the time and the whole experience was disorienting. It made me uneasy. I stuck close to the mom of the family and set the table. There didn't seem to be any rules, and no one told me what to do. In fact – get this – they told me to do whatever I wanted, and have a good time. Nobody ever said that to me before, and the screen just went blank; not knowing what to do, I did nothing."[26] Collective recognition of norms and behaviours, a type of cottage-country "culture," further binds cottage-property owners into a community.

If the image of the cottage as an image of Canadian society, especially in central Canada, has endured and been nurtured in the popular press, its most disturbing aspect is that cottaging continues to be a highly selective activity. Drawing on his research on "second homes" in Britain and Europe, Clout observes that "it is, of course, ironic that city dwellers who endure the worst environmental conditions are least likely to be able to purchase [cottages] or have access to them."[27] To an extent these are "landscapes of power," where participation in the folklore through ownership of a cottage confers status.[28] Again, Wolfe summarizes this point in his remark that "the ability to own and maintain an inessential house (the term is F. Scott Fitzgerald's) is an important index of having arrived."[29] The folklore adds symbolic meaning to cottaging, as "summering at the cottage is a symbolic act ... In former times, it symbolized the exclusion by the elect of those not fortunate enough to own the 'inessential houses': today it symbolizes, in its democratized form, the sense of belonging that all of us feel the need to demonstrate in one way or another."[30] The leisure time to go cottaging must be combined with having the economic resources to afford the purchase and maintenance costs of these "inessential houses."

This discussion of the folklore of cottaging highlights some critical gaps in the geographic imagination of cottage-country residents. One of the most important of these gaps involves issues of sustainable use and environmental values. This problem has much less to do with the contribution of a single cottage to local pollution levels than with the general idea of cottages. There is the serious issue of the alienation of land for use by the limited segment of the population able to afford it; of the closure of public access to large numbers of lakes ringed by a narrow band of private cottage properties; and of the environmental costs of having, maintaining, and travelling to and from these occasional-use retreats. Despite the importance of cottages in the landscape and economy of rural areas, relatively scarce attention has been paid to their form and function.

The long history of cottaging, of going to a resort landscape in the wilderness, has been important in creating a folklore now intimately attached to both the cottage and the act of cottaging. This folklore continues to define the image of a lifestyle and a landscape for cottaging areas that is clearly separate from the rural milieu within which it is set. The image involves issues such as the symbolism of family, a focus upon a landscape of leisure, and the confirmation of status through participation in cottage ownership. All these issues mark cottage country as a self-contained milieu where the rural landscape is only something to be passed through in travelling to the cottage. The social and economic implications of cottages for the small-town and rural areas within which they are set are the important flip-side of this subject. The folklore of cottaging and cottage properties is an essential element in understanding the rural-recreational countryside as a geographically and socially divided landscape.

COTTAGES

It is important to recognize at the outset that cottaging, and the implications of cottage ownership, are international phenomena.[31] Examples from France, Great Britain, Czechoslovakia, and Australia stand as testament that the phenomemon is widespread and that

Table 1
Wolfe's Estimates of Cottagers in Canada, 1941 Cross-section

	Canada	Ontario	BC
Cottagers within jurisdiction[1]	61,072	28,159	3,006
Cottaging activity in Canada (%)	100	46.1	4.9
Cottagers as % of households within jurisdiction[2]	2.3	2.9	1.3

Source: R.I. Wolfe (1951), "Summer Cottagers in Ontario," Economic Geography 27(1), 10–32.
[1] Total number of households Wolfe identified by post office data as cottaging within Canadian provinces; includes cottagers whose permanent home is in either Canada or the United States.
[2] Calculated by author: Wolfe's estimates of cottagers were divided by number of permanent households identified in the 1941 census for each jurisdiction. This is to offer an estimate of the comparative distribution of households using summer cottages, taking into account differences in jurisdictional size.

there are important commonalities. Among these commonalities, the first is a noted lack of information by which to gauge accurately the scale or scope of the impacts of this type of activity. A second is that patterns of cottage ownership show strong regional or metropolitan dominance of cottaging areas in their hinterlands. Third is that cottage ownership is strongly identified with socio-economic status. Despite the importance of these issues, research to date has made only tentative attempts to tie together the importance of cottaging in the rural-recreational countryside, the accessibility of cottage ownership, and the role of cottage communities within the wider rural community. Who then are these cottagers? To seek an answer to this question we turn first to historical and contemporary information on cottagers in Ontario and British Columbia.

Wolfe's early evaluations of the extent of cottaging across the Canadian recreational landscape focus upon an overview of "activity," defined as the use of a cottage property that is not necessarily correlated with ownership.[32] Wolfe's data are derived from lists of cottagers registered at either regular or summer-only post offices. He concedes that cottagers whose permanent homes are nearby their cottages may not be recorded, as they are likely to continue receiving mail at their permanent homes rather than having it redirected to the cottage.

Using data for 1941, Wolfe demonstrates how Ontario then dominated in terms of cottaging activity at the national level, with 46 per cent of cottagers in Canada active within that province (see Table 1). British Columbia ranked fifth among the provinces by capturing approximately 5 per cent of Canadian summer-cottager activity.

Table 2
Vacation Homes in Canada: Estimated Number of Households Owning Vacation
Homes

Year	Canada[2]	Ontario[3]	BC[4]
1973[1]	449,000	164,000	26,000
1974	476,000	188,000	31,000
1975	–	–	–
1976	476,000	195,000	30,000
1977	–	–	–
1978	473,000	186,000	27,000
1979	–	–	–
1980	495,000	185,000	25,000
1981	–	–	–
1982	523,000	196,000	32,000
1983	–	–	–
1984	–	–	–
1985	545,000	209,000	27,000
1986	–	–	–
1987	551,000	214,000	27,000
1988	568,000	227,000	35,000
1989	552,000	195,000	38,000
1990	558,000	212,000	30,000
1991	560,000	216,000	41,000

Source: Statistics Canada, "Household Facilities and Equipment," cat. no. 64-202.
– Vacation-home question not asked in HFE survey for this year.
[1] First year vacation-home question included in HFE survey.
[2] Statistics Canada estimates the standard error in this survey data is 2.6 to 5.0 per cent; no error
estimate available for 1973 and 1974.
[3] Statistics Canada estimates the standard error in this survey data is 2.6 to 5.0 per cent in 1976, 1978,
1982, and 1985, and 5.1 to 10.0 per cent in remaining years, with no error estimate available for 1973
and 1974.
[4] Statistics Canada estimates the standard error in this survey data is 5.1 to 10 per cent in 1976, and
10.1 to 16.5 per cent in remaining years, with no error estimate available for 1973 and 1974.

Particularly striking in Table 1 is that in Ontario and in British
Columbia only a very small proportion of the population, 2.9 and 1.3
per cent respectively, participated in cottaging.

Table 2 updates this attempt to gauge the extent of cottaging by
introducing vacation-home ownership estimates generated by Statistics Canada's Survey of Household Facilities and Equipment (HFE).
Since 1973 the annual HFE survey has included a question on vacation-home ownership.[33] It should be noted that the HFE survey
makes no distinction between summer/winter/year-round vacation
homes. In 1991 the HFE estimate of the number of vacation homes in
Canada was 560,000, of which 216,000 were in Ontario and 41,000
were in British Columbia.

The 1973, 1980, and 1985 HFE data must be read as including all Canadian households that own a vacation home outside of Canada. In 1988 the HFE survey added a supplementary section to the vacation-home question, identifying the home's location either by region in Canada or outside of Canada. As a result, the 1990 data exclude 66,000 households that own a vacation home outside of Canada. In comparing HFE data with Wolfe's post-office data, it must be remembered that the HFE question focuses on ownership, while Wolfe's data derive from activity regardless of ownership.[34]

The HFE estimate of the percentage of Canadian households owning vacation homes has been relatively static since 1973. This is a surprising result given that the period from 1970 to 1990 is widely interpreted as one marked by increasing wealth, leisure time, and pursuit of recreational opportunities. Clearly a range of factors, including demographics and changing tastes or preferences in leisure activity, influence interest in vacation-home ownership. Another explanation for this apparent contradiction may be found in the introduction of restrictions on waterfront cottage-lot creation and the resultant pressures on the cottage property market. When these are combined, the effect is to limit access to cottage ownership on economic grounds.

When we compare the provincial distribution of vacation-home ownership, we find that Ontario continues to account for the largest share, 37 per cent of the Canadian total in 1973 and 38 per cent in 1990. Taken together, Quebec and Ontario account for most of Canada's cottage owners. British Columbia captures a much smaller share, 6 per cent in 1973 and 5 per cent in 1990, although these figures may not be an accurate reflection of summer-home ownership. In amenity regions such as Vancouver Island and the Okanagan Valley, a new form of housing development involving self-contained retirement communities is appearing in small urban centres, and these developments may play the same role as rural cottages in Ontario for the retirement-age "snowbird" population. This provincial distribution of ownership mirrors the general pattern of activity described much earlier by Wolfe. On the issue of participation, in 1991 approximately 6 per cent of Ontario households – and approximately 3 per cent of British Columbia households – owned vacation homes. While this is a larger share than appears in Wolfe's 1941 data, it is still a very limited segment of the Canadian public.

Wolfe also compared the relative shares of cottager activity in terms of whether they were Canadian or American.[35] Ontario, with the largest number of summer cottagers in Canada, also records the largest number and proportion from the United States. Wolfe's 1941 data suggest that 5,520 cottagers in Ontario, or 19.6 per cent, were

American. This compares to 11.1 per cent for Canada as a whole and 2.6 per cent for British Columbia. Updating this question for the Rideau Lakes and Cultus Lake areas, I found a generally low level of cottage ownership by residents from outside Canada. In the Rideau Lakes area, 9.2 per cent of the questionnaire sample of seasonal-use cottage properties listed permanent mailing addresses in the United States. As with Wolfe's finding that most cottagers from the United States came from states bordering on the Lower Great Lakes, the Rideau Lakes sample shows that 44 per cent of cottage owners from the United States have a mailing address in New York State, with an additional 22 per cent coming from Pennsylvania. A review of all cottage properties in the Cultus Lake area determined that only 1.1 per cent were owned by residents of the United States. In this case, all were identified as having a permanent address in Washington State. No owners of seasonal-use properties were identified as having permanent mailing addresses outside of Canada or the United States.

Rideau Lakes

In reviewing the spatial origins of cottagers across Ontario's recreational landscape, Wolfe reported a distinct "regionalization" of activity based upon cottage-area proximity to metropolitan centres and/or to the United States.[36] In terms of metropolitan impacts, he identified cottagers from the Toronto area as dominating activity in the Kawartha and Muskoka Lakes regions north of the city.[37] For the "Frontenac Axis" region, which includes the Rideau Lakes area, increasing distance from Toronto and greater proximity to Kingston, Ottawa, and upstate New York leads to an expectation that these places will be important sources of cottage-property owners. Using property-owner address information for a sample of cottage properties in the Rideau Lakes area, we may explore this issue of metropolitan influence on recreational hinterlands, as well as integrate comparative information on cottage ownership by local residents.[38]

The issue of ownership is important since the control of property by either local or non-local owners has implications in debates concerning a community's future. It must be recognized that many factors can be associated with the concept of property control, including local government land-use regulations, zoning, taxation, and land-title restrictions. "Control" is conceptualized here as the ownership of property, something that confers on the seasonal or periodic "resident" the right to participate in local elections and politics. The political rights conferred by ownership and the exercise of those

Table 3
Distribution of Cottage Ownership[1]

Location of permanent residence of cottage owner	Percentage of cottage properties	
	Rideau Lakes	Cultus Lake
Internal[2]	6.2	1.9
Adjacent towns[3]	21.6	18.1
Adjacent rural / small town[4]	6.9	4.9
Adjacent metropolitan areas[5]	43.3	71.2
Other Canada	13.1	2.9
United States	8.9	1.1
Sample size	295	375

Source:
[1] The Cultus Lake sample includes all seasonal-use cottage properties within the study area. The Rideau Lakes sample is based on property-owner address information collected for the random sample of seasonal-use cottage properties identified for the questionnaire survey.
[2] Within the respective study-area boundaries.
[3] Cultus Lake = Chilliwack; Rideau Lakes = Perth, Smiths Falls, and Westport.
[4] Covers the region between each study area and the adjacent metropolitan area(s).
[5] Rideau Lakes = Ottawa and Kingston; Cultus Lake = Vancouver.

rights to promote locality-based interests underscores debate over community change. In the Rideau Lakes area it is clear that local-area owners account for more than one-quarter of all cottage-property ownership (see Table 3). Approximately 6 per cent of these cottage properties are owned by residents living within the rural townships surrounding the Rideau Lakes, while an additional 22 per cent are owned by residents of Perth, Smiths Falls, and Westport, three small towns immediately adjacent to the lakes.

One explanation for these local-ownership levels around the Rideau Lakes lies in the alienation of lakefront lands and limited public access to the waterfront. Along the Rideau Lakes the single tier of privately owned cottage properties necklacing the recreational waterways effectively limits public access. Only a few public-access points now exist along the entire lake system, most of these associated with government parks and boat-launching ramps. A number of local residents commented that they purchased a cottage lot simply to ensure family access to the lake.

The suggestion that proximity to major metropolitan areas imparts a distance-decay effect on cottaging activity is also reflected in the pattern of cottage ownership described in Table 3. With the added distance from Toronto, only 5 per cent of cottage properties are owned by Toronto-area residents. However, residents from the adjacent urban

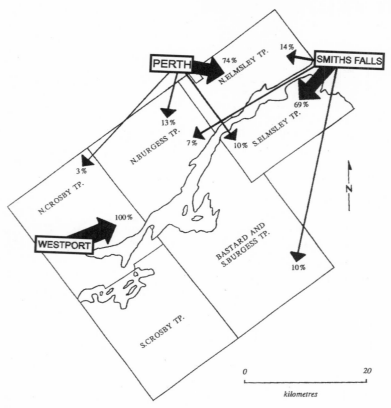

Figure 3
"Local" cottage-property ownership.

areas of Ottawa and Kingston account for 43 per cent of these cottage properties. This ownership pattern supports the contention that an adjacent urban area plays a significant role in controlling seasonal-use properties within its recreational hinterland.

To pursue spatial patterns of local area control further, I examined cottage-property owners in the Rideau Lakes sample who are identified as living in one of the three local towns of Smiths Falls, Perth, and Westport. The overwhelming finding is one of an intensely local relationship between permanent residence and cottage property. Of the 31 cottage-property owners identified as living in Perth, 74 per cent owned their cottage property in North Elmsley Township, and a further 13 per cent owned theirs in North Burgess Township. Of the 29 cottage owners who live in Smiths Falls, 69 per cent owned their cottage property in South Elmsley Township, while an additional 14 per cent owned theirs in North Elmsley Township. All six of the identified cottage owners who live in Westport owned their cottage property in surrounding North Crosby Township.

Cultus Lake

A similar distribution of cottage-property ownership can be noted for Cultus Lake (see Table 3). In this case, about 20 per cent of cottage properties are owned by residents whose permanent address is either within the study area or in the immediately adjacent municipality of Chilliwack. The importance of metropolitan-area control is clear in the approximately 71 per cent of cottage properties owned by residents of Vancouver. Again, the magnitudes continue to support the contention that metropolitan areas exercise considerable control of recreational activity within their surrounding hinterland. There is also, however, clear support for recognizing the importance of local-area residents in cottage-property ownership.

Implicit in urban-field and city-countryside models is an assumption that cottage properties within the rural hinterland of cities are almost exclusively controlled by urban residents. Case-study findings[39] in the Cultus Lake and Rideau Lakes areas confirm that while a large proportion of cottage properties are owned by residents of adjacent metropolitan areas, rural-area residents are also active as cottage owners. Reasons for the large number of cottage-property owners from within the local area are varied. Along the Rideau Lakes several residents remarked that since private cottage ownership has effectively cut off public access to the lakes, they purchased a cottage lot in order to ensure access for their family. At Cultus Lake the cottaging areas began as recreational retreats for local residents; only over time have non-local residents been able to supplant local residents' ownership of property within the cottage market.

ECONOMIC BOUNDS ON COTTAGE OWNERSHIP

Gauging the economic accessibility of cottage ownership is a difficult problem. No national statistics clearly identify the cottage-property sub-market, and in the Rideau Lakes area disparities in the property-assessment base years and "per cent of value" calculations make even the comparison of changes in assessed values of cottage property unreliable. In the absence of price data, I used two surrogate measures, assessed cottage-property value and household income of

Table 4
Cultus Lake: Average Property Assessments[1] (current dollars)

	Lindell Beach			Cultus Lake Park		
	land	house	combined	land	house	combined
1981	22,517	19,228	41,805	15,022	16,200	31,222
1986	33,353	20,429	53,782	16,486	18,196	34,682
1991	61,580	41,700	103,280	40,700	36,330	77,030

Source: British Columbia Assessment Authority.

[1] Average assessed values for 1981 correspond to the 1980 assessment year; the 1986 assessed values correspond to the 1984 assessment year; and the 1991 assessed values correspond to the 1990 assessment year. The average land values include all residential properties, while the average house values include only those properties with residential units. Assessed value set by British Columbia Assessment Authority at 100 per cent of market value calculated on a two-year-update basis.

cottage owners, to explore the contention that cottage properties are becoming more expensive relative to other residential properties, and that this increasingly makes them affordable only to a restricted subset of the Canadian population.

The first of these surrogate measures traces changes in the assessed value of cottage properties at Cultus Lake, where property-value assessment is based on 100 per cent of market value and is updated every two years, and compares the relative level of change to an index of residential price change in Vancouver and at the national level. In Table 4, the average assessed values for cottage properties at both Cultus Lake Park and Lindell Beach is listed for 1981, 1986, and 1991. For both of these Cultus Lake cottaging areas, the average property assessment (land and house combined) increased approximately 150 per cent between 1981 and 1991, and for both, most of this increase was in the value of the land (approximately 175 per cent increase) rather than the value of improvements (approximately 123 per cent increase). At Cultus Lake there is a locally recognized distinction between Cultus Lake Park and Lindell Beach, one that suggests Lindell Beach is a higher-status cottage area. Assessed-value data suggest that market demand for both areas is increasing and that the differences in property sizes (average lot size being larger at Lindell Beach) likely explain most of the difference in assessed values.

Figure 4 shows Canada Mortgage and Housing Corporation (CMHC) price-index data for the total selling price (land and house combined) of new housing for Vancouver and for Canada. Figure 5 shows indexes developed from average property-value assessments for Cultus Lake Park and Lindell Beach. Even allowing for the limitations in comparing the types of data upon which the two figures

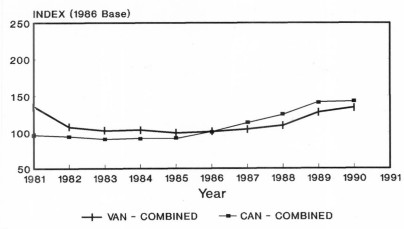

Figure 4
New-housing price indexes, Canada and Vancouver.
Source: Canadian Housing Statistics.

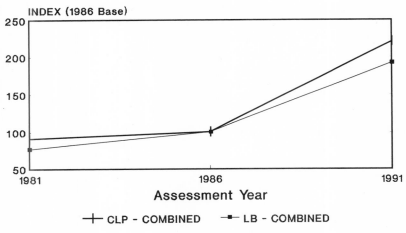

Figure 5
Property-assessment indexes, Cultus Lake.
Source: BC Assessment Authority.

are based, it would appear that at Cultus Lake prices have risen faster than for Vancouver or Canada since 1986. The evidence lends some support to the argument that cottage properties have been increasing in price relative to other residential housing.[40]

The second surrogate measure used to probe the changing economic accessibiliy of cottage ownership involves the average household

Table 5
Vacation Home Owners: Average Household Income (current dollars)

Year	Canada[1]	Ontario[2]	BC[3]
1982[4]	37,832	39,977	41,333
1985	47,513	51,487	48,710
1987	52,117	62,015	53,001
1988	55,297	61,311	54,573
1989	55,518	63,928	63,793
1990	61,916	76,858	54,707
1991	62,210	72,466	73,068

Source: Statistics Canada, "Household Facilities by Income and Other Characteristics,"
cat. no. 13-567 and 13-218.
[1] Statistics Canada estimates the standard error in this survey data is 2.6 to 5.0 per cent.
[2] Statistics Canada estimates the standard error in this survey data is 2.6 to 5.0 per cent in 1982
and 1985, and 5.1 to 10.0 per cent remaining years.
[3] Statistics Canada estimates the standard error in this survey data is 10.1 to 16.5 per cent.
[4] First year that a "vacation home" data cross-tabulation by household income was published by
Statistics Canada.

income of cottage-property owners. These data are, unfortunately, available only at the national and provincial scales. The data must be read with caution, as issues including duration of ownership tenure, cottage-property inheritance, and the substitution of access-to-use for of access-to-ownership can greatly complicate the relationship between income and prices.

Table 5 lists the average household income of vacation-home owners, as estimated from the HFE survey. This income cross-tabulation is published by Statistics Canada but is not, unfortunately, available for each year the vacation-homes question appeared in the HFE survey. The current-dollar comparisons show that the average household income of vacation-home owners has nearly doubled between 1982 and 1991. Within the estimated margin of error in the survey data, the average household incomes of vacation-home owners are consistently higher in both Ontario and British Columbia than the national average. In 1985 the estimated average household income of vacation-home owners across Canada was approximately 28 per cent higher than the average Canadian household income as reported in the census. In Ontario the average income of vacation-home owners was approximately 26 per cent higher than the average for all households in the province, while in British Columbia vacation-home owners had average household incomes approximately 31 per cent higher than the provincial average.

In Table 6 the average household income is expressed in 1986 constant-dollar values to control for the effects of inflation.[41] It is

Table 6
Vacation Home Owners: Average Household Income (constant [1986] dollars)[1]

Year	Canada[2]	Ontario[3]	BC[4]
1982[5]	45,200	47,762	49,382
1985	49,493	53,632	50,740
1987	49,920	59,401	50.767
1988	50,918	56,456	50,251
1989	48,700	56,077	55,959
1990	51,813	64,316	45,780
1991	49,295	57,422	57,899

Source: Statistics Canada, "Household Facilities by Income and Other Characteristics,"
cat. no. 13-567 and 13-218.
[1] Calculation of household income into 1986 constant dollars uses conversion factors from Statistics Canada's Consumer Price Index, and the formula [(Current Year $) × 100] / (Conversion Factor) = Constant $.
[2] Statistics Canada estimates the standard error in this survey data is 2.6 to 5.0 per cent.
[3] Statistics Canada estimates the standard error in this survey data is 2.6 to 5.0 per cent in 1982 and 1985, and 5.1 to 10.0 per cent remaining years.
[4] Statistics Canada estimates the standard error in this survey data is 10.1 to 16.5 per cent.
[5] First year that a "vacation home" data cross-tabulation by household income was published by Statistics Canada.

clear that the average household income of vacation-home owners increased between 1982 and 1991 in constant-dollar terms even with the significant lag effects described above. Allowing for sampling error, this increase at the national level is in the order of 11 per cent over the intervening nine-year period. The relative increase is approximately the same for British Columbia, while in Ontario the increase is in the order of 20 per cent.

Both surrogate measures used to probe the question of whether cottage-property ownership is increasing in exclusivity are imperfect. However, there is a strong suggestion through these surrogates that 1) cottage-property values are increasing relative to other residential housing,[42] and 2) cottage-property owners are more upwardly mobile in economic terms than the rest of the population.

The cost of cottage property is a significant barrier that can limit access to ownership. However, there are further ownership costs even after a property is purchased. Taken together, cottage expenses include "the original cost of land and dwelling, taxes, electricity, furnishings ... possessions and activities ... [and also] the expense of travelling to and from the cottage."[43] The questions of land-use planning, property rights, and local-area taxation on cottage properties continue to generate serious, and sometimes heated, debate between cottagers and local governments or school boards.[44] Many of these costs, such as maintenance, annual investment in improvements, and travel between the permanent and seasonal residences, can vary widely among owners. However, the role and potential impacts of three important economic issues are further reviewed here. These include availability of mortgage financing, property taxation, and capital-gains-tax exemptions.

The availability of mortgage financing is dependent upon the amount financed and the applicant's financial status as determined by the lending institution. In both the Rideau Lakes and Cultus Lake areas, conventional mortgages with 25 per cent of purchase price as down payment are available for privately owned cottage properties. Depending upon the customer, some institutions suggest they may even approve high-ratio mortgages on cottage property, that is, mortgages with less than a 25 per cent down payment. Among the range of local banks and credit unions, some institutions charge a rate 0.5 per cent higher than similar mortgage rates for permanent residences; others charge an additional 1.0 per cent premium if the cottage is under 1,000 square feet in size; and some insist that cottage properties proceed with a collateral mortgage at personal-loan rates. Not surprisingly, nearly all mortgage officers interviewed prefaced their comments on rules and premiums with the proviso: "well, it does depend on who the customer is."

The situation is much different with leased properties, as at Cultus Lake Park in British Columbia and along the Beaubassin coast of New Brunswick, and elsewhere.[45] In these cases, banks are restricted in their ability to offer mortgages. In the Cultus Lake area, First Heritage Savings Credit Union and Fraser Valley Credit Union handle most mortgage activity for leased lots. High-ratio mortgages are generally not available, and the rates for conventional mortgages are between 0.5 and 1.0 per cent higher than for owned cottage property.

In both the Cultus Lake and Rideau Lakes study areas the purchase price of cottage property varies greatly depending upon the location, size, and quality of the dwelling-unit. However, for either leased or owned cottage properties the costs of financing the purchase are proportionally similar to, though perhaps slightly higher than, those for urban or small-town residences.

As in urban property markets, questions of property taxation (including school taxes) and capital-gains taxes when selling property are important issues for cottage owners. Property taxation generates some of the most intense rhetoric and debate among the cottager population. In both Ontario and British Columbia the assessment of property for taxation purposes makes no distinction between seasonal or permanent occupancy. Current-year market assessment,

Table 7
Rideau Lakes: Examples of Taxation Revenue Shares,[1] 1992 Estimates

	South Elmsley %	South Crosby[4] %	North Crosby %	North Burgess %
Local government	18.4	22.2	27.4	14.8
Senior government[2]	11.7	11.5	10.3	15.7
School boards[3]	69.9	66.3	62.3	69.5

Source: Annual financial statements of selected townships.

[1] Calculated from 1992 township budget statements to local residential property taxpayers.

[2] County level.

[3] Includes public and separate school boards.

[4] Does not include calculation of additional approximately 14 per cent "special area rate" levied on property owners in Elgin Police Village.

often incorrectly described in popular debate as market-value assessment, is being introduced in the Rideau Lakes study area. Both the Federation of Ontario Cottagers' Associations (FOCA) and several local-area cottagers' associations have been vocal in their opposition to its implementation.[46] The concern is that prices for waterfront properties have been rising much faster than for other properties and that updating the base year at which assessed values are calculated will shift the tax burden more and more on to these high-value properties. Interviews with cottagers' associations that have already experienced reassessment suggest that in fact this expectation of higher taxes has been realized.

Leaseholders in Cultus Lake Park are more upset at paying property taxes to the Regional District of Fraser-Cheam (RDFC) – the local "municipal" government – when most of their services are in fact provided by the Cultus Lake Park Board. In 1992 a six-month entitlement lease along the waterfront at Main Beach involved an annual fee of $506, while on the backlots in the Main Beach area the fee was $485, and on the larger lots along Mountainview Drive the fee was $631.[47] A twelve-month entitlement annual lease fee was $622, $594, and $788 respectively for these same lots. In terms of property taxes paid to the RDFC, a typical small, seasonal-use cottage in a desirable location in Cultus Lake Park paid over $900 in 1990.

The second property-taxation issue, and the one that most inflames tempers in the Rideau Lakes area, concerns local school taxes. In both Ontario and British Columbia school taxes are collected via the municipal property-tax bill. When we compare Tables 7 and 8, we find that a larger share of property taxes in the Rideau Lakes area is paid to the local school boards than at Cultus Lake. The relationship

Table 8
Cultus Lake: Examples of Taxation Revenue Shares,[1] 1991 Estimates

	Lindell Beach %	Cultus Lake Park[3] %
Local government	21.7	16.6
Senior government[2]	22.8	24.3
School boards	55.5	59.1

Source: British Columbia Assessment Authority.
[1] Calculated from mill rates table.
[2] Provincial government and various agencies, including hospital, Assessment Authority, and Municipal Finance Authority.
[3] Does not include the $105.25 flat-rate sewer-charges levy on each lot.

between local school-board budgets and local property taxes is much more complicated; however, a significant portion of the Rideau Lakes taxpayer's taxes goes to schools. Seasonal-use property owners have consistently argued that they pay school taxes twice and do not receive benefit from the second taxation.[48]

One of the most significant cost issues concerning cottage ownership is the implications of capital-gains-tax calculations. Until recently two important capital-gains-tax exemptions, the taxpayer's principal residence and a lifetime $100,000 exemption, had important implications for cottage ownership. Prior to 1982 it was possible for both spouses to claim a separate principal-residence exemption by arranging "property ownership such that the city home [was] in one spouse's name and the cottage [was] in the other spouse's name."[49] Beginning in 1992, application of the $100,000 exemption to cottage properties was restricted. The FOCA lobbied against this tax change, arguing that there is considerable concern among cottage owners that the sale of their appreciating recreational property, or its transfer by gift or inheritance to family members, is threatened.

The costs of owning cottage property may not only act to limit access to ownership but may also work to generate a significant push factor behind the conversion of cottages into year-round or retirement homes. The implications of capital-gains taxes as an incentive for cottage conversion are clear. In the case of a near-retirement-age household, sale of the city home would cash out equity on a long-standing principal residence. A permanent move to the cottage would then identify it as the permanent residence for much of the household's retirement years, a length of time that would be important in reducing future capital-gains implications.

When these issues are considered together, there are clearly a set of costs involved in owning a cottage. When the cottage is also a second home, some of these costs may be paid twice, and the property owner must be able to afford these additional costs in order to own the second home. A household living in a metropolitan area who decide to sell their urban home and relocate to the lake at retirement will be able not only to cash-out the equity of their urban residence but also to reduce substantially some of those costs at a converted lakeside property.

SUMMARY

Cottaging is much more than the physical act of going to a recreational property for rest or enjoyment. There is an intricate symbolism attached both to cottaging and to cottage ownership, a symbolism that not only accords and defines a certain status but also defines a unique place – cottage country. In the rural-recreational countryside this legacy has evolved into a folklore associated with cottaging. The issue that permeates this folklore is that the cottage, and the cottaging area, are conceived of as entirely separate from the rural milieu in which they are set. The rural countryside is not just separate; it is largely invisible. The rural landscape is, at best, a back-cloth for cottage scenery, and rural places are often little more than local supply depots. Cottage conversion as a pressure behind community change is occurring within a landscape that clearly is socially and geographically divided. The implications of this division for interpreting public debates over community change need to be examined.

The ownership of cottages is bounded by a number of economic factors. These factors can impose costs that limit access to cottage ownership to particular segments of the Canadian population. As a reflection of such economic limits, the cottage-owner cohort clearly stands out from the provincial population in terms of household income in Ontario and British Columbia. Patterns of cottage-property ownership by location of permanent residence demonstrate some mixing of geographic origins between local-area residents and those from adjacent urban and metropolitan areas. These issues suggest two sources of pressure behind cottage-conversion activity. The first is from higher-income, non-local residents who have gained considerable local familiarity through long-term ownership of a cottage property and are now seeking an amenity residence, perhaps coincident with retirement planning. The second includes locally generated pressures, involving either upper-income households relocating to the lake for reasons similar to those of residents from metropolitan areas, or those with perhaps lower income levels seeking an affordable local housing option. These suggestions now require testing and clarification.

3 Community Change in the Rural-Recreational Countryside

This study of community change and local contention over that change in the rural-recreational countryside is organized around four closely connected conceptual frameworks. The first is concerned with the role of *spatial orientation*. This is a critical issue because the decision to view local change from within the rural community or from outside affects the type of questions asked. The second framework is concerned with defining the *rural-recreational countryside* and establishing the relative status of change as an integral aspect of that countryside. Third is the nature of *community* itself, including the need to transfer the community question to the rural-recreational-countryside setting. Finally, there is the question of *conflict*. If the pressures of community change are contentious, then the interaction between and within local community groups and institutions is an important part of the expression of such contention. It is important to set out from the start how this study is organized with respect to these conceptual frameworks, for its organization affects both the scope and focus of the research as well as the conclusions drawn from it.

SPATIAL ORIENTATION

Spatial orientation refers to the privileging of either an urban- or rural-focused perspective and the potential biases that choice imposes on the research design. Halseth and Rosenberg have argued that geographic research on small towns and rural areas in Canada tends to develop within one of three spatial orientations.[1] The first focuses on specific interactions between an urban system and the adjoining rural hinterland.[2] This overwhelmingly urban-centric perspective views interactions and changes as being driven from within the urban system. With the exception of an interest in farmland conservation, little attention is paid to impacts on the rural community itself. A second orientation fixes on the small towns and villages within the rural milieu.[3] Concentrating upon individual places as "points" on an otherwise barren isotrophic landscape, the immediate interface between the small settlements and the surrounding rural milieu is not developed. A third and, I would argue, less well-developed orientation includes specific attention to the rural milieu within particularly defined regions or jurisdictions.[4]

Most published research in Canada maintains a predominantly urban orientation to the study of changing rural geographies. Within the rural–urban-fringe literature, considerable research on rural population change focuses upon the movement of an exurban population from the cities to the countryside.[5] However, as Simmons argues, the questions are framed with a distinctly urban bias, with the result that little attention is paid to the consequences of that change on the local rural community.[6] Troughton counters that this bias is understandable given that the urban fringe "begins at the city edge; and there is little doubt that urbanization is the dominant process at work."[7] Coppack, agreeing with Troughton, contends that the "set of conditions called urbanization" has an overriding importance in understanding change in the rural-urban fringe.[8]

Much of the intellectual foundation for the rural–urban-fringe literature derives from the "urban field" construct.[9] An evolving conceptualization of the urban field has employed cultural, economic, and ecological notions of the region to situate small towns and rural areas within the hinterland of urban centres. In their seminal paper Friedmann and Miller employ an ecological formulation to argue that the "idea of an urban field is similarly based on the criterion of interdependency ... [and] represents not only an approximate geographic limit for commuting to a job, but also the limit of intensive weekend and seasonal use ... for recreation."[10] The distinct urban-centred focus of this research is explicit in its recognition of the functional interaction between the rural and urban components, and its concern for the use of, and expansion into, the non-urban landscape by the urban system.[11] Too often, research employing this urban-centric orientation loses sight of the interdependency so central to Friedmann and Miller's concept. Despite their broad formulation of the urban field, most rural–urban-fringe researchers have not taken up the challenge of integrating recreational land uses into current research.

Research focused specifically upon small towns or villages in the non-metropolitan areas of Canada is less well developed. The intellectual lineage for much of this research is drawn from the "dispersed city" model of interrelationships between small towns. Hayes suggests that it is the absence of a single dominant urban centre that is important in the formation of a system where higher-order functions are dispersed throughout a number of separate communities within an otherwise rural region.[12] Dahms adds that there is a "form of spatial organization of small settlements in the countryside which collectively provide some of the economic functions normally found in the city."[13] A critical difficulty with published research is the emphasis on settlements to the exclusion of the surrounding landscape in which they are set. The identification of research subject by the criterion that it bear a place-name may be useful for data-collection purposes, but it fails to capture important processes, changes, and activities not centred on named towns or villages. In some cases such named communities may actually be more a reflection of historical accident than of contemporary importance. I would argue that cottage development and conversion is an important element of change in the rural-recreational countryside, and that the processes and implications are not captured within a dispersed-city framework.

Perhaps the least developed of the three research orientations within rural geography is the literature that works from a rural-area perspective. One developing body of literature probes "perceptions" in quality of life as residential change occurs in rural places. Walker, for example, has used the metaphor of an "invaded countryside" to describe the social and political changes in a sample of rural–urban-fringe locations north of Toronto.[14] Fuller and Leckie have shown an interest in the changing agricultural community, while Mackenzie traces a finer current of change in the constitution of the agricultural community.[15] The exciting aspect of recent work by researchers such as Leckie and Mackenzie is its engagement with contemporary theoretical debate in an effort to develop new interpretations of rural landscapes and livelihoods. While concerned with a general "rural community," however, these contributions are often not studies of change within particular localities.

Working from a tradition that has emphasized an urban bias towards rural studies, the research described in this book clearly situates itself within the local rural community. This includes the dispersed rural-agricultural landscape, the clusters of cottage development, and the small towns and villages located within the study areas. This geographic setting not only provides the spatial context for experiencing processes and pressures of change; it is also the locale that is modified by the outcomes of these pressures. As well, it is the local residents who are affected by, and are in some cases effecting, these changes and must develop strategies to deal with them as part of their daily lives. The local community forms the context in which pressures of residential change are represented and contested.

RURAL-RECREATIONAL COUNTRYSIDE

A critical issue in the study of residential change involves defining the specific geographic context within which this change occurs. A central argument of this book is that a locally constructed recognition of a separation in social and geographic space of the rural and cottage-property areas is an important organizing principle for area residents. In a somewhat different rural context, Fitchen elaborates upon the importance of these types of locally constructed understandings of separation:

The contrast between "city people" and "farm people" is a leitmotif in local perception of population changes. These are categories, not descriptions of individual people, but as categories they serve to explain and order people's perceptions of other people. Even though the opinions and feelings of farm people vary as widely as do the individual people from any city, and even though individual farm people and city people may actually be good friends, the perceptual categories are a ready party of the collective belief system and the communal lexicon.[16]

Drawing upon the conceptual work of Cloke and Halfacree, a working definition of "rural" must clearly recognize, first, the physical or spatial setting, and second, the need to integrate personal and sociological behaviour within that setting.[17] In the geographic literature concerned with defining the "rural" much attention has been directed to physical or spatial settings, especially by research aimed at refining empirical measures of urban and rural based upon the application of population-density or non-farm-development scales.[18] Critical issues include the size of geographic units for which data are available, the classification and mix of settlement types in each unit, and the quality, reliability (including definitional changes), and temporal availability of data.[19]

The physical or spatial setting is a crucial aspect of the rural-recreational countryside. In its most general form the Friedmann-Miller urban-field model includes a generally dispersed rural countryside surrounding the urban centre. Daily commuting to work or weekend recreational travel are utilized as alternative criteria in establishing the outer bounds of the urban area's influence. Under this model, the rural area is most often defined in terms of the use to which it may be put by the urban population,[20] or is negatively defined in terms of what it lacks in the way of services or infrastructure in comparison to urban areas.[21]

The notion of rural also has a sociological element, which operates within the physical setting. Several decades ago the sociologist. Wirth suggested "modes of association" as an approach for investigating differences in individual and group behaviour between rural and urban communities, even while de-emphasizing the notion of rural-urban ideal types, in recognition that North American rural and urban experiences follow a pattern of gradation into each other.[22] The value of such an approach rests upon continuing differences between these groups. This may no longer be applicable, or relevant, as a result of the continuing integration of norms and values, assisted by the various media, that Hodge and Qadeer term "social convergence."[23]

As an update of this sociological line of enquiry, Lewis and Leckie introduce concerns for rural community change that emphasize changing social institutions and social cohesion in the face of externally generated pressures.[24] Cloke attempts to bridge the empirical and the social definitions of rural by proposing that the rural system is characterized by extensive land uses, small and generally low-order settlements, and a way of life that recognizes "the environmental and behaviourial qualities of living as part of an extensive landscape."[25]

In this book, however, we are interested only in one particular cross-section of the rural hinterland, areas that feature large numbers of lakeside recreational properties and cottages. This particular rural-recreational-countryside setting incorporates a striking juxtaposition of intensively developed cottaging landscapes together with lower-density farming and rural landscapes. For these rural and cottage residential areas, it is the availability of a recreational amenity (i.e., the lake) that identifies candidate areas, while proximity to urban centres influences the relative strength of cottage-development pressure.

The Importance of Change

Building upon the identification of the particular context within which change is occurring, this research argues that the issue of change itself must be placed at the very centre of our understanding of the countryside. In both the Rideau Lakes and Cultus Lake areas, the beginnings of the current settlement pattern emerged in the early 1800s. Changes in activity ranging from forestry to farming to cottage development and residential speculation have worked at different times to transform the landscape. Current pressures from exurban development and cottage-conversion activity need to be evaluated as forces that are part of a long history of change in both social and spatial configurations of communities within the rural-recreational countryside.

Researchers interested in communities and community change outside of urban settings have struggled against the perception of the rural as an unchanging entity. Such a perception has often become reified in the writings of researchers whose theoretical foundations develop from ideas about *Gesellschaft* or *anomie*. But for more than a century, change has been as fundamental to the meaning of countryside as it has been to the meaning of urban. In his historical review of the rural English village, Newby argues that the rural community of popular nostalgia never existed in static form but has been undergoing a continual process of change.[26] Harper updates this argument, suggesting that across contemporary Britain the rural countryside is "in a state of metamorphosis."[27]

In North America attention within rural sociology has moved from the origins of a distinct rural community to concern about its survival in an increasingly urbanized social context.[28] As early as the 1930s Sanderson recognized that "the rural community is an emergent group; it is in the process of becoming."[29] Fitchen suggests that contemporary rural America continues to face change and uncertainty, and that it is only being immersed in these changes that "makes the past appear stable and unchanging by contrast."[30]

Recent research in Great Britain has shifted the focus towards understanding the structures of community and community change.[31] Important here has been work that highlights the role of incoming residents as critical to changing the very nature of rural communities. Empirical results from current research reflect, to a degree, the findings and implications of earlier studies. However, several researchers have theorized that these changes in Britain are closely connected with a "commodification of rural idylls and rural lifestyles."[32] Emerging from a political-economy critique, this argument suggests that commodification pressures underlie the movement of new residential groups into rural places. Changes wrought by this influx of new residents affect not only the economic and social relations within localities but will also have important political consequences; they will affect the types of issues brought forward for debate and decisions on community priorities. In effect, rural politics becomes "a complex modality of power, contest and participation, reflecting change both in the wider political economy and in localized social relations; change in both the wider colonization of the politics of a commodified environment and in the localized politics of those who have colonized a slice of that environment."[33]

The political pressures inherent in the commodification of the rural landscape and the invasion of new resident groups generate community struggle. This is not just a struggle for access to or development of rural lands; the struggle is also a contest for control of local decision-making power – control over the future of the locality. In many cases this contest is played out in the very public forum of land-use planning debate, a forum where alternative visions for the future of the community clash.

COMMUNITY

Before we can talk about the details of community change, we must identify what is meant by the term *community*. I would argue for an interest in community as a set of relationships rather than as a concrete entity. To begin, it must be recognized that communities are both defined by the researcher, as a lens through which to examine the impacts of residential change, and are self-defined by the people living in the area, as a reflection of their local participation. While both "top-down" or "bottom-up" formulations of community are problematic, four aspects of community may be identified as crucial to evaluating the local implications of residential change. The first concerns who is living in the area, and is pursued in this study through a socio-economic comparison of residents. The second aspect concerns the local/non-local integration of the residents themselves, namely their urban or rural origins and efforts at maintaining ties to former communities. The third involves the local activities and participation patterns of residents. Fourth, local social-group interactions provide examples of community institutions that reflect the ways residents organize themselves and their commitments to the local community.

As a term, community is at once both clear and complex.[34] Its principal characteristics have been formulated, reformulated, summarized, and debated within sociology, psychology, and geography. Agreement on a general conceptualization of community includes that it is the social and spatial framework within which individuals experience and conduct most of their day-to-day activities, that it is bound together by a shared sense of belonging, and that the group defines a distinctive identity for its members.[35] In this general formulation, community is clearly seen as something that is defined from the bottom up by its members. However, these definitions have largely focused upon the identification of criteria by which to label entities called communities. Such criteria are often employed as a "checklist" for classification; any flexibility in interpreting the sense of community is often lost.

A second, top-down formulation of community is based on the imposition of boundaries designed to enclose some part of a local area. Common examples include the jurisdictional boundaries of local governments and their planning units, or the data collection, service provision, or management regions of governments and agencies. In the rural-recreational countryside it may be that, as household needs are increasingly met at the local government level through a range of functions from the general welfare rolls to sponsorship and naming of youth sports teams, these jurisdictions qualify as a type of community for residents. But such jurisdictional communities suffer important limits. An administrative formulation of community may be very far removed from the way people structure their social and interactive lives, failing to capture those outside the physical boundaries who also consider themselves part of that community while including those within who consider themselves separate. I argue that in debates over residential change, attention to local government jurisdictions is important in evaluating how differing social conceptions of communities and interests are represented in political debates on land-use planning issues.

To explore the impacts of residential change within the rural-recreational countryside, a more flexible conceptual framework for understanding community organization within localities is needed. The search should not be limited to identification of community as a thing, but rather as a relationship. Critical issues concerning the meaning of community are reviewed below through research on the confluence of spaces, places, and social structures that goes into the local construction of community.[36] The incorporation of both spatial setting and social behaviour presents an important challenge for research into community change.

One formulation of this social-spatial challenge concerns identification of socially distinct population groups within a geographically defined locality. Gans and Suttles both examine urban neighbourhoods that reflect clear internal social and spatial divisions despite being externally defined as single communities.[37] The differences are rooted in the separate bases of community identification used; the top-down jurisdictional partitioning by local governments and planning boards, as compared to the bottom-up creation of social bonds and interactions.

A second formulation focuses on the separation of the spatial into local and non-local components. McClenahan[38] introduced the notion of "communality", and Webber[39] extended this into "community without propinquity," as early definitions of a new conception of community life based on a loosening of the friction of residential distance. Drawing upon this work, Lee illustrates how "interest based communities rather than place based communities" are useful in differentiating between sets of interests and values within a locality.[40] Yet clearly, even a community without propinquity has a geography, and connections between this geography and group behaviour patterns are therefore open to investigation. In such a case the organization of residents within particular areas may include participation in differing interest groups or different patterns of neighbouring and social contact with friends. The incorporation of "place-bounded" relationships in "communities of interest" is an important part of examining local community change. Changing social institutions are as important as population flows and economic linkages. This book argues that in the rural-recreational countryside, the added complexity of cottage development requires that we give further consideration to changing groups within the local population.

Fitchen states that the influx of new residential groups presents a fundamental challenge to social cohesion in the rural community. This echoes earlier suggestions by Pahl, who noted that urban-to-rural movements within the metropolitan fringe introduce newcomers and pressures that in turn generate new social geographies.[41] For Lewis, changing social institutions provide one mirror of social change in rural communities, a perspective that Leckie's examination of farm-family participation in agricultural associations demonstrates by highlighting the importance of institutions to continued cohesion within communities experiencing change.[42] In this book, two forms of local institutions are examined. The property-based residents' or cottagers' associations and interest-based groups such as the Women's Institute have very different organizing and operating mandates; however, as a current expression of long-standing local institutions, these groups may provide one avenue for insight into community change.

In the rural-recreational countryside, the issue of residential change through the specific mechanism of cottage conversion needs to be drawn into debates on community change. Helleiner introduces the notion of community into a cottaging setting by suggesting that the perception of shared or common interests can infuse collections of relatively isolated cottages with a sense of unity.[43] Dilley, and Helleiner and McGrath, extend this search for community in cottaging areas by arguing that the role of cottage conversion in introducing new permanent residents into an area needs more investigation.[44]

Dilley's study of planning controversy near Thunder Bay, Ontario, highlights the role of retirement planning as an impetus to cottage conversion. His research must be interpreted in terms of the growing literature exploring the relationship between the broader demographic processes of retirement and aging, and the migration and housing decisions of the elderly.[45] Longino and Biggar introduce the issues of regionally focused moves to amenity locations, the role of the affluent elderly, and deliberate return migration later in the life-cycle. Meyer and Speare suggest that migration to amenity destinations by the elderly is limited by variables that include age (the younger elderly), family structure (married), and social status (affluence). As Gober, McHugh, and Leclerc point out, the continuing pressures of this type of migration to amenity towns will increase the contrasts from place to place across the rural landscape and will affect the "economies, sociologies, and political geographies of contemporary non-metropolitan America."[46]

Hallman's study of new condominium developments within an established tourist area near Collingwood, Ontario, suggests a keen market awareness of the role of retirement- and amenity-property demands within particular segments of the population.[47] Yet Beck and Hussey can suggest an expansion of cottage-property sales as an economic stimulus in northern Alberta without incorporating any of the suggested impacts and costs of later conversion of some of these properties.[48] Clearly, a sound basis for research has been laid, but the process of conversion and community change in the rural-recreational countryside needs to become more visible in the research.

COMMUNITY CONFLICT

Local debate and contention over residential change within the rural-recreational countryside can greatly complicate our understanding of both the processes of change and their outcomes. A framework for understanding local debate and contention within this particular context is developed from the three separate bodies of community-conflict literature. The first of these developed within rural sociology during the 1920s and 1930s and details the importance of both individuals and community groups in small localities. The second body of literature involves a set of debates within sociology and political studies over the issue of community power and differential access to decision-making. The third has emerged from the radical critique of locational analysis in urban geography and describes the foundations of a "politics of turf." Together, these three literatures lend insight to the evaluation of change within the contemporary rural-recreational countryside.

Rural Community Conflict

An important background literature involves research published in rural sociology. Through the 1920s and 1930s researchers in rural sociology were engaged in a sustained research effort concerned with understanding the changes occurring in rural America. The intellectual commitment to this effort was considerable, and the legacy of published theoretical and applied case-study research is impressive. In fact, many of the questions raised and insights offered are being echoed by community-conflict researchers in the 1990s. A hallmark of the rural-sociology research is its concern both with understanding the rural community and with preparing community workers to assist rural communities through change. The interventionist nature of this assistance, labelled "community organization work," affects the organization and style of published research, which commonly includes an introductory interpretive section followed by a prescriptive concluding section. The presumptiveness subsumed in this duality of purpose is evident in a major treatment of rural community organization published by Sanderson and Polson.

Community conflict, as understood by Sanderson and Polson, is "one of the major social processes in community life ... [something that] can be expected to appear when groups or individuals are making adjustments to meet new conditions."[49] Within the local community, conflict and competition may develop between individuals over differences in opinion or between groups where one stands to gain and another to lose. Sanderson and Polson codify a set of eight "typical rural community conflict" situations (see Table 9). Among these situations, conflict and competition between local organizations or leaders, or between newcomers and old-timers, are evident in land-use planning debates over residential change in the rural-recreational countryside.

Sanderson and Polson identify a set of "basic drives" that stimulate local community conflict. These drives include issues of economic or social security; adjustments to social change or to the environment; and desires to protect or promote personal or local prestige or recognition. When these are combined with the range of

Table 9
Typical Rural Conflict Situations

1	School principals
	– versus ministers
	– the school board
	– the parent-teacher association
2	Conservative churches versus liberal churches
3	Between local organizations for local people and funds
4	Newcomers versus old-timers, particularly when newcomers enter politics
5	Old-line Americans versus foreigners
6	Rivalry between local leaders or organizations
7	Those for and those against community improvements and local spending
8	Farmers versus merchants

Source: Summarized from Sanderson and Polson (1939), *Rural Community Organization.*

typical rural community-conflict situations, a series of flashpoints for local debate, competition, and conflict occur. The most obvious situations precipitating conflict involve antagonistic personalities, especially where local groups or leaders are bypassed in the decision-making process. Differences in opinion between leaders often result in the alignment of other individuals or groups, the continued recurrence of which may entrench local rivalries. A second situation involves a challenge to the security of a group by a competing group, the natural response to which is usually a strong defensive posture. In the rural-recreational countryside this defensive posture in established community groups is evident in debate over new cottage-development proposals, while the outrage of cottagers' associations at not being central players in the planning of new waterfront-development regulations is also evident.

Perhaps the most interesting point brought out in the early rural-sociology literature concerns the need to distinguish between "true" and "derivative" issues in community conflict. Sanderson and Polson argue that the immediate subject of debate is not always the essential, underlying issue of contention. This discrepancy can greatly complicate analysis of the situation. Citing evidence from community-development debates, they note that individuals "in a community controversy may realize their objections do not carry sufficient weight to defeat a proposal and will consciously or unconsciously create substitute issues."[50] For Sanderson and Polson the sorting out of true and derivative issues rests upon assessing who will gain/lose relative to their set of typical conflict situations. This remains a fundamental challenge for the evaluation of local debate.

Community Power

Identification of who gains and who loses in local competition and conflict leads directly to the kinds of questions asked within the community-power debate. Dahl's initial question, "Who governs?" has an exceedingly broad scope.[51] Polsby "broke down the question 'who runs this town?' into 'who participates, who gains and loses and who prevails in decision-making?'"[52] The form and timing of this reformulation during a period of pronounced quantification within the social sciences cannot be divorced from its obvious implications as a more structured set of criteria for empirical investigation. In the analysis of debates over residential change in the rural-recreational countryside, the question can be recast again, this time in terms of who gains access to power and decision-making, and whether the geography of property ownership structures this access.

The recasting of the community-power question in terms of who gains access to decision-making power has important implications for building a geography of residential change within the rural-recreational countryside. If there is a social and geographic division of the countryside between cottage and rural property areas, then the question of whether one group has been historically excluded from local land-use planning and decision-making must be evaluated. In recent debates, how are these separate sets of property owners inter-acting within the decision-making process? If there is a change in relative access to decision-making, then we can try to suggest who gains and who loses. In this study of community change, contention over land-use planning and residential change is part of a nego-tiation or struggle for access to, participation in, and exertion of con-trol over the decision-making process by property-owner groups organized around the cottage/rural-property division in the rural-recreational countryside.

A literature interested in the elucidation of community power has developed from debates within sociology and political studies over the broad issue of local political contention.[53] Dahl's general question identified an object of study for researchers interested in the organi-zation of community change and debate over local political implica-tions of that change. The answer to Dahl's initial question has been largely dependent upon the model of community power to which the researcher subscribed.

Two separate models of community power generally predominate in the literature. The basic premise of an "elitist" model is the sug-gestion that there is a small group of power-brokers effectively ruling the community.[54] The "interlocking, duplication and overlapping of leadership roles tend to channel community policy into relatively few hands, and it results, at the level of the personalities of the leaders, in some degree of community coordination."[55] The elitist model mirrors closely the "important local individuals" who so interested the rural sociologists. A competing "pluralist" model argues that there are multiple centres of community power and that local history, socio-economic conditions, and value patterns will influence the local form and organization of that power within the community. The pluralist argument suggests that these multiple centres are not completely independent but are limited to varying degrees by one another. However, "a pluralist structure of leadership is not in itself adequate evidence that the political system is serving the interests of the many."[56]

Differences in which model of community power the researcher adopts does not appear to have a significant impact upon the method of study employed. The fundamental task is to reconstruct the debates and their outcomes to identify successful initiation of or opposition to proposals. Using a range of techniques – interviews, observation, questionnaires, and analyses of public records – researchers seek to "penetrate behind official positions, reputations, or participation ... to weigh and compare the power of different individuals or groups."[57] My own research recognizes from the outset that the reconstruction of public debates over local land-use development issues is a difficult and problematic undertaking. Given this recognition, the methodology is multi-layered and involves the incorporation of a range of sources of information. These include newspaper reports and published letters to the editor, interviews with people who were active participants in the debates as well as those who were observers, and review of local government documentation of these debates.

Politics of Turf

Interest in questions of community power led, during the 1980s, to research that drew upon alternative theoretical frameworks. The third body of community-conflict literature informing this study of contention within the rural-recreational countryside emerged from what has become known as the "politics of turf" critique. Three issues with respect to this critique are important to this study. The first concerns the identification of four constituent elements of local debate: the role of externalities, the fact that land is a fixed commodity, the role of local government, and the participation of interest groups. While it must be recognized that these elements will most often interact with one another, their separate delineation assists in distinguishing particular arguments within public debates. Second, the conflict situations envisaged by politics-of-turf researchers are generally single-event, limited-duration debates. Residential change through cottage conversion in the rural-recreational countryside is, however, part of an ongoing process of community change and contention, and negotiation over that change. Finally, while much of the research on the politics of turf developed as a class-based analysis, the identification of conflict at the local level has garnered a wider currency among researchers interested in using both local historical precedents and social relations to evaluate current debates.

Originally developed as part of the radical critique of urban geography through the 1970s and 1980s, the focus of research on the politics of turf is clearly with neighbourhood-level conflict over the siting of facilities and services.[58] However, many of the issues central to understanding these locational conflicts have gained wider currency in the analysis of access to local politics[59] or of disputes between residential groups in the rural community.[60]

For Cox the key element to the emergence of a politics of turf is that residents come to understand their interest in land as something more than a simple interest in an environment for living. This "something more" is an understanding of property as a commodity, such that conflict is conceptualized as a mobilization by local residents to protect their use rights from disturbance by capital seeking to extract additional profit. This research strongly suggests that socio-economic status and home-ownership are correlated with local activism. The research objective, then, "is to shed light on the forces – expressed at an individual level – which engender a politics of turf."[61]

Tracing an interest in the response of local residents to neighbourhood change from Tiebout and Orbell and Uno,[62] Cox translates their individual-choice analysis into a fundamentally class-based framework. When development pressures are experienced at the neighbourhood level, Orbell and Uno suggest, residents have three broad alternatives. The first is "resignation," where no action is taken; the second is to leave the neighbourhood; and the third is to stay and voice opposition in an attempt to make challenges. In the study of local conflict, research interest will focus on those residents who stay and engage in active debate. The reason for this local mobilization, and thus its explanation, will rest in the conscious awareness of these residents of the commodification of their neighbourhood.

The evaluation of success for area residents in local conflicts is an important issue. Success needs to be evaluated in terms of both expected and relative returns to local residents, depending on their starting position in the decision-making hierarchy. Success may range from defeat of a contentious proposal to a recognition by the decision-making body that the resident group represents a constituency and has a valid voice in the debate. In the rural-recreational countryside, where cottagers' associations have traditionally not participated in local government, the ultimate bargaining tool appears to be the threat to participate in local elections, which can pose a fundamental challenge to the local government power structure.

Evaluation of the debates themselves, however, is problematic. Many community-conflict researchers have warned of the difficulty of distinguishing the overt language of the debate from the underlying issues of contention. Cox warns that in debates over turf, statements about "property values" often mask "racial" or other concerns for social exclusivity. The use of property value as a surrogate for social exclusivity reflects in part the fact that legislation governing land-use planning at the level of local government is phrased in such terms. Sifting out underlying issues requires clear identification of the threat to the residential community – that is, identification of the perceived change. Some of the motivations identified resemble the list of threats suggested by Sanderson and Polson, including an invasion of new resident groups, local power struggles between individuals, and a fear of a loss of control/participation in local decision-making.

The range of elements that can structure or initiate urban politics of turf have been summarized by Cox and Johnston under four general themes. The first focuses upon external effects, where local activism is directed at reducing negative and accruing positive externalities. For local homeowners a "net balance of positive externalities ... [will generate] an increase in property values."[63] A second set of elements involves the appropriation of rent from property. Since land is a fixed commodity, its value can be greatly affected by the spillover costs/benefits of roads, services, or noxious uses. As a result, landowners are likely to pay close attention to the land-use planning activities of their local governments. A third set of elements involves specific conflicts around these local government activities. In this case, it is government institutions themselves that are the focus of contention. Jurisdictional fragmentation is an important issue here, as a lack of local government co-ordination in response to issues affecting a broad area may result in calls for a more appropriate spatial organization of decision-making. In the Rideau Lakes area, co-ordination of watershed policy suffers under the current structure of local government, while the lake-based cottagers' associations appear to provide a more coherent jurisdictional focus. Cox and Johnston identify the fourth set of structural elements in local debates according to the participation of interest groups and the process of negotiation over mandates, constituencies, and bargaining positions. Where local residents' groups exist, they form ready and effective two-way channels for information and opinion. In many urban and suburban residential locations, however, such groups are not commonplace. This is also the case across much of the rural-recreational countryside. Where groups do not exist, they tend to form only on issue-specific bases. The energy required to form and open information channels may preclude later attempts to reconstitute the organization over a subsequent issue.

Clarke and Kirby agree with the basic politics-of-turf premise that "the uniqueness of local politics centres on conflicts over land as a commodity ... [and that] places can be viewed as contested areas, across which processes of investment and disinvestment operate."[64] However, they also develop an argument for a much broader conceptualization of debate over community change. They suggest that the "bases for local political organization [by residents] and conflict ... are not restricted to the economic dimensions ... [and go beyond 'class' factors to be as well] sensitive to splits between culturally distinctive groups over quality-of-life issues and the allocation of surplus wealth."[65]

This broader conceptualization is key to understanding local contention over residential change in the rural-recreational countryside. A central goal of this book is to identify this countryside as a socially and geographically divided landscape. Part of this argument will rest on an economic differentiation based upon ability to afford cottage property, while an equally important part is the socially constructed image of a cottage community as something apart from the rural milieu. Both the economic and social structures are necessary in the evaluation of contention and debate over land-use planning at the local level.[66]

Cloke and Goodwin have recently offered a summation of the pressures of change in rural areas.[67] Building upon the integration of economic and social forces identified in urban community-conflict research, they argue that "the commodification of rural idylls and rural lifestyles [has generated] a new theatre of consumption ... [where] social and cultural change has not been merely the result of economic change, but has often been a precondition."[68] Citing in-migration based on "recreation, leisure and tourism," Cloke and Goodwin suggest that "this can lead to the occurrence of 'two nations' in the same rural place ... [with] a contesting of local political power ... [and] local cultural images."[69]

This discussion of three frameworks that have informed community-conflict research has identified a set of questions concerning the participation and access to decision-making of interest groups and local residents. As detailed in the chapters following, these questions have been refined here to focus upon who gains access to local decision-making. Residential landscapes may be internally divided along a range of criteria, and one fundamental division in the rural-recreational countryside is between the cottage and rural-residential areas. In this setting, a geography of community conflict must depend on understanding the changing access of residential groups to local decision-making power, and contention between groups in the competition for this access.

QUESTIONS

The results of traditional studies of community conflict argue that research on residential change at the intersection of rural and cottage landscapes must be attentive to both physical and social constructions of space. From this tradition I derive five sets of questions that explore community change and contention in the rural-recreational countryside. The first explore the foundations for a social geography of local communities. They address specific changes, such as who is arriving locally, how the local population mix is changing, and the scale of local population change through comparisons of family structure and other socio-economic characteristics. In this study, information about individual households has been derived from a questionnaire survey of Rural Residents, Converters, and Seasonal Occupants.

The second set of questions concerns the social organization and activity networks of local residents. Again soliciting household-level information, these questions explore the scope and range of residents' social networks and their level of participation in community organizations. The purpose of these first two sets of research questions is to identify the characteristics of Converters and to note their differences from the local rural population.

The third set of research questions focuses more specifically on households involved in cottage conversion. Issues such as mobility and previous residential location can be compared to models of exurbanization, while questions on the quantity and quality of housing consumed explore differences between Converters and Rural Residents across the two study areas.

The fourth set of questions focuses on the issue of community groups. The central interest is in the formation, operation, and mandate of these groups and their ongoing interactions with other local groups and governments. Particular attention is directed to whether certain groups form a community reference-point for a collection of residents, especially where such groups are able to lobby and argue on behalf of the collective on issues of community change. Layered geographically, do individuals associate and identify more with their neighbours, those within a small area, or those within a broader region? Also, how does the existence of political jurisdictions at the local level affect an individual's sense of community? What is the effect of jurisdictional fragmentation? Are there several levels of community with which people identify strongly?

The final set of questions focuses on conditions in which community change becomes contentious. Public debates involving individuals and groups are incorporated into an evaluation of contention over cottage-conversion activity within the rural-recreational countryside. Such an evaluation rests on arguments developed earlier respecting numbers and characteristics of residents and their organization into community groups within the geographic and institutional boundaries imposed on the landscape. If the rural-recreational countryside is a geographically and socially divided landscape, then we might expect that such a division would be reflected in differing positions regarding the future of the local area. In such debates the questions of who has access to the decision-making process, and whether their access changes as a result of participation in the debates, also become important issues.

METHODOLOGY AND DATA

In this book I have adopted a comparative approach to the study of residential change. Three methodological issues inherent in a comparative approach are central to the research plan. The first concerns the relative merits and difficulties of a comparative design. The second concerns the localities selected for comparison, including the practical and theoretical issues involved with that selection. Finally, the focus on residential change arising from the interaction of identifiable population groups within the rural-recreational countryside raises questions about group definitions and the assignment of households to these groups.

Comparative Research

A comparative research design is used to avoid locality-bounded explanations. Generally, the aim of comparative research is to build a foundation for generalization that extends beyond conditions found in particular places at particular times. Three benefits of a comparative research design have been suggested.[70] The first concerns a greater attention to the delineation of the specific from the general. The second concerns the inherent requirement to make plain the criteria for selection of comparable cases in terms of critical similarities and differences. Finally, this attention to specificity of criteria extends to the conduct of the research itself, with the central issues being directly connected with, and deriving from, the research questions asked. While a comparative research design has the drawback of limiting the amount of time available for a detailed examination of each case, it provides a wider base of experience from which to interpret and evaluate specific research findings.

Debate on comparative research design is well developed within the discipline of history. Bloch's early arguments suggested comparative research as a systematic and explicit way of explaining phenomena by showing their interrelations.[71] Sewell expanded upon Bloch's ideas during the 1960s. He suggested that "placing a study in a comparative framework not only invalidates purely local explanations for what are in fact general phenomena, but also separates out those phenomena which are genuine peculiarities of the locality, phenomena which, of course, will have to be explained by local conditions."[72] Comparative research is valuable as "a tool for dealing with problems of explanation" by allowing for a refinement of explanation not available in a single historical or geographic setting.[73] While Bloch recognizes that comparative research does not consist of rigid or pre-arranged sets of procedures, he suggests two fundamental pre-conditions for the application of a comparative design: "a certain similarity or analogy between observed phenomena ... and a certain dissimilarity between the environments in which they occur."[74] An important caution is that the juxtaposition of two parallel analyses is not adequate without binding them together to address some explanatory problem.

As the underlying tenets of comparative research require, this book works to separate clearly the local from the general. The general process under examination, residential change through cottage conversion, is only one element of local community change. To explore the locality-specific impacts of conversion, a range of questions needs to be asked. What is the level of conversion activity in each study area, and how does this compare to local population growth? How is the conversion actually carried out, and who is doing it in each study area? In the debate on local community change, what organizations represent different local interests? How well are cottagers and converter households integrated into community groups? These questions form the basis for starting to separate out the local impacts of general processes from local peculiarities.

A second benefit of a comparative-research design is the attention focused on the selection of case-study localities. The inherent requirement to make plain critical similarities and differences requires clear specification of the units of analysis under investigation. The selection of units, geographical, social, or political, must be suited to the questions asked. In this book the two study areas selected for comparison are relatively small regions set within similar social, cultural, and temporal contexts. In each case there is an immediate juxtaposition of rural landholdings with cottaging properties, some of which are being converted into permanent homes.

A third benefit of comparative research is the requirement to specify more clearly those issues central to the comparison. These include the appropriateness of categories and classifications, the usefulness of information from divergent sources, and the meanings attached to objects and processes within different cultures and societies. There is a need to be alert to differences that require explanation or interpretation. Again, small study areas within generally similar sociocultural milieux are more suited to avoiding the potentially enormous pitfalls of unfamiliarity and definitional uncertainty. In this book attention to land development requires attention to the regulation of that development by local governments; as well, the attention to residential groups requires attention to the organization of social groups within localities.

Localities

Arguments for the evaluation of "local" as involving change both through time and in place have a long tradition in geographic thought. Vidal de la Blache's regional "genres de vie" and Sauer's "areally localized cultures" represent broad ecological formulations of this interest, while Hartshorne's "chorology" detailed a more narrowly defined interest in regional differentiation.[75] More recently, research recognizing the operation of general processes in particular places re-emerged in geography with the waning of the "quantitative revolution." Arguing from what has become the foundation for both the "new regional geography" and the "new industrial geography," Massey writes, "'General processes' never work themselves out in pure form. There are always specific circumstances, a particular history, a particular place or location. What is at issue ... is the articulation of the general and the local."[76] The placement of geographic context at the very centre of the research design recognizes that the local region not only establishes the spatial context for experiencing pressures of change but is also modified by the outcomes of these pressures.[77]

Regions of differing social, economic, cultural, institutional, and physical characteristics can be expected to experience, respond to, and be modified by broad pressures of change in differing ways. Hodge and Qadeer recognize the potential for local outcomes to general processes, arguing that while small towns and rural areas are "linked to extensive networks of production, distribution, and socialization," local historical, cultural, and social circumstances allow communities to interpret and react to these broad forces in unique ways.[78] The connection between the specific (local) and the general (theory) is, however, not straightforward nor unproblematic.

A recent industrial-restructuring case-study has attempted a sophisticated rendering of the connection between local outcomes and general explanations. Barnes and Hayter examine community response to industrial restructuring in the small lumber-mill town of Chemainus in British Columbia. Their introductory theoretical framework is provided by the restructuring and flexible-accumulation thesis that has been important to debates in industrial geography. However, in their interpretation of the local response to economic trauma the authors employ additional notions of periphery and resource-industry towns originally developed by Innis to connect these local outcomes back to a general explanatory framework.

The locally exerted pressures of industrial restructuring involved the closure of a large sawmill (the town's major employer) and its replacement two years later by a new and largely automated mill. The community's response, which was to develop a thriving tourist industry, Barnes and Hayter interpret as a local "flexible restructuring" of civic interests within the opportunities of a peripheral resource-town. In "tempering Marx by Innis [the authors] thus seek to contribute to a specifically Canadian political economy."[79] In part they illustrate the assertion that peculiarity of place needs to be explained through local conditions. As well, they demonstrate a willingness to reconnect local outcomes to general frameworks of explanation. If their case-study is lacking in any way, the fault lies in not giving enough attention to local geography. While the community of Chemainus is small, it is located in the most densely populated region of British Columbia. The choice of a tourism-industry alternative is not surprising given Chemainus's location on the Victoria-Nanaimo highway, one of the most heavily travelled tourist corridors in the province.

Following Barnes and Hayter, this book examines one general process of residential change within the rural-recreational countryside – cottage conversion. Attention to the specificity of cottage-property ownership in this context is extended through incorporation of the folklore and social symbolism that is a very powerful part of cottaging activity. Together, cottage conversion and the folklore of cottaging form the basis for interpreting this particular form of local residential change. This framework is also important in explaining contention and debate over residential change in the rural-recreational countryside, a setting in which cottage-property ownership and the associated folklore ground a locally constructed recognition that this is a geographically and socially divided landscape.

Unfortunately, there is no formula, no calculus that can guarantee the translation of case-study analysis into more general theoretical synthesis. Rather, such translation is an interpretive exercise by the researcher – interpretive within the bounds of the criteria and definitions set for the research. The challenge is to determine if the peculiarities of place are simple variations on more general expectations or direct challenges to them. This disentangling of local context and general processes is critical to the examination of community change in the rural-recreational countryside because of inherent pressures in privileging either the urban or rural perspective. Attention to historical and regional context is therefore regarded as central to a research design interested in the processes of change, and changes in these processes, that produce the present landscapes.

Residential Groups

To determine if cottage conversion is a contested issue within the rural-recreational countryside, this study focuses on two groups of local residents, Rural Residents and Converters. This distinction between local residents based on use and location is a significant departure from the standard farm/non-farm treatment of rural populations used in much of the rural-studies literature.[80] *Rural Residents* are defined simply as the local population not living within the cottaging areas of either study area. Their residential landscape consists of permanent-use housing stock occupied by year-round residents.

Converters are defined as those within the cottaging areas who have converted a seasonal-use property into their permanent home. Their residential landscape is tightly restricted to the set of small-lot cottage properties located along the lakefront. There is a mix of both permanently and seasonally occupied properties such that the area's population, and the individual Converter's neighbours, vary through the year. The housing stock, which began as cottages, now contains dwellings that range widely in levels of investment and suitability for year-round occupancy. Local commitment by property owners may also vary widely depending on patterns of use and investment. Converters form the critical group for examining change by allowing a focus upon who is arriving in the area and their local participation and patterns of activity. It is at this intersection of rural and cottage residential landscapes that distinct communities are constructed within the wider community.

A third residential group, *Seasonal Occupants*, is included in part of the analysis to introduce a sense of latent conversion pressures into the discussions. Seasonal Occupants also own property within the small-lot cottaging areas along the lakefront; however, they are distinguished by the seasonal or periodic pattern of occupancy and by the maintenance of a permanent residence elsewhere.

Questionnaire

A questionnaire survey of local residents is the principal source of household-level data used in the analysis.[81] In each study area, the small-lot cottage-area properties could easily be distinguished from surrounding agricultural and rural-residential properties. As well, the use of these cottaging properties in terms of seasonal or permanent occupancy could also be readily ascertained using property-assessment records. The questionnaire pursues information on four topics: basic socio-economic and demographic characteristics of the household, including individual, family, and employment-status questions; recent residential histories, including property descriptions, location and timing of last residential move, and strategies for home improvement; opinions on local service-provision needs and the responsiveness of local government in meeting those needs; and community participation, including membership in local interest or volunteer groups, and household-activity patterns such as shopping for daily and specialized goods, recreation, and basic household services.

The questionnaire sample of Converters included all households identified within the cottaging areas that had actively converted a seasonal-use property into their permanent home during the period from 1980–81 to 1990–91. The Seasonal Occupant sample was randomly drawn from the remaining subset of cottage properties where use continued to be seasonal. The Rural Resident sample was randomly drawn from the set of remaining residential properties not located within the cottaging areas. To enable direct comparison

Table 10
Summary of Sample Sizes and Response Rates, Rideau Lakes and Cultus Lake Study Areas

Study areas	Sample size	Number of replies	Response rate %
RIDEAU LAKES			
Converters	295	154	52
Seasonal Occupants	295	112	38
Permanent Residents	294	124	42
Total	884	390	44
CULTUS LAKE			
Converters	120	45	38
Seasonal Occupants	120	40	33
Permanent Residents	104	39	38
Total	344	124	36
Combined total	1,228	514	42

Source: Resident Survey, 1991.

between groups, the size of the Rural Resident and Seasonal Occupant samples was directly determined by the number of Converter households identified. Sample sizes and response rates are listed in Table 10, and may be an illustration of the argument posited by Sosdian and Sharp that response/non-response to mail surveys may reflect levels of interest or identification by respondents with the research question.[82] There is no information to suggest that non-responses are systematically organized, and the response rates do compare favourably to those summarized in Feitelson's review of survey research methods.[83]

Interviews

Harper argues for incorporating humanist methods into the study of rural social change.[84] While this research does not explore Harper's "subjective place centredness," it does recognize the need for local interpretation of change within a community. Schoenberger agrees with this need for interpretive information, stating that the potential value of interview-based research derives from the "richness of detail and historical complexity that ... allows one to reconstruct a coherent representation of how and why particular phenomenon came to be."[85] In this book interview information is important in the interpretation of questionnaire results and in the reconstruction of land-use planning debates.

Interviews with local community leaders in both study areas were conducted. Leaders were defined as those persons now or previously active in local government, resident associations, or similar local groups. In some cases these people were politicians, in others, simply volunteers with a local service club. They were identified through local governments, newspapers, and service organizations; often a key-informant strategy came into play, with interviewees suggesting other individuals better suited to provide views or opinions on particular aspects of the research. Interviews consisted of a short series of open-ended questions about local conversion pressures and community change. All were arranged for times and places convenient for respondents; in many cases this was their own home, and the hospitality offered was universally gracious. To protect anonymity, not all members of any individual group were interviewed, and no comments or direct quotations that can be identified with particular individuals are included.

A recent debate within economic geography concerning open-ended interviews as a research strategy has brought a number of important issues to the fore. Both Schoenberger and McDowell agree that the dynamic relationship between the interviewer and the subject is of critical importance.[86] Considerable discussion centres on what McDowell describes as "power relations" and the "exercise of control." Schoenberger warns that the interviewer is in a position of authority and must be wary in setting both the agenda and the questions themselves so as not to guide the respondent to answers the interviewer wants to hear. In the corporate-interview setting that informs their debate, McDowell questions the ability of the interviewer to establish any real control, suggesting that "the interviewer is more often in the position of a supplicant, requesting time and expertise from the powerful."[87] When the researcher imposes upon the time and hospitality of local residents, a certain level of respect and consideration must be maintained. Further, it is commonly recognized that in open-ended interviews some respondents may misunderstand questions and provide answers or opinions on a topic very different from that intended by the researcher. Rather than following, as suggested in the conventional literature, a strategy of pressing until all areas of ambiguity are clarified, the researcher must exercise judgment.[88] In interviews with rural residents, perhaps older and perhaps female, it is not difficult to create scenarios where such pressing of detail begins to constitute abuse. At the same time, it became clear during the course of this research that tangents introduced by respondents offered new windows on the experience of local life or community change not anticipated by the researcher.

It became plain in many of the interviews that respondents had a specific agenda to communicate. As part of this agenda, respondents usually placed themselves and/or their organization in a favourable light compared to perceived opposing organizations. Liberal commentary on these opposing individuals or groups was often offered, especially by members of local organizations that had been subject to public criticism in the recent past. The degree to which these agendas affected the individual interviews is a matter of interpretation, but in some cases they became a dominating theme. The incorporation of the agendas of particular groups represented not only a dialogue constructed at a particular time with the interviewer but also formed part of an ongoing and evolving dialogue and debate within the community at large. These interviews were valuable, then, not so much as individual sets of data but rather as part of the collection of local interpretations available for each study area. Factual information obtained through such interviews has some checks and balances. Dates of events, names of participants, legislative requirements, and similar items of information can all be cross-referenced in the public record. The opinions, perceptions, and views gleaned, however, have fewer checks and balances. It is only when a number of interviews are pieced together that the range of individual comments and interpretations can be balanced and interpreted to provide, perhaps, a clearer sense of positions, actions, and relationships. The representations constructed from the interviews may still fail to identify the "reality," but then such reality may never be completely static or knowable.

Local Government Records

Local government records form the third principal source of information used in the analysis. Two sets of records, lists of building permits issued and the public record of recent land-use planning debates, are central to the research. While building-permit data are available in generally comparable form for both the Rideau Lakes and Cultus Lake areas, information on land-use planning debates is less uniformly available.

Hamilton, Capozza, and Helsley recognize that building permits are an imperfect reflection of housing construction, renovation, and reinvestment activity.[89] Halseth adds that building permits are also an imperfect reflection of cottage-conversion activity.[90] Therefore, building-permit data are used here in two ways, first as an indication

Table 11
Issued Building-Permit Data Availability

Location	Data years[1]
CULTUS LAKE	
RDFC[2]	1980–1990
CLPB[3]	1985–1990
RIDEAU LAKES	
Township of South Elmsley	1980–90
Township of North Elmsley	1987–90
Township of Bastard and South Burgess	1977–90
Township of North Burgess	1980–90
Township of South Crosby	1977–90
Township of North Crosby	1985–90

[1] Complete years.
[2] Regional District of Fraser-Cheam.
[3] Cultus Lake Park Board.

of levels of activity between and within the study areas, and second as a marker of relative levels of conversion activity where the methodology allows.

The most serious challenge presented by building-permit data for the rural-recreational countryside is the degree of undercounting – that is, the amount of construction, renovation, and reinvestment that occurs without formal permit.[91] Two possible explanations have been suggested for undercounting. The first is a general ignorance of the requirement for building permits. This may especially be the case at Cultus Lake or along the Rideau Lakes, as both permanent settlement and cottaging are of long standing, while local government involvement in building permits and inspections had existed for only five to fifteen years. A second factor is the conscious decision not to obtain a building permit where, under existing land-use regulations, a rejected application would only serve to notify the local government of a possible by-law infraction. Restrictive land-use regulations on the conversion of summer homes to permanent residences along sections of the Rideau Lakes is just such an impediment.

Table 11 lists the availability of building-permit data by study area and issuing jurisdiction. Given the problem of underreporting, it seems reasonable to conclude that where such services are new, the impact on the data may be important. Any interpretation of change over time must recognize that such change will also reflect a growing awareness of permit requirements.

The public record of debates on land-use planning matters from the second set of local government records consulted. Such debates can include questions over immediate land-use designations, such as those raised during rezoning hearings, or can arise over major reviews or revisions of the existing long-term "community plan."[92] Three issues concerning the public record of local planning and development debates are important. The first is the requirement to consult the public and, in doing so, to provide a formal forum for debate. Municipal jurisdictions in both the Rideau Lakes and Cultus Lake study areas are required to consult the public over land-use planning matters. The form of consultation undertaken, however, is subject to wide interpretation. Perhaps no greater contrast in the interpretation of public consultation can be illustrated than that which occurs in the Cultus Lake study area. At Cultus Lake Park, perhaps as a result of its vague legislative mandate and its legacy of Park Board control, not only are public-hearing reports not maintained but the Park Board feels no obligation to discuss planning or development issues with the leaseholder population. In contrast, the RDFC is required under provisions of the Municipal Act to take all zoning and community-plan by-laws to public hearing as part of the approval procedure.[93] The RDFC has extended this requirement through a policy of extensive consultation at public information meetings on many development issues and community-plan initiatives. The result is a wealth of recorded minutes from these public hearings and information meetings.

Secondly, the availability of public-debate records varies widely across jurisdictions. The RDFC maintains public-hearing records, and following their receipt by the Regional Board they become part of the public record. Most jurisdictions in the Rideau Lakes area do not, however, maintain any form of public-hearing records beyond a note identifying date, time, place, issue, and names of attending council members. In this situation the public debate must be reconstructed from local newspaper accounts and interviews with individuals in attendance.

A third methodological issue is that public-hearing reports must be evaluated cautiously as representations of publicly expressed views. A first concern is with the authorship of the minutes and the need to be wary of biases introduced, consciously or unconsciously, by writers whose agendas are potentially different from those who spoke. This issue is more easily resolved with the RDFC minutes because of the district's policy of keeping verbatim transcripts of spoken arguments and attaching all written statements in the form in which they were originally submitted. A second concern is with the interpretation of comments divorced from the context in which they were made. In this case the researcher is reviewing material at arm's length. It is important to recognize that people bring their histories into these meetings, histories that can extend back many years or may be strongly influenced by striking recent events. Attention must not only be paid to local-area history but also to the individuals, especially those speaking on behalf of interest groups. In this sense, previous experience, stated views, and personal disputes all must be considered in the interpretation. The possibility that a more reserved rural audience may leave the public-hearing floor to the more outspoken residents creates an interpretive problem for researchers, planners, and elected officials alike. This represents one of the central issues identified in the literature on community conflict and is more problematic in the Rideau Lakes area, where newspaper reports and interviews used to recapture the public debate are already one step removed from the meeting context.

In summary, this study adopts a comparative research strategy to examine issues of community change provoked by cottage-conversion activity in the rural-recreational countryside. Such a research design demands that attention be given to separation of the local from the general in evaluating outcomes of particular processes of change in particular places. A comparative strategy also demands that attention be given to the selection of study areas and to the choice of criteria and data to be used in support of the research. A questionnaire survey of residents within both cottaging and rural-residential areas is used to obtain household-level information on local demographics and to probe impressions of cottage conversion and local residential change. Interviews with selected community leaders are used to develop further the understanding of local social and institutional relations. Finally, recent land-use planning debates involving new lakeside developments or regulations are examined. These debates form the context in which contention and conflict over local residential change can be evaluated.

PART TWO

Communities and Change

4 Rideau Lakes and Cultus Lake Study Areas

This chapter sketches the local geographic and historical context in which community change in the rural-recreational countryside can be interpreted. It begins by reviewing the historical development of the Rideau Lakes and Cultus Lake study areas. With particular attention to the cottaging areas where conversion pressures are experienced, historical patterns of local development are reviewed to provide one setting against which recent patterns of residential change can be evaluated. A second discussion provides an overview of local and regional population changes using recent census data. Finally, the chapter closes with an argument for understanding the amenity values of each study area as regionally important recreational assets. These are important issues, as geographic and historic factors that make one area similar to or unique among other rural-recreational areas establish limits on the extent to which generalizations may be made beyond the case-study. In other words, place is important; if we are interested in community change, we must be aware of the local context within which this change is occurring.

RIDEAU LAKES

The Ontario study area comprises six rural townships located along the Rideau Lakes in the central portion of the Rideau Canal Heritage Waterway. These townships of North Elmsley, South Elmsley, North Burgess, Bastard and South Burgess, North Crosby, and South Crosby

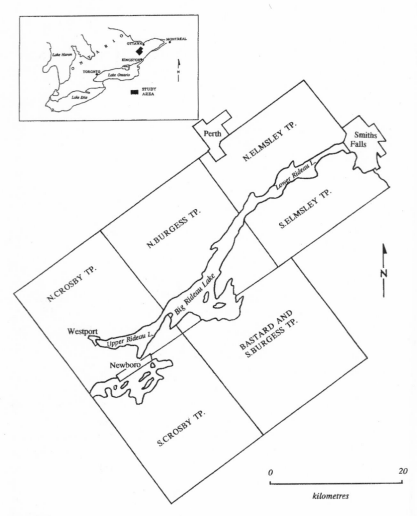

Figure 6
Rideau Lakes study area.

cover approximately 1,010 km² (390 mi²) of land in Lanark and Leeds
& Grenville counties.

The Rideau Lakes region was largely uninhabited by white settlers
prior to the War of 1812. This changed dramatically following the
British military engineers' construction of the Rideau Canal and the
adoption of a policy to settle British immigrants and discharged soldiers along the canal's route for security reasons.[1] Never used for the

military purposes for which it was intended, the canal was from its opening through to the 1920s primarily a commercial shipping route. Logging and milling activity along the waterway generated considerable traffic in the form of barges towing rafts of timber to Ottawa or Kingston. During this initial period of settlement many newly arrived farmers contributed their winter labour and their land-clearing activities to the logging industry. As settlers found the soils and climate of the Canadian Shield could support only marginal agricultural activity, the land was increasingly logged and then often abandoned.

The decline of logging in the region through the 1930s coincided with an increase in tourist and recreational use. In their study of canal lock-station records, Osborne and Swainson document this shift by reporting that by 1934, ten thousand pleasure-boats made use of the canal, outnumbering commercial boats five to one.[2] Limited tourist and recreational activities were, however, available along the canal almost from its opening. There were resort hotels like the Opinicon at Chaffeys Lock and the Kenney at Jones Falls, which catered to an elite who could afford the time and expense of hunting and fishing in this newly accessible wilderness.[3] Increased accessibility over time, first by ferryboat service, then for a brief time passenger rail service, and more recently by a quality road network, has opened the Rideau Lakes to a wider public.

Cottaging was well established along the Rideau Lakes prior to the 1880s. Lock stations such as Jones Falls Locks, Davis Lock, and Chaffeys Lock and narrows such as Seeleys Bay, Newboro, and Rideau Ferry were initial points of cottage development. Kennedy and Brown describe cottaging during these early years as a way for upper-class families to spend their summers in the countryside while the husband or father would travel to Ottawa or Kingston during the business week.[4]

Recreation has grown to become a very important component of the regional economy. Cottaging has become the dominant land use along the lakes and waterways.[5] Increasing intensification of lakefront development is noted in South Elmsley, while across the region most cottage development is clustered along the south shore of the Rideau Lakes and the lock stations through South Crosby. Accessibility to the water is the key attractive feature of these cottaging properties, and this appears to have been the principal reason behind this clustering. The historic development of roadways into the area is also important, as Highway 15 along the southern shore provides high-quality year-round access, while along the northern shore, road access remains more limited.

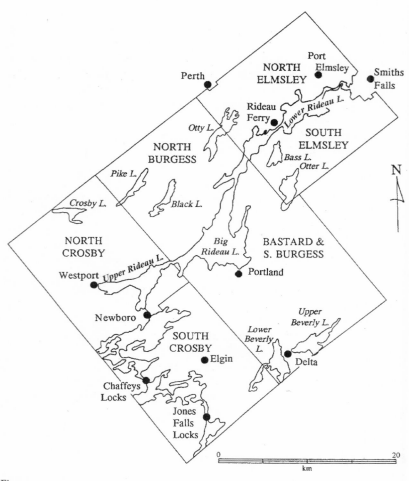

Figure 7
Rideau Lakes place names.

Patterns of recent development are associated with proximity to either the town of Perth or the town of Smiths Falls. It is clear that much of the recent growth in North Elmsley and South Elmsley townships is the result of residential-development spillover from Perth and Smiths Falls. This growth pressure includes the conversion of some cottage properties into year-round homes.

Unlike at Cultus Lake, where a small number of distinct localities can be identified, the settlement pattern through the Rideau Lakes area is generally composed of three distinct elements. The first is a scattered set of small communities and hamlets, usually located at a principal crossroad or historic transshipment or milling point, and characteristically containing one to four commercial businesses and between 10 to 40 residences. Examples would be places such as Rideau Ferry, Lombardy, Portland, Elgin, and Phillipsville, settlements that also serve as local reference-points for the rural population. The second settlement element is composed of individual residences dispersed along the local road network. Many of these are farms associated with dairying or other more marginal agricultural activities. The remainder are rural residences associated with local employment, local retirees, and more recently, exurban settlement or hobby farming. The third settlement element is the cottage-property areas. Comprising cottages, permanent residences, and a few recreation-focused commercial businesses, they form a distinctive linear pattern along the margins of the lakes and waterways. In most cases the depth of development does not exceed a single row of properties. There is also an element of dispersion, as the pattern is an irregularly broken line rather than a continuous string of individual properties. This is not unlike the form of cottage development Bielckus documented along the Danish coast, a form that can seriously inhibit public access to waterfront.[6] These three local settlement elements can readily be seen across South Elmsley Township.

Two tiers of linkages operate within the Rideau Lakes area. The first involves internal interactions among the local small communities, including Rideau Ferry, Delta, Phillipsville, Seeleys Bay, Portland, the village of Westport, the town of Smiths Falls, and the town of Perth. These provide generally low-order commercial activities, support facilities for agricultural activities, as well as employment opportunities for a portion of the local population. As is fairly typical of such rural landscapes, a significant proportion of both local employment and local shopping occurs within this network of small communities.[7]

The Rideau Lakes region is also within an hour's driving time of the Kingston and Ottawa metropolitan areas. At this distance, afternoon and weekend recreation opportunities for urban residents are easily within reach.[8] In addition, parts of the study area fall within commuting range of Kingston or Ottawa, providing the possibility for some local residents to commute to jobs in these urban centres. In a larger framework, the study area is within three to four hours' driving time of Toronto and Montreal.

The historic pattern of recreational land use and cottage development mirrors that of other central Canadian resort areas such as the

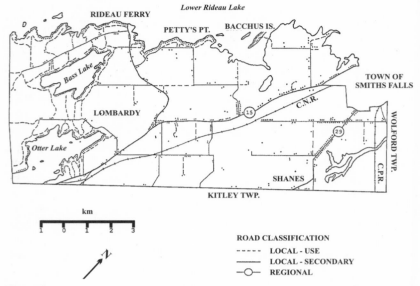

Figure 8
Settlement pattern, South Elmsley Township.

Muskoka Lakes and the Trent-Severn Heritage Canal. Wall describes a pattern of cottage development in the Muskoka Lakes region that compares to the Rideau Lakes in terms of the time-period of initial cottaging, intensification of use as access improved, and development of a single row of cottages along the waterfront.[9] Triantis describes the economic importance of cottaging in the Muskoka Lakes area and the addition of economic functions in the local communities to serve seasonal customers.[10] In as much as the development history of cottaging areas is similar, the precedents to current pressures may allow some generalization.

Lakeshore-development pressures along the Rideau Lakes have been recognized by local, provincial, and federal governments and authorities. In 1982 the Canada-Ontario Rideau Trent Severn (CORTS) agreement was jointly signed by the federal government and the Province of Ontario.[11] This policy document was to serve as a co-ordinating mechanism for federal and provincial action and to provide a guide to assist local governments in their land-use planning and decision-making. Individual policy directions within CORTS include heritage preservation and tourism promotion, and recognition of the national historic significance and recreational amenity values of the canals. Land-use policy directives focus squarely upon environmental-risk management by advocating local planning in an "environmental context." Policy suggestions include development restrictions on flood-plain areas and open-space requirements in environmentally sensitive areas.

Cottage-development and service-provision issues are discussed under the Pollution Abatement and Water Management sections of CORTS. Foreshadowing recent local debates over water quality and septic-tank pollution, CORTS identified a serious pollution concern along parts of the Rideau Canal during the summer months. Thin soils and the presence of rock near or at the surface create problems for private septic-tank systems. High construction costs and a dispersed user group impede the provision of community sewer systems. As the length of stay of occupants at cottage properties increases, so too will the potential for increased pollution of the lakes. A central land-use and development planning issue identified in CORTS is the need to differentiate seasonal use from permanently occupied waterfront properties. In this respect CORTS implicitly recognizes the importance of cottage conversion as a pressure on the lakeshore environment.

The CORTS agreement presents a dilemma to local governments. As a federal-provincial agreement, the policies are presented only as guides for local governments. Yet all municipal zoning and community-plan by-laws require provincial approval before they come into effect. By-laws that do not conform to CORTS policies are not likely to receive approval from the provincial ministries under the existing review procedures, which suggests that the province in fact has a fairly strong hand in enforcing CORTS. This said, however, the CORTS agreement has not established any mechanisms for review or continued consultation at the senior government level, nor for formal liaison with the local governments that are supposed to implement the suggested policies. Thus, while CORTS remains an important document, its effectiveness as a planning tool has been severely undermined.

After a lengthy study and review period, in 1992 the Rideau Valley Conservation Authority (RVCA) published its new *Rideau Valley Conservation Strategy.*[12] This report was developed from in-house and public consultation processes as well as the input received from commissioned background papers, including the *Rideau Lakes Basin Carrying Capacities and Proposed Shoreland Development Policies.*[13] Concurrently, Parks Canada has been involved in updating its Rideau Canal Management Plan.[14] The details of these planning exercises as an extension of the CORTS initiative are reviewed in chapter 9 in the context of debate over community change and cottage development along the Rideau Lakes.

The settlement pattern along the Rideau Lakes creates unique problems for local government in its provision of basic residential services. First is the general issue of the additional costs imposed by distance in servicing a rural landscape of dispersed customers.[15] Second, many of the private access routes to cottage properties have not been constructed to public roadway standards and as such pose access difficulties, especially in winter, for service equipment. Should ownership of these private routes be transferred to the public sector, then the burden of improvement and maintenance costs would be borne by all taxpayers to the advantage of specific cottage owners. For this reason the Official Plan for the Township of South Elmsley recommends that private roads remain privately owned wherever possible, a policy expressed in most other local community plans as well.[16]

The Ontario provincial government has recognized the increasing pressure for expanded lakefront residential development, and the potential costs this type of development generates for local governments. In 1978 the Ontario Ministry of Housing published its Discussion Paper on Seasonal Residential Conversions, which investigated the potential impacts and possible methods of managing seasonal-to-permanent conversion activity in cottage areas.[17] The report advocated the introduction of "staged servicing" residential zones, where conversion of uses would be permitted but where definitive levels of services, either existing or to be made available, would be recognized.

The ministry argued that this type of zoning would do three things. First, it would let property owners know the limits to existing property-servicing commitments on the part of local governments and would provide a mechanism for applications to increase the expected servicing level. Second, applications for rezoning would act as a formal notification that conversion activity was occurring and would allow local governments to track the location and rate of such activity. Third, the rezoning application might generally be accompanied by a processing fee. While this fee would never make up the costs generated in the municipal-services budget, it would shift at least part of the costs to the property owner rather than the local tax base as a whole.

Along the Rideau Lakes, South Elmsley was the first jurisdiction to recognize cottage conversion as a concern. Local initiatives have included adoption of revised community-plan and zoning by-laws

Table 12
Study Area Population Change

Jurisdiction	1971	1976	1981	1986	1991
Rideau Lakes study area[1]	7,875	9,010	9,895	10,764	12,168
N. Elmsley[1]	1,568	1,954	2,118	2,360	2,827
S. Elmsley[1]	1,445	1,994	2,525	2,735	3,065
N. Burgess[1]	542	608	664	812	1,021
Bastard & S. Burgess[1]	2,285	2,314	2,386	2,429	2,610
N. Crosby[1]	638	673	728	815	968
S. Crosby[1]	1,397	1,467	1,474	1,613	1,677
Cultus Lake study area[2]	na	na	1,430	1,465	na
Lindell Beach[3]	49	62	86	70	na
Cultus Lake Park[3]	554	470	481	434	na
Columbia Valley[4]	na	na	863	961	na

[1] Statistics Canada, Census of Canada, 1971, 1976, 1981, 1986, 1991 (100 per cent sample).
[2] Special tabulations, Regional District of Fraser Cheam, from Statistics Canada census data.
[3] Statistics Canada, Census of Canada, 1971, "Population, Unincorporated Settlements" (92-771, sp-1); 1976, "Population of Unincorporated Places" (92-830); 1981, "Place Name Reference List" (E-484); 1986, "Unincorporated Places" (92-105).
[4] Columbia Valley population estimate includes Parkview development area.

incorporating the ministry of housing's "staged services zones" in an attempt to control conversion activity through management of residential service levels. By 1992 at least three Rideau Lakes townships had adopted a zoning by law incorporating the staged residential service-zone alternative.[18]

Contemporary Census Overview

The pattern of population distribution within the Rideau Lakes area is closely tied to development pressures from the adjacent incorporated towns. Tables 12 and 13 describe the pattern of local population change using census data from 1971 to 1991.

South Elmsley has the largest population and highest rate of growth among the six townships. A population change from 1,445 in 1971 to 3,065 in 1991 represents an increase of 112 per cent. North Elmsley recorded a 1971 population of 1,568, which increased by 80 per cent to 2,827 by the 1991 census. Local officials suggest that much of this growth is the result of residential spillover from Perth and Smiths Falls, much of which has involved intensive cottage-conversion activity and small-lot residential subdivisions around the communities of Rideau Ferry and Port Elmsley.

Table 13
Population Growth Rates

Jurisdiction	1971–76 %	1976–81 %	1981–86 %	1986–91 %	1971–91 %	1981–91 %
Rideau Lakes study area[1]	14.4	9.8	8.8	13.1	54.5	22.9
N. Elmsley[1]	24.6	8.4	11.4	19.8	80.3	33.5
S. Elmsley[1]	37.9	26.6	8.3	12.1	112.1	21.4
N. Burgess[1]	12.2	9.2	22.3	25.7	88.4	53.8
Bastard & S. Burgess[1]	1.3	3.1	1.8	7.5	14.2	9.4
N. Crosby[1]	5.5	8.2	11.9	18.8	51.7	32.9
S. Crosby[1]	5.0	0.5	9.4	3.9	20.0	13.8
Cultus Lake study area[2]	na	na	2.4	na	na	na
Lindell Beach[3]	26.5	38.7	−18.6	na	na	na
Cultus Lake Park[3]	−15.1	2.3	−9.8	na	na	na
Canada	6.6	5.9	4.0	7.9	26.6	12.1

[1] Statistics Canada, Census of Canada, 1971, 1976, 1981, 1986, 1991 (100 per cent sample).
[2] Special tabulations, Regional District of Fraser Cheam, from Statistics Canada census data.
[3] Statistics Canada, Census of Canada, 1971, "Population, Unincorporated Settlements" (92-771, sp-1); 1976, "Population of Unincorporated Places" (92-830); 1981, "Place Name Reference List" (E-484); 1986, "Unincorporated Places" (92-105).

Population and growth rates of South and North Elmsley stand in marked contrast to changes occurring in the remaining townships. Bastard and South Burgess, which was the most populous local township in 1971, had a growth rate of only 14 per cent during the period to 1991 and now ranks as third most populous. For South Crosby, a 1991 population of 1,677 represents an increase of only 20 per cent since 1971. North Crosby and North Burgess have much smaller populations, reflecting a historical pattern of underdevelopment along the north shore of the Rideau Lakes, tied to the physical geography of the lakeshore and the pattern of early road development. Along the north shore of Upper Rideau Lake and parts of Big Rideau Lake, steep rock cliffs limit access to parts of the lakeshore. The early roads came up from the south, and the later placement of Highway 15 along the southern shore contributed further to the north shore's lag in residential and cottage-lot development.

Regional Recreational Asset

The Rideau Lakes area, as part of the Rideau Canal Heritage Waterway system, is a regionally significant recreational amenity and a

Table 14
1986 Rideau Canal Boater Survey: Geographic Origin of Users Surveyed

	Boater Origin %
Ontario	66.0
Ottawa	35.0
Eastern Ontario[1]	19.0
Southwest Ontario	5.0
Central Ontario	3.0
Toronto	4.0
Montreal	11.0
Hull/Western Quebec	2.0
USA	20.0
Other	1.0
(n = 589)	

Source: Environment Canada, Parks Service (1988), *1986 Rideau Canal Boater Survey*, prepared by Market Facts of Canada Ltd.
[1] Includes the Kingston area.

nationally significant heritage asset.[19] In 1986 a survey of boat users on the Rideau Canal was conducted for the National Parks Service. The survey sampled users along the four major divisions of the Rideau Canal: Ottawa, Rideau River, Rideau Lakes, and Cataraqui. Canal use was measured at the lock stations by the numbers of boats locking through each facility. From this survey the Parks Service estimated that more than one-third of all canal use occured within the Rideau Lakes division.

A summary of the geographic origin of surveyed boaters is shown in Table 14. Approximately 54 per cent were identified as being from Ottawa or Eastern Ontario (including Kingston). The United States and Montreal were the next most important points of origin. Table 15 lists the distribution between first-time and repeat users of Rideau Canal facilities. Approximately 61 per cent of surveyed boat users had previously been on the Rideau Canal system.

A 1987 survey of land-based users of Rideau Canal facilities presents an even clearer portrait of a regionally significant recreational asset. Most visitors to the Jones Falls lock station were from Ottawa, Kingston, or Eastern Ontario, and most were making repeat/return visits. Taken together with the boater-use survey, these results suggest a regionally significant recreational asset.

Table 15
1986 Rideau Canal Boater Survey: Repeat Users of Canal Facilities

	%
First time users	39.0
Previously used	61.0
(n = 589)	

Source: Environment Canada, Parks Service (1988), 1986 Rideau Canal Boater Survey, prepared by Market Facts of Canada Ltd., Ottawa.

Recreational accommodation along the Rideau Lakes is largely provided by the private sector. The Parks Service provides only a limited amount of overnight moorage at its Rideau Canal facilities, while Murphy's Point Provincial Park has approximately 200 campsites and about 100 day-use sites (see Table 16). The RVCA conservation areas provide about 125 day-use sites but no overnight accommodation, while Lower Beverly Lake Township Park, operated by the Bastard and South Burgess Recreation Committee, provides about 180 campsites. Available listings of privately operated accommodation in cottages, motels/inns, and campsites identify over 1,500 units. Table 16 lists just over 264 rental cottages, 200 rooms in motels or inns, and 1,000 campsites. It should be noted that many more cottages are rented out or loaned on a more informal basis. In a study of commercial recreation and tourist accommodation, Hinch estimates that between 10 and 15 per cent of visitor person-nights in Ontario are spent at privately owned cottages.[20] He argues that the use of these private cottages has a negative impact on the viability of other commercial accommodations.

CULTUS LAKE

Located in the Lower Fraser Valley, just 90 kilometres (60 miles) east of Vancouver, the Cultus Lake–Columbia Valley district contains a sharply contrasting landscape of intensively developed cottaging areas and lower-density farming and rural-residential areas. The study area is bounded on the south by the international border with the United States and on the north by the regional service centre of Chilliwack. Access to the Cultus Lake area is funnelled through a single road. Although they share the same valley, socially distinct and geographically separate residential areas have emerged. Two cottaging areas, Cultus Lake Park and Lindell Beach, are located one at each end of Cultus Lake, while an agricultural and rural-residential

Table 16
Recreational Accommodation, Rideau Lakes Study Area

Recreational facility supplier	Number of cottages	Number of rooms	Number of sites/units
PARKS SERVICE			
Overnight moorage			See n 1
PROVINCIAL PARKS			
Campsites			189
Day-use sites[2]			94
RVCA[3]			
Day-use sites[2]			125
TOWNSHIP RECREATION COMMITTEES[4]			
Campsites			180
PRIVATE OPERATORS			
Rental cottages[5]	264		
Rooms[6]		206	
Campsites			1,065

Sources: AAA-CAA (1992), Tourbook: Ontario (Heathrow, Fl.: American Automobile Association); local newspapers; Ontario Ministry of Tourism and Recreation (1990), Camping, and Accommodations.
[1] Within the study area, the Parks Service provides just over 2,550 linear feet of overnight boat moorage at its 7 lock stations/facilities along the Rideau Canal, accommodating between 60 and 120 boats.
[2] Picnic sites identified per parking spaces.
[3] Rideau Valley Conservation Authority.
[4] Lower Beverly Lake Township Park operated by the Bastard and South Burgess Recreation Committee.
[5] Cottage rental operations conducted as a licensed business; does not include cottage owners who might rent out their own cottages for part of the season, a phenomenon that is considered to be widespread.
[6] Includes rooms in bed and breakfasts, hotels, and motels.

area lies in the Columbia Valley. The degree of local distinction among these relatively close areas should not be underestimated. In fact, many residents of Columbia Valley and even Lindell Beach would object to my labelling the entire study area Cultus Lake.

Compared to the Rideau Lakes area, the distinct local communities that have developed around Cultus Lake also function with a more distinct set of external linkages. Here the localities undertake a minimum of interaction with each other, and relations are more directly structured with Chilliwack or the remainder of the Lower Mainland.

The Cultus Lake area is geographically smaller than the Rideau Lakes study area, covering approximately only 47 square kilometres

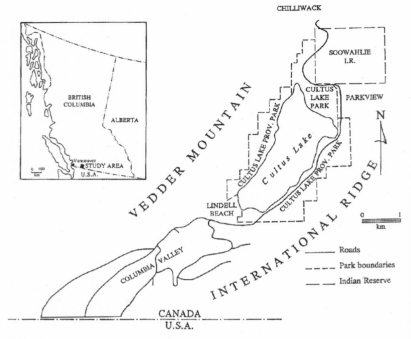

Figure 9
Cultus Lake study area.

(18 square miles). More importantly, the morphology of cottage development is very different in the two areas. Rather than the single-property-wide linear band of cottages evident along the Rideau Lakes, Cultus Lake Park and Lindell Beach contain dense clusters of cottage properties, reflecting in part the restrictions of topography upon development but also a different land-use management policy respecting the alienation of lakefront lands. This difference in settlement morphology may be useful in extending and challenging previous cottage-area research focused upon the linear pattern.

Despite its smaller size, the Cultus Lake area is a much more complex jurisdictional landscape. Immediately surrounding the residential and agricultural areas are four additional jurisdictions. The Soowahlie Indian Reserve (I.R. 14), part of the Sto:lo Nation lands, covers approximately 470 hectares adjacent to and just north of Cultus Lake Park. Cultus Lake Provincial Park, under the jurisdiction of the provincial Ministry of Environment, Lands and Parks, straddles nearly all of the lake itself. Most developed facilities, day-use, and camping sites within the park are located along the eastern shore coincident with the only road along the lakeshore. Most of the remaining lands on the mountainsides bordering the lake are Crown lands under the jurisdiction of the provincial government. On Vedder Mountain commercial forestry is the main activity, while along International Ridge the areas outside of the provincial park have been designated part of the International Ridge Recreation Area. Finally, the federal Department of National Defence (DND) has facilities and conducts military exercises on a number of properties located throughout the Cultus Lake–Columbia Valley area.

The entire Cultus Lake area falls under the jurisdiction of the Regional District of Fraser-Cheam (RDFC). Incorporated in 1967 under a provincial program to introduce a regional level of local government, the RDFC covers an area from Chilliwack eastward to the central Fraser Canyon near Boston Bar. Since no part of the Cultus Lake study area has been formally incorporated as a separate local government, it bears the appellation of "unorganized" territory for jurisdictional purposes. The unorganized territory around Cultus Lake makes up about half of the RDFC's Electoral Area "E." Since its inception the RDFC has introduced basic zoning, building, and development controls to the unorganized territory within its jurisdiction. As will be detailed in following chapters, the simple existence of many of these controls has provided the flashpoint in several of what might otherwise appear to be more narrowly focused development debates.

Cultus Lake Park

Cultus Lake Park has a unique status within the jurisdictional framework. While technically still within the RDFC's Electoral Area "E," the park has developed and continues to operate as a near-autonomous community. Its development as a recreational retreat began just before the turn of the century. Through the early 1900s the north end of Cultus Lake became an increasingly popular picnic and, later, camping area for Chilliwack-area residents.[21] Over time, improvements to the trail leading up to the lake helped to reduce the trials of the journey and increased the ties between Chilliwack and the wilderness beaches. Concern that railway logging activity around Vedder Mountain would eventually reach and destroy the beach areas prompted the neighbouring municipal governments of the City of Chilliwack and Township of Chilliwhack to negotiate the purchase of lands at the lake "for public park and recreation purposes."[22] The initial timber leases were purchased in 1924, and a joint committee of councils began operating the former Provincial Forest Service campsite the following summer. Over the next number of years most remaining timber leases near the beach areas were purchased as the park approached its current 260 hectares.

The allocation of "lease" rights to the camping lots began in 1924, when applicants submitted their names and drew lot numbers from a hat. Demand for camping lots was not heavy at the time, and the first drawing was carried out over a number of weeks.[23] In the end, most prominent local families had secured a site. With only a couple of exceptions, all available lots were allocated to Chilliwack-area residents.

Since the original drawing of lots, much has changed. Cultus Lake Park remains outside municipal boundaries. The land is, however, still owned by the District of Chilliwack (the former city and township having amalgamated in 1980). Day-to-day management of the park was delegated to the Cultus Lake Park Board (CLPB) in 1932 under the provisions of a private member's bill, the Cultus Lake Park Act, in the provincial legislature.[24]

The original camping sites have been replaced by about 450 cottages and year-round homes, some with combined land-improvement assessments well above $250,000. There is no officially registered plan of these properties; however, a site survey conducted for the Park Board in 1982 demonstrates that these lots are small. Along the waterfront they are about 7.5 metres by 20 metres (25 feet wide by 65 feet deep), while back lots average about 12 metres by 18.5 metres (40 feet wide by 60 feet deep). Crowding is a dominant visual feature, as lot coverage on many sites now exceeds 90 per cent.

Property tenure continues by individual lease agreement with the Park Board, although the original one-year leases have recently been replaced by terms of twenty-one years.[25] Most leases are no longer held by Chilliwack-area residents. Rights to lease renewal have always been regarded as matter of fact, even though some residents have pointed out that the legislation and lease documents are not so clear on the issue. None of the leases is registered in the provincial Land Title Office. Despite questions about the security of these leases, local real estate and assessment officials suggest the sale and investment patterns of Cultus Lake Park properties appear much as in a condominium or strata-title development.[26]

This legacy of development, property tenure, and current management contributes to what has been described as a fundamental chasm between the Park Board and the leaseholder population. There is undoubtedly a large block of leaseholders who are unconcerned with their relationship to the Park Board and simply pay their

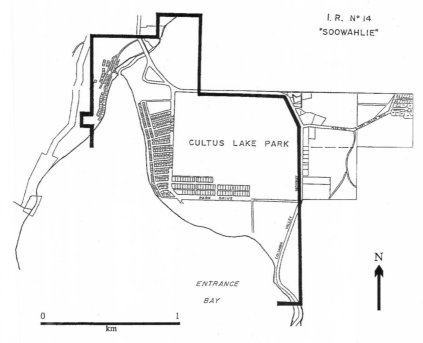

Figure 10
Cultus Lake Park.
Source: Base map from RDFC.

annual lease fees and ensure that they sign a lease renewal from time
to time. There have been, however, several difficult debates between
the leaseholders and the board. In evaluating current planning
issues, the RDFC's 1983 Official Settlement Plan for Electoral Area
"E" identified persistent frustrations over the "need for a face-lifting
of the Park, the planning of the approximately 80% of Park land
which remains undeveloped, and the need for a clearer administrative structure which permits and encourages public input."[27] Debate
over development, housing, and conversion activity within Cultus
Lake Park is, therefore, subsumed within a legacy of difficult relations between the Park Board and the leaseholders.

The final recreational-use issue of importance at Cultus Lake Park
involves the Sunnyside campground located at its southeast corner.
The campground contains about 600 tenting and travel-trailer sites,
many of which are available for full-season leasing. A pattern has
emerged whereby some sites are leased by the same campers for numbers of years in succession. Interviews suggest that many of these

leased sites become quasi–summer homes since they are only a short drive to work and shopping opportunities in Chilliwack. As well, these long-term leasing patterns are the foundations for the formation of summertime neighbourhoods in sections of the campground.

While campsite leaseholders at Sunnyside are given first opportunity to reapply for the same site each year, the Park Board stipulates that all tents and travel-trailers must be removed when the campground closes each fall. This requirement has two directly observable impacts on the landscape. The first is that a recreational-vehicle storage site has opened on the Soowahlie Indian Reserve just across from Cultus Lake Park and appears to be doing a good business. The second is that a walk through the Sunnyside campground in the late fall presents an intriguing image of landscaped patios, pyramid cedar borders, locked garden sheds, and raised landings and steps, all quietly awaiting the return of trailers to their summer parking places to complete the scene.

Lindell Beach

The second cottaging area, Lindell Beach, is located on an alluvial fan at the south end of Cultus Lake. As at Cultus Lake Park, Lindell Beach has developed as a dense cluster of properties. Unlike Cultus Lake Park, Lindell Beach is a private development of owned properties. As Cultus Lake Park developed through the 1920s and 1930s, Lindell Beach remained farmland. Improvements in road access along the lake, however, led to increased development pressure.[28] Originally developed in 1945 as a collection of 62 cottaging lots, Lindell Beach expanded over the following fourteen years through the creation of an additional 82 lots. Since 1954 the only development has been the division of some of these lots into two. In 1990 the Lindell Beach area contained 150 properties.

Since the original sale of cottage lots at Lindell Beach, an active residents' association has been responsible for most local organizational and service-provision needs. Property owners pay an annual fee to the association, which in turn operates and maintains a water system, a cable-television system, a collection of recreational facilities, and a local volunteer fire department. The Residents' Association is also the registered owner of several large parcels of land surrounding the cottage area that have been designated a privacy greenbelt. An annual association fee of $200 is viewed by many property owners as "a very good deal" for the levels of benefits received. The Residents' Association has also emerged as an important voice for local property owners in dealings with the RDFC and

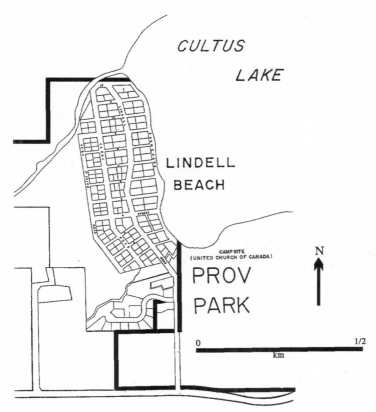

Figure 11
Lindell Beach.
Source: Base map from RDFC.

a number of provincial government agencies. In this role the Residents' Association is very similar to the cottagers' associations found along the Rideau Lakes, developing internally through the need to provide services to properties and property owners, and externally through mediations and representations on behalf of property owners.

The structure of planning and development control for the Lindell Beach area has evolved through two distinct phases. The first essentially concerned self-regulation by the cottage-property owners. When the first cottage lots were created in 1945, the previous property owners registered a restrictive covenant on all property titles, subsequently extended to all other cottage lots as they were created. The covenant agreements contain standard clauses respecting issues

Figure 12
Lindell Beach, entrance and lakeshore.

of access on to property by the Residents' Association, for example, in order to conduct repairs to collective services; as well, they contain guarantees of peaceable enjoyment of the property by its owners. The control these covenants extend to the Residents' Association is remarkable. Interviews suggest that most powers have not been exercised, but their presence is an important local symbol.

The second phase of planning control began in 1967 with the establishment of the RDFC, even though the first land-use regulations for Electoral Area "E" were not enacted until 1976. Since that time Lindell Beach has confronted three tiers of local government regulations, the Official Regional Plan, the Official Settlement Plan for Electoral Area "E," and the Zoning By-law for Electoral Area "E."[29] Within the framework established by these regulations and provincial legislation, additional regulations pertaining to building permits, subdivision approvals, and the creation of campground-holiday parks have also been implemented by the RDFC. However, it is the building-permit requirements that have had the most immediate impact and caused continuing frustration for Lindell Beach property owners.

Following the original cottage-lot subdivision in 1945, the greater Lindell Beach area began a slow transformation from farming to commercial recreation. Beginning in 1955, a series of campgrounds

Figure 13
The agricultural landscape of the Columbia Valley. The cut line in the forest cover
on the right marks the Canada–United States International Boundary.

and recreational trailer/vehicle parks were established. As well, an
eighteen-hole golf course and restaurant facility was developed. In
1986 a strata-title subdivision creating 14 lots was approved adjacent
to, but not directly connected with, the original Lindell Beach cottage
area. In 1990 the Lindell Beach area included approximately 164 cottage properties and 865 camping or holiday park sites.

The Columbia Valley

The history and settlement pattern of the Columbia Valley is distinct
from the Cultus Lake cottage areas in that it is an agricultural and
rural-residential area whose earliest ties were to the United States.
Two themes recur in the history of the Columbia Valley. First is the
overriding sense of "sought isolation" – the isolation of the valley
within the Cultus Lake area and also the isolation of families within
the valley itself. In structuring local relationships, the family bond is
of fundamental importance. The second theme is the value of community cohesion. While this may seem at odds with the theme of
isolation, such cohesion really emerges only when there is a perceived challenge or threat to the local community.

Local histories recall that the first pioneer families came to the
Columbia Valley in 1888[30] from the United States. From Limestone
Junction, Columbia Station, and Maple Falls in Washington State, the
Columbia Valley extends northwards for thirteen kilometres, into
Canada for only the last five. Pioneer pathways into the valley were,
however, part of a long-standing communications route within the

Sto:lo nation territory.[31] Trails through the valley and alongside Cultus Lake connected Sto:lo villages in the Chilliwack area with those along the Nooksack River in Washington State.

Local folklore has it that when the international border was re-surveyed and cut through in 1905–06, the pioneer settlers were surprised to find that they had "become" Canadians. This representation may, however, need careful interpretation, as a British Royal Engineers survey team working with the Boundary Commission of 1858–62 had camped at Lindell Beach and marked the 49th parallel in the valley by erecting a cairn and cutting timber for some distance on each side along the parallel.[32]

Connections with Cultus Lake and Chilliwack developed slowly over time. In 1916 a wagon road was pushed through along the eastern shore of Cultus Lake, although mail was still collected at Maple Falls and children continued to go to school in Sumas and Mount Baker in Washington State (RDFC, 1983b).

The first extensive clearing of the valley lands came in 1920, when railway logging companies began local operations. Employment with the Campbell River Timber Company provided additional income opportunities for members of many pioneer families, continuing until the late 1920s and early 1930s, when a succession of fires further reduced remaining stands of timber.[33] A remnant of this activity persists at Henderson's Mill, located at the intersection of the Columbia Valley Highway and Henderson Road, near the international border. As well, many of the local roads have been built upon the former railway track beds, the last of which was used in completing the Columbia Valley Highway.

The harsh settlement conditions for the farming families who followed logging in the Columbia Valley are poignantly described in Knight's *Stump Ranch Chronicles*.[34] Soil and moisture conditions prevented settlers from ever earning a bountiful livelihood from agriculture. Knight describes the role of employment outside the valley as a necessary supplement to the family income. In the local history developed for the RDFC's Official Settlement Plan, the sense of family combines with a sense of isolation, evoking a pioneer community where men left the valley farms "for logging work in the active logging areas of the lower mainland, returning periodically to their families. They left a small, insular community which maintained a subsistence level farming economy to support the nuclear families which remained on the farm."[35] The sense of family has passed from necessity to legacy: the inscription on the pioneers' plaque in front of the Columbia Valley Community Hall reads, in part, "although there was little money, there was great love of home."

With the phasing-out of railroad logging activity, Columbia Valley residents began to orient themselves more towards the Chilliwack area. The international border, which had been wide open prior to the 1920s, became a regulated crossing during the railroad logging era and was closed following the demise of the industry. The last schools in the valley closed around 1950, and local children continue to be bussed to schools at Cultus Lake Park and Chilliwack.[36] The road around Cultus Lake was widened and paved in 1958, solidifying, and easing, access to Chilliwack. The Columbia Valley general store and post office were destroyed by fire in 1959, and have never been replaced.

There continues to be a small turnover of residents; however, many Columbia Valley properties are still held by members of long-time pioneer families. Soil and irrigation conditions continue to limit agricultural activity. One response has been the introduction of intensive animal operations, in an effort to generate farm-based income. The RDFC reported that in the early 1980s ten intensive swine farms, representing as much as 4 per cent of Lower Mainland production, were established in the valley. In 1991 four major operations remain, producing over ten thousand hogs per year. A number of extensive tree and berry farms characterize the remainder of the significant agricultural investment. As well, many of the small rural-residential landholders also engage in some form of small-scale agricultural activity. Local residents cite the continued uniqueness, and even quirkiness, of the Columbia Valley as partial explanation for the recent inclusion of fallow deer, pheasant, and ostrich ranching as local agricultural experiments.

Parkview

The Parkview area, adjacent to Cultus Lake Park, includes a collection of 80 residential and 6 commercial properties. While the commercial areas are somewhat older, having developed to service the summer tourist traffic to the provincial park, most residential properties were developed in the early 1980s. Three mobile-home parks, containing approximately 180 sites, are located adjacent to the area. Due to the high turnover and widely fluctuating vacancy rates, these mobile-home parks are not included in most of the following analysis.

Contemporary Census Overview

The utility of census data in tracing internal patterns of population growth within the Cultus Lake area is limited (see Tables 12, 13). In the 1971 census only Cultus Lake Park was identifiable as a single enumeration area; the rest of the study area was combined with several other rural areas such that local population could not be delimited. In the 1976 census the Columbia Valley, Lindell Beach, and the Parkview area were all combined into a separate enumeration area. By 1981 the Cultus Lake Park, Columbia Valley, Lindell Beach, and Parkview areas were each identified as separate enumeration areas.

Two issues concerning local population change are important. First, the year-round population level in each cottaging area has remained relatively stable, a result of a long history of cottage conversion and winter rentals. Second, the cottaging areas contain approximately one-third of the local population. In contrast to the recent and rapid growth experienced in some Rideau Lakes townships, population growth in the Cultus Lake area has been much more stable.

Regional Recreational Asset

The Cultus Lake area is a regionally significant recreational asset and destination. I probed its status as such through the results of two surveys conducted within Cultus Lake Provincial Park in 1990.[37] The user surveys sampled visitors to both the provincial park campgrounds and day-use picnic areas. Table 17 shows the clear predominance of users from the Vancouver-centred Lower Mainland of British Columbia: approximately 74 per cent of campground users and 85 per cent of picnic-area users come from the Vancouver, central Fraser Valley, or local Chilliwack areas. Not surprisingly, the campground captures slightly larger shares of users from outside the Lower Mainland area.

The trip length of users surveyed indicates that over two-thirds of the picnic-area users are visiting the Cultus Lake area for the day only. Among campground users, approximately 58 per cent are staying in the area for only one to three nights. An explanation for these brief visits is the large proportion of repeat users: Table 18 shows that just over 53 per cent of the campground sample and over 72 per cent of the picnic-area sample report previously visiting the Park. This sketch of park use lends support to the argument that the Cultus Lake area is a regionally significant recreational asset.

Recreational accommodation at Cultus Lake is dominated by a mix of privately and publicly operated campgrounds (see Table 19). Approximately 1,500 campsites are available to visitors, as are approximately 700 day-use sites. Privately owned recreational property includes approximately 275 recreational-vehicle sites and approximately 620 cottage properties.

Table 17
Cultus Lake Provincial Park 1990 User Survey: Geographic Origin of Users

	Campgrounds %	Picnic areas %
British Columbia	84.7	91.0
Vancouver CMA	55.3	41.0
Central Fraser Valley[1]	9.3	37.0
Local[2]	9.3	7.0
Other BC	10.7	6.0
Alberta	8.0	2.0
Other Canada	2.0	1.0
USA	4.6	3.0
Other	0.7	3.0
(n =)	(150)	(100)

Source: British Columbia Ministry of Lands and Parks (1990a), *Visitor Satisfaction Survey: Cultus Lake Provincial Park*.
[1] The Central Fraser Valley area is that area of the Lower Mainland of British Columbia lying between the Vancouver CMA and the municipal boundaries of Chilliwack or Kent.
[2] Local refers to the District of Chilliwack, Cultus Lake, and Columbia Valley areas.

Table 18
Cultus Lake Provincial Park 1990 User Survey: Repeat Users of Park

	Campgrounds %	Picnic areas %
First-time users	46.8	27.7
Previously used	53.2	72.3
(n =)	(154)	(101)

Source: British Columbia Ministry of Lands and Parks (1990a), *Visitor Satisfaction Survey: Cultus Lake Provincial Park*.

DISCUSSION

The distribution of population varies markedly within the two study areas. The geographically larger Rideau Lakes area contains a number of small settlements, dispersed farm residences, and year-round occupied waterfront properties, with two immediately adjacent incorporated towns and two small incorporated villages. The

Table 19
Recreational Accommodation, Cultus Lake Area

Recreational-area facility	Number of properties	Number of sites/units[1]
CULTUS LAKE PARK		
Leased properties	450	
Sunnyside campground		600
LINDELL BEACH		
Residential subdivisions		
Lindell Beach	150	
strata-subdivision	14	
Holiday parks		
Cultus Lake Holiday Park		227
Leisure Valley		49
Campgrounds		
Thousand Trails		326
Tee-Pee Campground		263
CULTUS LAKE PROVINCIAL PARK		
Campsites		296
Day-use sites		716
Totals	614	2,477

[1] These estimates are subject to fluctuation over time.

Cultus Lake area also contains distinct settlement clusters as well as dispersed farm residences, but it is located adjacent to a single large municipality, the District of Chilliwack.

Table 20 lists population data for the study areas and the immediately adjacent incorporated places. The first item of note is that the total population surrounding Rideau Lakes is much smaller than that surrounding Cultus Lake, 28,000 compared to 50,000. When only the population within the study areas is considered, the pattern reverses. The Rideau Lakes townships have a much larger population (12,000) than that of the Cultus Lake area (1,500). At comparatively three times the population density, the Cultus Lake study area is, however, much more intensively settled. In 1987 Yeates proposed a scale of four population-density classification levels – sparse, rural, semi-urban, and urban – as a way of evaluating the degree of urbanization of areas adjacent to a developed core.[38] On this scale, the Rideau Lakes area (approximately 12 persons per square kilometre) is at the threshold of sparse to rural, while the Cultus Lake area (approximately 30 persons per square kilometre) is well within the semi-urban classification. From these differences in population levels

Table 20
Study Area Population

Jurisdiction	1971	1976	1981	1986	1991
Rideau Lakes study area[1]	7,875	9,010	9,895	10,764	12,168
Perth[1]	5,537	*5,675	*5,655	5,673	5,574
Smiths Falls[1]	9,585	9,279	*8,831	9,163	9,396
Westport[1]	601	644	621	694	664
Newboro[1]	296	259	260	282	282
Total area population	23,894	24,867	25,262	26,576	28,084
Cultus Lake study area[2]	na	na	1,430	1,465	na
Chilliwack[1]	9,135	8,623 }	40,609	41,337	49,531
Chilliwhack[1]	23,740	28,421 }			
Total area population	na	na	42,039	42,802	na

[1] Statistics Canada, Census of Canada, 1971, 1976, 1981, 1986, 1991 (100 per cent sample).

[2] Special Tabulations, Regional District of Fraser Cheam, from Statistics Canada census data.

* Intervening boundary change.

} City of Chilliwack and District of Chilliwhack amalgamated in 1980 as District of Chilliwack.

and densities we might expect that residential-development pressures would be greater in the Cultus Lake area and that, with relatively limited areas for new housing, these pressures would likely be experienced as cottage-conversion activity.

The physical form of cottage-property areas is also very different in the two study areas. Along the Rideau Lakes there is a single row of cottage properties along the margins of the recreational lakes and waterways, while at Cultus Lake all cottage properties are located in two densely developed clusters. As a result, the two areas are very different cottaging environments. Along the Rideau Lakes, cottages remain relatively isolated within a landscape that appears "rural." At Cultus Lake the clustered cottage-property areas convey much more the sense of an urban place surrounded by rural space.

While cottages are a relatively long-standing part of the landscape in both study areas, cottage-conversion activity is not. Cottage development was established along the Rideau Lakes by 1880, while at Cultus Lake such development did not really begin until the 1920s. However, cottage-conversion activity at Cultus Lake first began during the 1940s, spurred by a shortage of wartime housing in Chilliwack, while large-scale conversion activity along the Rideau Lakes is much more recent.

There is a further contrast to be found in levels of local government recognition of cottage development and conversion pressures in the two study areas. Along the Rideau Lakes, recognition of cottage conversion as an important element of local residential change has been very uneven among individual townships, despite some longer-standing interest in the issue on the part of the provincial and federal governments. One outcome of the recent planning exercises conducted by the Parks Service and the RVCA is that most Rideau Lakes townships are currently working to implement new planning policies and regulations for lakefront development. In the Cultus Lake area the RDFC has recognized that there are a range of development pressures that impact upon resort areas and has introduced planning policies to manage these pressures. This longer experience with permanent residential settlement in the cottaging areas, and with policies directed at cottage-development and conversion issues, suggests there may be a maturity of both the organizations representing cottage property-owner interests and the local governments in supporting a mixed seasonal and permanent population.

Both the Rideau Lakes and Cultus Lake areas are regionally important recreational assets. In terms of the origin of recreational users, both serve a regionally concentrated market that includes the local area and adjacent metropolitan centres. The strength of this regional concentration conforms to expectations that metropolitan areas tend to dominate recreational activity within their hinterlands. Complimenting this pattern, each area also serves many return visitors. Compared to the Cultus Lake area, the Rideau Lakes may also serve a more international market. It remains to be examined whether these patterns of regionally concentrated recreational users also act to structure patterns of cottage-property ownership.

In terms of recreational accommodation, both areas contain large numbers of public camping/day-use facilities. At Cultus Lake these facilities account for most of the available recreational accommodation. Along the Rideau Lakes, however, it is the commercial accommodation industry, as well as an unmeasured contribution from the private cottage-rental sector, that accounts for most recreational accommodation.

Both the Rideau Lakes and Cultus Lake study areas contain well-established cottage-property areas set within a rural/farm landscape. However, there are also a number of distinct differences with respect to population growth, cottage development, conversion activity, and local government intervention in the two study areas. These differences will be important in the interpretation of residential change, and contention over that change, in each local area.

5 Respondent Profiles

To sustain the argument that differences among residential groups in the rural-recreational countryside are critical to the organization of local debates over community change, it is important to delineate the specific differences. This chapter compares the socio-economic profiles of Rural Resident, Converter, and Seasonal Occupant groups in the Rideau Lakes and Cultus Lake areas. The analysis is based on responses to questionnaire surveys carried out in both locations in 1991. For the most part the discussion focuses on the Rural Resident and Converter groups, introducing Seasonal Occupants to highlight latent conversion pressures. However, a specific summary of Seasonal Occupant data is presented to reinforce earlier arguments about the continuing exclusivity of cottage-property ownership. A second discussion focuses specifically upon the Converter group, outlining issues of local/non-local integration and maintenance of ties to former place of residence. Finally, local participation and activity patterns for both Rural Resident and Converter respondents are compared. The central theme of this chapter is that the Rural Resident and Converter groups are very different in their profiles and activities, and that these differences have varying impacts within their respective study areas.

POPULATION PROFILES

Rideau Lakes

The first socio-economic measures focus on family structure, including age distribution, marital status, whether there are children living in

Table 21
Respondent Profiles: Family Structure

	Rideau Lakes			Cultus Lake		
	Rural %	Conver. %	Seas. %	Rural %	Conver. %	Seas. %
RESPONDENT GENDER						
Female	50.9	51.6	53.4	45.7	53.7	55.1
Male	49.1	48.4	46.6	54.3	46.3	44.9
(n =)	(226)	(304)	(189)	(70)	(67)	(69)
AGE STRUCTURE (years)						
25–34	10.2	6.4	2.7	11.4	5.9	1.5
35–44	23.6	17.0	18.9	24.3	17.7	10.3
45–54	22.2	20.0	23.2	20.0	13.2	20.6
55–64	19.6	26.4	22.7	28.6	13.2	26.5
65–74	17.3	26.1	21.6	11.4	44.1	32.4
75+	7.1	4.1	10.8	4.3	5.9	8.8
(n =)	(225)	(295)	(185)	(70)	(68)	(68)
MARITAL STATUS						
Single	2.4	2.5	3.9	10.3	18.2	0
Married	81.5	87.0	80.6	82.1	52.3	76.9
Widowed	9.7	6.2	10.7	0	20.5	20.5
Div./sep.	6.4	4.3	4.8	7.7	9.1	2.6
(n =)	(124)	(162)	(103)	(39)	(44)	(39)
CHILDREN AT HOME						
Yes	53.7	28.0	41.2	45.9	7.3	28.9
(n =)	(121)	(157)	(102)	(37)	(41)	(38)
HOUSEHOLDS BY NUMBER OF CHILDREN AT HOME						
1	34.9	50.0	30.9	41.2	0	45.5
2	46.9	40.5	47.6	47.1	66.7	45.5
3	10.6	9.5	16.7	0	33.3	9.1
+3	7.6	0	4.8	11.7	0	0
(n =)	(66)	(42)	(42)	(17)	(3)	(11)
AGE OF CHILDREN AT HOME (years)						
Up to 6	26.2	29.9	4.9	32.3	14.3	0
7–12	27.0	34.3	17.1	25.8	28.6	44.4
13–18	30.2	26.9	37.8	29.0	42.8	22.2
19–24	7.9	8.9	29.3	9.7	14.3	22.2
25+	8.7	0	10.9	3.2	0	11.1
(n =)	(126)	(67)	(82)	(31)	(7)	(18)

Source: Resident survey, 1991.

the home, and the number and ages of these children (see Table 21). Notable in the age structure of respondents is the difference in relative shares between a younger and an older population by resident group. Among Rural Residents, 56 per cent of respondents are aged 25 to 54 years. Among Converters, approximately 57 per cent of respondents are aged 55 years and over. The Seasonal Occupant group is relatively older than Rural Residents, with an age distribution that more closely approximates Converters.

The marital status of survey respondents indicates a predominance of traditional married couples among all groups. However, comparing respondents by whether there are children living in the home suggests an important difference between Rural Residents and Converters. More than half of Rural Residents report having children living at home, compared to just over one-quarter of Converters. In part these findings reflect noted differences in the age distribution of these two groups.

Family size is small even where there are children living in the home. Only 18 per cent of Rural Residents, 10 per cent of Converters, and 21 per cent of Seasonal Occupants have three or more children living at home. The distribution of children's ages is similar among Rural Residents and Converters despite the very different age profiles of household heads. There are of course far fewer (67) children living in Converter households. In summary, Converters tend to be older and are less likely to have children living in the home than are Rural Residents.

When we turn to measures of socio-economic status (see Table 22), we find that approximately 55 per cent of Rural Residents have up to a high-school level of education, while approximately 54 per cent of Converters have at least a university-level education. Seasonal Occupants stand out markedly, as 73 per cent of respondents have at least a university-level education.

Comparison of respondents by household income suggests that Rural Residents fare more poorly than the other groups. Just over 20 per cent report a gross household income of less than $20,000 per year, while approximately 39 per cent report an income over $50,000 per year. For Converters, only 7 per cent report household incomes of less than $20,000 per year, while just over half report an income of over $50,000 per year. Seasonal Occupants were even more strongly skewed towards the higher-income categories.

Any review of income must allow for the income of retired households, which is not always a good reflection of household wealth. When retired households are excluded from the analysis of household income, all groups increase in the proportion earning more than

Table 22
Respondent Profiles: Socio-economic Status

	Rideau Lakes			Cultus Lake		
	Rural %	Conver. %	Seas. %	Rural %	Conver. %	Seas. %
EDUCATION						
Public	8.9	1.6	2.7	7.1	1.5	2.9
High school	46.5	44.6	24.3	53.5	43.3	36.2
University	40.7	53.1	71.4	35.2	53.7	55.1
Other	3.9	0.7	1.6	4.2	1.5	5.8
(n =)	(226)	(303)	(189)	(71)	(67)	(69)
HOUSEHOLD INCOME ($000s)						
<20	20.5	7.3	4.2	26.3	23.3	12.1
20–29	13.4	10.6	7.4	15.8	20.9	3.0
30–39	14.3	17.9	11.6	18.4	20.9	9.1
40–49	12.5	13.9	11.6	18.4	20.9	9.1
50+	39.3	50.3	65.2	21.1	14.0	66.7
(n =)	(112)	(151)	(95)	(38)	(43)	(33)
HOUSEHOLD INCOME ($000s) (retired not included)						
<20	13.3	2.9	0	14.8	5.9	0
20–29	9.3	5.7	2.0	14.8	29.4	6.7
30–39	14.7	12.9	6.1	18.5	5.9	0
40–49	14.7	11.4	10.2	25.9	35.3	6.7
50+	48.0	67.1	81.6	25.9	23.5	86.7
(n =)	(75)	(70)	(49)	(27)	(17)	(15)
OCCUPATION						
Professional	19.4	21.9	32.4	20.6	18.5	26.5
Service	20.4	19.2	12.6	23.5	12.3	13.2
Primary	10.7	0	0.6	7.4	0	1.5
Secondary	11.1	4.6	2.8	11.8	1.5	4.4
Other	8.3	4.6	8.2	8.8	4.6	10.3
Retired	30.1	49.7	43.4	27.9	63.1	44.1
(n =)	(216)	(302)	(182)	(68)	(65)	(68)

Source: Resident survey, 1991.

$50,000 per year. Among Rural Residents the proportion earning more than $50,000 per year increases from 39 to 48 per cent; among Converters from 50 to 67 per cent; and among Seasonal Occupants to 82 per cent. When households who identified themselves as retired are excluded, the relatively poorer income performance of Rural Residents compared to the other two groups is made even more clear.

The final socio-economic measure concerns occupation. While the Rural Residents and Converters are similar in terms of employment in professional and service occupations, a greater proportion of Rural Residents are employed in primary, secondary, and other occupations.[1] The retired category reflects some of the age-structure differences detailed above: 30 per cent of Rural Residents compared to half of Converters report being retired. While a large proportion (43 per cent) of Seasonal Occupants are retired, most of those employed are in the professional category.

Across these measures of socio-economic status, Converters tend to be better educated, have higher incomes, are less likely to be employed in primary or secondary activities, and are more likely to be retired than are Rural Residents. As a group, Seasonal Occupants are also better educated and have higher incomes than Rural Residents.

Three issues emerge from this discussion. The first is the importance of age and the role of retirement in cottage-conversion activity. Although retirement is an important variable along the Rideau Lakes, it may be somewhat restricted to the younger and fitter retirement years. Second, Seasonal Occupants mirror Converters across a number of family-structure and socio-economic measures. Seasonal Occupants may represent a form of latent or potential future conversion pressure, and as such it seems clear that the socio-economic bases for a separation of rural and cottage residential areas are not likely to diminish. Third, residential-development and population-growth patterns in the townships adjacent to Smiths Falls and Perth suggest that some conversion activity is the result of young-family moves, an extension of small-town spillover growth. This finding is reflected in the age, retirement, and family-structure variables. Together these issues suggest an emerging dichotomy within the Converter population between young families with small children and retired/empty-nest households.

Cultus Lake

The most striking aspect of the age distribution of Cultus Lake area respondents again concerns the elderly age groups (see Table 21). The distribution approximates a normal curve for Rural Residents, while Converters are skewed strongly towards the older cohorts. One-half of Converters are 65 years of age or older, compared to only 15 per cent of Rural Residents. This elderly component of Converters is, however, tightly clustered in the 65–74-year age group. Seasonal Occupants fall between these two extremes but more closely approximate the age distribution of Converters. In this case, approximately 41 per cent of Seasonal Occupants are aged 65 or older, and a further 27 per cent are in the pre-retirement 55–64 group.

As along the Rideau Lakes, there is a predominance of traditional married couples among Rural Residents at Cultus Lake. Converters, by contrast, are less likely to be married and more likely to be single or widowed. Among Converters reporting single or widowed, 61 per cent are female and 85 per cent are living alone, with the distribution between single and widowed accurately reflecting the distinction between younger and older respondents. Seasonal Occupants fell between these two groups, with three-quarters reporting being married and most others reporting widowed.

At Cultus Lake just under half of Rural Residents report having children at home. By comparison, nearly all Converters report no children at home. Family size for all groups is generally small, usually limited to one or two children. Among Rural Residents with children at home, more than 87 per cent of the children are school age or younger. Across these family-structure measures, Converters at Cultus Lake tend to be older and are less likely to have children living in the home.

By our first measure of socio-economic status, approximately 61 per cent of Rural Residents have up to a high-school education, while approximately 55 per cent of Converters and 61 per cent of Seasonal Occupants have at least a university-level education (see Table 22). The similarity between Converters and Seasonal Occupants does not carry through to household-income comparisons, where the profile of Converters is not much different from Rural Residents. This continues to be the case even when retired households are dropped from the analysis. It is clear that most Seasonal Occupants have significantly higher education and income levels than Rural Residents, and that when conversion occurs with a retirement move, the pattern of income tends to even out.

Comparisons by employment highlight again the role of retirement as an important characteristic among Converters. Only 28 per cent of the Rural Residents identify their employment status as retired, compared to 63 per cent of Converters. Seasonal Occupants also record a high proportion of retirees. For those respondents who are not retired, Converters are much more likely to have professional occupations, compared to the prevalence of service occupations among Rural Residents. Across the measures of socio-economic status, Converters at Cultus Lake are more likely to have a higher level of education and be retired than are Rural Residents.

Discussion

In summary, clear differences emerge in the population profiles of the Rural Resident and Converter populations. In terms of family structure, the age distributions for Rural Residents are generally similar between the two study areas. While Converters at Cultus Lake are much more concentrated in the older age groups, in the Rideau Lakes area there is an emerging dichotomy between a younger and an older set of Converter households. In terms of marital status, one striking difference is the much larger proportion of widowed or single Converters at Cultus Lake than at Rideau Lakes. For older, widowed households, the climate, pattern of property development, proximity of neighbours, and distance to medical services may differentially affect the ability to live independently at a converted cottage. This outcome may be connected with patterns identified by researchers studying the migration associated with elderly retirement to amenity locations and later return to care-giving locations.[2] As with the Rideau Lakes respondents, Cultus Lake area households with children living at home report generally small family sizes, involving either one or two children. Very few Converters at Cultus Lake, however, report children at home. This is an important difference from the Rideau Lakes area, where Converters are more evenly divided between older retired households and younger households with small children.

Across measures of socio-economic status, Converters in both study areas report generally higher levels of education than do Rural Residents. In terms of household income, however, there is little difference between the two groups in both areas. This similarity in income levels is largely the result of the smaller annual incomes common in retired households, and is a reflection of a research question focus on income, a measure that does not account for other aspects of wealth. In terms of occupation, the principal difference from the Rideau Lakes area is that retired households account for a much larger share of the Converter population at Cultus Lake.

"COTTAGERS"

Measures of family structure for seasonal-use cottage-property owners are also presented in Table 21. There is remarkable similarity across these measures among Seasonal Residents in both the Cultus Lake and Rideau Lakes areas. Over half of all respondents are 55 years of age or older, and over three-quarters are married. Perhaps because of the slightly older age profile, a higher proportion of Cultus Lake respondents are widowed. Fewer than half of these Seasonal Residents have any children living at home. Not surprisingly, Cultus Lake has a lower proportion of children living at home.

As with the family-structure measures, there is considerable similarity among Seasonal Residents in terms of socio-economic status variables (see Table 22). More than half of Seasonal Residents have a university education. Along the Rideau Lakes this proportion reaches nearly three-quarters. More than two-thirds of Seasonal Residents report an income of over $50,000 per year. When retired households are dropped from the analysis, the proportion reporting annual incomes of less than $20,000 falls to zero in each area. As well, a large proportion of Seasonal Residents report that they are retired, an expected outcome in light of the age structure. Of those who are not retired, the clear majority are employed in professional occupations.

There are relatively few studies of cottage-property owners with which to compare the profile developed here. Hodge undertook a probe of cottagers living in the Toronto urban field in the early 1970s and argued that cottagers tended to be families, particularly those with young children, and to be clustered within the higher income categories.[3] The predominance of higher incomes and associated higher levels of education and occupational status compares favourably with the profile of cottage-property owners developed here. In terms of family structure, however, the Cultus Lake and Rideau Lakes profiles differ markedly from that suggested by Hodge, in that there is a pattern of older households without children living at home. A more recent study by Gill and Clark developed a socio-economic profile for second-home owners in the mountain resort of Whistler, British Columbia.[4] They found that second-home owners tend to have high income and education levels and that they tend to be employed in professional occupations. The second-home owners surveyed by Gill and Clark are, however, concentrated between ages 35 and 54, not the retirement years. This may be an indication of important differences among types of cottage/resort areas in the rural-recreational countryside and types of households drawn to different recreational landscapes. These differences may have significant implications not only for determining who purchases property but also for the future costs of service provision to very different populations.[5] The findings of my research suggest a clear distinction between cottager and converter populations. Also, while married couples are a noted characteristic of exurban households,[6] the prevalence of retirement-age households suggests conversion involves different pressures and processes.

LOCAL/NON-LOCAL INTEGRATION

The questionnaire uses former residential location to highlight differences in local/non-local integration of Rural Residents and Converters. This includes evaluating patterns of local and non-local newspaper subscription and location of respondents' best non-local friend. These questions of integration into local places are important in developing a portrait of the degree to which residents are involved in and committed to their locality.

Rideau Lakes

Local/non-local integration is described through household newspaper subscription and non-local friendship patterns (see Table 23). Following arguments developed by Fischer, these spaces are defined as something that residents must expend some effort in order to create and maintain.[7] In the Rideau Lakes area nearly all Rural Residents and Converters subscribe to a local newspaper. A large number of newspapers were cited as local in origin, including the *Smiths Falls Record News* and the *Perth Courier*, which offer bi-weekly editions; the *Westport and Rideau Valley Mirror* and the *Athens Laker*, which offer weekly editions; and the monthly *North Leeds Lantern*.[8] Newspaper subscription to non-local newspapers was much lower for both groups, with 58 per cent of Rural Residents and 63 per cent of Converters reporting subscriptions. While this suggests some general interest in non-local news and information, both groups express through local newspaper subscriptions a high level of interest in local news and information.

If these newspaper-subscription patterns are probed for Converters across former place of residence, however, a difference between those who last moved from an urban residence and those relocating within the local area begins to emerge. Approximately 90 per cent of local-based Converters compared to 72 per cent of exurban Converters report subscribing to a local newspaper. The difference is less marked with non-local newspapers, as approximately 63 per cent of local-based Converters compared to 67 per cent of exurban Converters subscribe.

The questionnaire explored non-local friendship patterns among Rural Residents and Converters by asking for the location of the respondent's best non-local friends. There is a clear difference between the two groups. Half of the Rural Residents identify a best non-local friend who is, in fact, living within the general Rideau Lakes area. For Converters, just under half identify their best non-

Table 23
Newspaper Subscription and Location of Non-local "Best" Friend

	Rideau Lakes		Cultus Lake	
	Rural %	Converter %	Rural %	Converter %
NEWSPAPER SUBSCRIPTION				
Local	89.9	81.2	77.8	73.8
Non-local	58.4	62.6	45.5	85.7
(n =)	(119)	(149)	(36)	(42)
NON-LOCAL "BEST" FRIEND				
Local[1]	50.6	30.9	51.9	30.8
Adj. rural[2]	12.7	7.1	3.7	7.7
Adj. metro.[3]	25.3	48.7	37.0	61.5
Other	11.4	13.3	7.4	0
(n =)	(79)	(113)	(27)	(26)

Source: Resident survey, 1991.

[1] In the Rideau Lakes area "local" includes the study area and the incorporated places of Smiths Falls, Perth, Westport, and Newboro. In the Cultus Lake area "local" includes the study area and the District of Chilliwack.

[2] In the Rideau Lakes area "adjacent rural" includes all rural and small-town areas of Eastern Ontario between Ottawa and Kingston, Westport, and the Quebec-Ontario border (excluding the study area). In the Cultus Lake area "adjacent rural" includes all rural and small-town areas of the lower mainland of British Columbia from the Vancouver CMA to the Town of Hope (excluding the Chilliwack–Cultus Lake areas).

[3] In the Rideau Lakes area "adjacent metropolitan" includes all of the Ottawa-Hull CMA together with the Kingston CA. In the Cultus Lake area "adjacent metropolitan" includes all of the Vancouver CMA.

local friend as living in an adjacent metropolitan centre. Interestingly, approximately 22 per cent of Converters who relocated from an urban area failed to identify a best non-local friend at all.

Cultus Lake

The comparison of newspaper subscription rates reveals that approximately three-quarters of both Rural Residents and Converters subscribe to a local newspaper (see Table 23), the local newspaper in this case originating in the neighbouring regional centre of Chilliwack. Subscription to non-local newspapers, however, highlights a considerable difference between the groups. Only 46 per cent of Rural Residents subscribe to a non-local newspaper, compared to 86 per cent of Converters.

These findings can be extended by examining newspaper subscription among Converters on the basis of former residential location. Local newspapers are subscribed to by approximately 63 per cent of Converters who last moved from an urban residence and by approximately 77 per cent of those previously living in the local area. The pattern, however, reverses for non-local newspapers, with approximately 87 per cent of Converters from an urban area compared to approximately 69 per cent of those from the local area subscribing.

While the respondents identify a distribution of friends across the southwestern corner of British Columbia, approximately half of Rural Residents identify their best non-local friend in the local rural and small-town area surrounding Cultus Lake, while nearly two-thirds of Converters identify their best non-local friend in metropolitan Vancouver. For Converters who relocated from a Vancouver area residence, 64 per cent of those identifying a best non-local friend identify one within metropolitan Vancouver. It should also be noted that approximately 42 per cent of all Converters from urban areas did not identify a best non-local friend at all.

The review of local/non-local integration highlights three important issues arising from cottage-conversion activity as an element of community change that have not been detailed in the published literature. First, subscription levels to local newspapers by Converters suggest a generally high level of interest in, and potential awareness of, local politics and activities in both study areas. As I suggest later in discussion of local debates, the interest of Converters in local government land-use and property-tax issues may be a central motivation of local newspaper subscriptions.

The second issue is the maintenance of ties to former place of residence through newspaper subscriptions. In each area Converters have a strong inclination to subscribe to non-local newspapers, often those from their former place of residence. If non-local newspaper subscription can be taken as an effort to maintain community awareness and ties beyond the local, then it is clear that Converters can readily be differentiated from Rural Residents and that, among Converters, there is an internal differentiation to be made based on former place of residence. This difference was, however, clearer at Cultus Lake than along the Rideau Lakes.

The third issue is maintenance of friendship networks following residential/retirement-move decisions. There is some clear evidence in both study areas that respondents tend to maintain best non-local friends according to notions of exurbanization – that is, former urban residents maintained some ties to friends in those urban locations. However, in both study areas, and especially in the Cultus Lake area, a high proportion of Converters who relocated from an adjacent metropolitan area failed to identify any best non-local friends at all. These results appear to modify Hodge's earlier suggestion of a tendency to maintain fairly close contact with relatives and/or friends in previous locations.[9]

LOCAL PARTICIPATION

The questionnaire aimed to examine issues of participation and interaction within the local area by comparing Rural Residents and Converters in terms of their use of a range of local services, their level of local volunteer activity, and their local friendship and neighbouring patterns. These latter two issues were pursued by the identification of the respondent's best local friend and by characterizing the level of social interaction with each of up to four immediately adjacent neighbours.

Rideau Lakes

Within the Rideau Lakes study area there is wide variability in terms of local patronage, between resident groups and across services types (see Table 24). For Rural Residents, commonly needed goods such as groceries are acquired locally by over 82 per cent of respondents, while less frequently purchased items such as clothes are routinely acquired locally by only about 39 per cent. While professional service needs are met locally for 79 per cent of Rural Residents, entertainment is locally obtained by only about 44 per cent. This general pattern holds true for Converters as well, although there is a slightly lower level of reported local patronage across the complete range of services listed.

Table 25 provides an overview of respondents' satisfaction with local services. In the Rideau Lakes area Converters are more generally satisfied with locally available services than are Rural Residents. While this result may be unexpected, it can perhaps be explained with reference to the baseline level of expectations among respondents. In this case, Converters may be more generally satisfied simply because their expectations of local services are lower.

The volunteering of one's time to local community groups can place a considerable demand upon an individual's energy and time. In the Rideau Lakes area there is little difference between levels of volunteer activity among Rural Residents and Converters: approximately

Table 24
Local Participation

	Rideau Lakes		Cultus Lake	
	Rural %	Converter %	Rural %	Converter %
USE OF LOCAL SERVICES				
Groceries	82.3	71.3	97.5	75.6
Clothing	38.7	28.8	92.5	64.4
Entertainment	44.3	38.6	94.7	82.2
Professional	79.0	63.5	97.5	71.1
(n =)	(124)	(160)	(40)	(45)
LOCAL VOLUNTEER				
Yes	44.3	36.2	49.3	30.9
(n =)	(235)	(304)	(75)	(81)
LOCAL "BEST" FRIEND				
Next door	22.3	19.6	10.8	32.6
<1 mile	26.9	28.5	24.3	44.2
1–5 miles	35.3	25.9	27.0	9.3
+5 miles	15.1	25.9	37.8	13.9
(n =)	(119)	(158)	(37)	(43)
NEIGHBOURING[1]				
Regular	36.6	34.2	17.5	44.3
Some	40.5	46.6	52.6	39.2
None	22.9	19.2	29.8	16.5
(n =)	(385)	(464)	(114)	(158)

Source: Resident survey, 1991.
[1] Average social contacts with up to four immediately adjacent neighbours.

44 per cent of Rural Residents and 36 per cent of Converters offer their time to local community groups or activities.

In Table 24, estimates of distance to best local friend suggest little difference between Rural Residents and Converters, with Converters demonstrating a slightly larger frame of reference for best local friend. While approximately half of both groups identify a best local friend within about one mile[10] of their homes, only 15 per cent of Rural Residents compared to approximately 26 per cent of Converters look beyond five miles for a best local friend. The distribution for Rural Residents may be a reflection of the dispersed rural landscape. For Converters, the linear single-tier pattern of waterfront lot development suggests that if a best local friend is not immediately adjacent, then some considerable distance is likely to be involved.

Table 25
Satisfaction with Local Services (shopping, entertainment, professional, etc.)

| | Rideau Lakes | | Cultus Lake | |
| | Rural | Converter | Rural | Converter |
Level of satisfaction	%	%	%	%
Satisfied	52.1	59.4	64.5	63.6
Neutral	9.4	13.3	19.4	12.1
Dissatisfied	38.5	27.3	16.1	24.3
(n =)	(96)	(128)	(31)	(33)

Source: Resident survey, 1991.

Levels of social contact and interaction with immediately adjacent neighbours can be used to clarify local social space.[11] Respondents were asked to describe their level of social interaction with each of up to four adjacent neighbours. The intensity of social interactions are averaged across the number of neighbours identified, to provide a summary statistic of neighbouring activity. As with the best local friend, there is little variation between Rural Residents and Converters, with approximately one-third reporting regular social contacts, just less than half reporting some social contacts, and the remaining respondents reporting no social contacts with their immediate neighbours.

Cultus Lake

The pattern of local-service patronage within the Cultus Lake area is generally much higher than in the Rideau Lakes area (see Table 24). Nearly all Rural Residents and about two-thirds of Converters regularly use local-area services. Commonly needed goods such as groceries are acquired locally by 97 per cent of Rural Residents, while less frequently purchased items such as clothing are routinely purchased locally by about 92 per cent. In contrast, Converters' patronage of these services was lower, ranging from 64 to 82 per cent, with entertainment receiving the highest local patronage and clothing the lowest. Comparing respondent satisfaction with locally available services, both Rural Residents and Converters are generally satisfied (see Table 25).

On the question of volunteering one's time to local community groups or activities, the difference between Rural Residents and Converters at Cultus Lake is a marked one. Approximately half of Rural

Residents compared to fewer than one-third of Converters offer their time to local volunteer work.

Comparison of friendship and neighbouring patterns around Cultus Lake outlines a more spatially constricted local community for Converters than for Rural Residents. Of Rural Residents, 65 per cent look beyond one mile for their best local friends, while 38 per cent look beyond five miles. Three-quarters of Converters identify best local friends living within a mile of their residence. While only 18 per cent of Rural Residents indicate regular social contacts with their immediate neighbours, nearly half of Converters claim regular social contacts with neighbours. Nearly one-third of Rural Residents, compared to only 17 per cent of Converters, have no social contacts with their immediate neighbours. These differences suggest a more local focus to social interaction among Converters. The geographic and social intensity of local friendship and neighbouring patterns for Converters stands out from those of Rural Residents.

Discussion

In terms of local service use, Rural Residents and Converters in both study areas demonstrate similar patterns of participation. For his sample of families in the Toronto urban field, Hodge found that most obtained basic services locally.[12] Since patronage of a nearest available service requires the least expenditure of effort, we may expect that for more routinely needed goods and services there will be higher levels of local patronage. Where more specialized goods and services are involved, there is likely to be a wider spatial range of choice exercised by these residents.[13]

The importance of tourist activity in supporting a wide range of locally available services has been noted in other research on cottaging areas.[14] As with Windley's[15] finding that older residents in rural areas are not necessarily restricted to "in-community" services, Cultus Lake area interviews suggest that for some elderly converters there are organized, often bi-weekly, group shopping trips to Seven Oaks Mall, a large retail centre between Chilliwack and Vancouver. This may account for some of the lower levels of local-service patronage by the Converter group. The entertainment category included meals at restaurants and other activities often taking place in the evening. Again, several of the elderly converters interviewed suggested a dislike of nighttime driving and a desire to do such activities close to home. Finally, the presence of two retail shopping malls in adjacent Chilliwack must be read into the comparisons with the

Rideau Lakes area, where a number of services are available in the small towns of Perth and Smiths Falls but where large shopping malls are located outside of the local area, in the urban centres of Ottawa and Kingston.

There is general satisfaction with local services among both resident groups, with this satisfaction slightly stronger in the Cultus Lake area than along the Rideau Lakes. Converters may be more satisfied than expected because of lowered expectations concomitant with the move into an area characterized by the availability of generally lower-order goods and services.

Volunteer and neighbouring activities suggest very different levels of local participation by Rural Residents and Converters at Cultus Lake. In terms of volunteering, where participation by the individual is important for community activities and where, therefore, the individual is depended upon by the community, the rural community in both study areas has a strong base-level of interaction to draw upon. This generalization, however, does not hold true for Converters around Cultus Lake. In the Columbia Valley the local Ratepayer's Association has a long-established tradition of community involvement: patterns of participation on committees such as those for the annual parade, recreation, and the Christmas pageant reveal scarcely a household in which one or both adults are not currently active in one volunteer activity or another. These kinds of local activities and groups have long been fundamental to the social life of rural areas, and the similarity between the Rideau and Cultus Lake areas is not surprising.[16] As a balance to this, one retired Converter commented that after fifty years of volunteer work and activity in their former community, he and his wife had earned some time to themselves.

The pattern of local social contacts for Rideau Lakes respondents is higher among Rural Residents but lower among Converters than at Cultus Lake. This pattern holds for both the best local friend and neighbouring measures. Together these measures sketch a much more uniform picture of local social activity and personal networks around the Rideau Lakes than at Cultus Lake. Converters at Cultus Lake demonstrate a more localized and intense social sphere of interaction with local friends and neighbours. This contrasts with geographically broader local friendship patterns and a less intense social sphere of neighbour interaction for Rural Residents in both areas, an extensive pattern that Walker has termed "neighbourhood territory."[17] The impact of the compact, densely developed cottaging areas of Cultus Lake Park and Lindell Beach, compared to the single strand of cottages necklacing the Rideau Lakes, must be considered when we evaluate these spatial-proximity results.

SUMMARY

As one form of local residential change, cottage conversion is introducing a new group of residents with some very distinct socioeconomic and local participation characteristics. These characteristics have implications for local community change. The age, marital status, and family structure of Converters is part of a longer-term trend in the Cultus Lake Park settlement area. Local residents recall the bustling of community-organized, child-centred activity groups that served the many young families living locally on property that was then more affordable than nearby Chilliwack. The passing of time and the increasing demand for these cottage-area properties worked to reduce their attractiveness to young families, with the result that many activities for youth ceased within the community. Participation in locally organized activities such as the swim club, the Scouting groups, and youth sports teams has disappeared and been replaced by participation in the Old Age Pensioners' card game and bingo afternoons. This shift suggests strong support for arguments about the importance of retirement in cottage-conversion timing.[18]

As well as identifying the characteristics of Converters and of the conversion process, the discussion has raised important issues with respect to defining the rural-recreational countryside as a socially and geographically divided landscape. Among these issues is the truncation of social ties to former urban communities experienced by ex-urban Converters, ties that are replaced somewhat by a localized social network focused within the cottage-property areas. A further discussion of the conversion process is developed in the next chapter, while local social organization at the group level is elaborated upon later in the chapter on community groups.

6 Housing Change and Conversion Pressures

The conversion of seasonal-use cottaging properties into permanent homes is responsible for introducing new residents and residential groups into the rural-recreational countryside. In this sense, conversion refers to the change from seasonal to permanent residential use of the property, which may be accomplished by renovating a cottage or constructing a new dwelling. In some communities this conversion activity accounts for a significant proportion of recent population growth and local development pressure. Residential change through cottage conversion, therefore, occurs within and has an impact upon the local housing stock. To evaluate both the scope and scale of conversion activity, and whether the housing of Converters is different from the local population, this chapter examines the Rideau Lakes and Cultus Lake study areas through four specific discussions. The first focuses on a broad regional overview of housing trends. The second uses local building-permit data to highlight variability in residential-development and cottage-conversion pressures within each study area. The third discussion examines the conversion process itself, with attention directed towards Converters' residential pathways, move timing, and yearly occupancy patterns. Finally, a comparison of housing quality of Rural Resident and Converter respondents is developed.

REGIONAL HOUSING FRAMEWORK

Housing development and change in the rural-recreational countryside operate within a broader regional framework. This section uses data

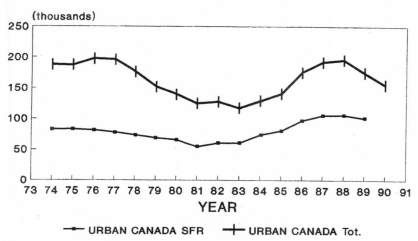

Figure 14
Canada, housing starts, three-year averages.
Source: Statistics Canada.

on housing starts to describe regional trends necessary for evaluating local construction and conversion activity. The data are presented using three-year sliding averages to help smooth the trend lines,[1] in order to recognize the important lag effects found in the residential construction industry. The Canadian trend in total residential housing starts between 1973 and 1991 suggests high levels of activity in 1976–77 and 1987–88, with a downturn concentrated in 1981–83.[2] For detached single-family-residence housing starts, the decline between 1978 and 1981 was less precipitous. As well, since 1983 detached single-family units account for a larger proportion of total housing starts. These "boom" and "bust" periods represent the national baseline against which to compare local/regional house-construction trends.

Rideau Lakes

Trends in housing construction in the Rideau Lakes study area must be interpreted within a regional housing framework. Limited data availability restricts this discussion of a regional housing framework to Kingston, Ottawa, and urban Ontario. Urban Ontario is defined as including all census areas or municipal jurisdictions in the province with populations over 10,000 persons. The Kingston and Ottawa areas are defined by their Census Agglomeration and Census Metropolitan Area boundaries respectively. The Ottawa data exclude those portions of the CMA in Hull, Quebec.

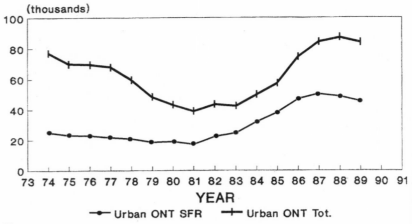

Figure 15
Ontario housing starts, three-year averages.
Source: Statistics Canada.

The general urban Ontario trends follow closely those described at the national level: a long decline in total residential starts bottoms out in 1980–83, a low period that lasts one year longer than at the national level. A strong recovery to a peak around 1987–89 also corresponds to the national trend. Again, as at the national level, the decline in detached single-family residences is less sharp preceding 1981 and the recovery more dramatic to 1987.

In Figure 16, housing starts for Kingston and Ottawa follow the general pattern described nationally and for urban Ontario. For total starts, a low period around 1980–81 is followed by a strong recovery to 1987–88. Following 1988 there is a noted drop in total housing activity. For detached single-family starts, the decline to 1980–81 is marked in Kingston but more ambiguous in Ottawa. In terms of the scale of recovery, detached single-family starts in Kingston increased 320 per cent to 1989, while Ottawa starts increased 260 per cent to 1988.

Cultus Lake

The broader regional framework for evaluating Cultus Lake–area housing and conversion pressures focuses on the Lower Mainland of British Columbia. Housing-starts data are presented for:

Chilliwack	the District Municipality prior to the 1986 census and the Census Agglomeration thereafter[3]
Metropolitan Vancouver	the Vancouver CMA
Urban British Columbia	census areas or municipal jurisdictions with populations over 10,000 persons

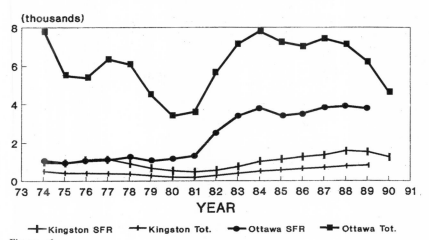

Figure 16
Ontario housing starts, three-year averages.
Source: Statistics Canada.

Housing starts for urban British Columbia and metropolitan Vancouver experienced two downturns in the 1977–78 and 1983–85 periods.[4] The recovery into the late 1980s is quite strong, representing an approximate doubling of activity to a peak around 1988–90. The general trend for detached single-family starts follows the total-activity pattern. This result is not surprising considering that these units consistently make up approximately half of all annual residential starts.

Housing starts for urban British Columbia and metropolitan Vancouver represent a two-peak trend generally similar to the Ontario example. The principal difference is that the high and low periods in British Columbia lag behind their counterparts in Ontario by several years. In both areas the recovery into the late 1980s is quite strong, approaching a doubling of activity. The 1987–88 Ontario peak is replaced in British Columbia by a 1988–90 peak.

Chilliwack-area housing starts generally follow those described for Vancouver and urban British Columbia, suggesting that provincial economic circumstances had a definite local impact. One important difference is that, rather than reflecting the mild provincial recovery of 1979–80, detached single-family starts in the Chilliwack area continued a slow downward trend until 1984. Chilliwack demonstrates a strong recovery from 1983 to 1989; however, by contrast with the trend in urban British Columbia and Vancouver, this recovery continues through 1991. Local officials acknowledge that the Chilliwack area has become an important destination for retired households relocating out of the metropolitan area. There is a consensus among these officials that this pressure continues to bolster local housing starts.

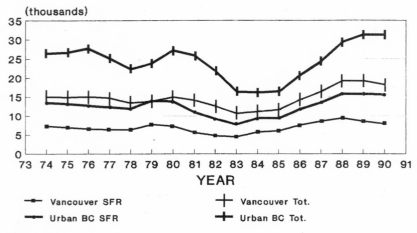

Figure 17
British Columbia housing starts, three-year averages.
Source: CMHC, Pacific Region Office.

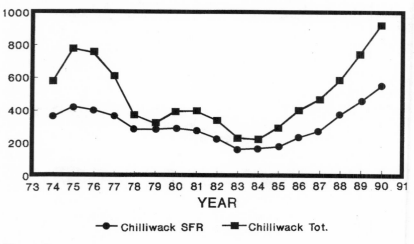

Figure 18
British Columbia housing starts, three-year averages.
Source: CMHC, Pacific Region Office.

LOCAL HOUSING CHANGE

This section reviews the status of, and patterns of change in, residential properties and the local housing stock. It begins with a comparison of the distributions of permanent-use, seasonal-use, and converted cottage properties in each study area. Using local building-permit data, it then highlights trends in local residential construction activity between 1980 and 1990.[5]

Building-permit records include issued building permits only. Data on rejected applications are not available. Also, it must be kept in mind that the classification procedure used to develop maps of building-permit patterns represents a third tier of categorization. The first is imposed by applicants in describing projects on their application forms; the second is the building-department staff interpretation on recording the application in the permit records. The records are remarkably consistent between jurisdictions in terms of the types of information applicants are requested to supply. Of interest to the examination of building and conversion activity is location, and type and intended use of the building or property. As a cautionary note, all jurisdictions except Cultus Lake Park have land-use zoning and community-plan by-laws in place, which may influence applicants' statements regarding intended uses.

Rideau Lakes

Table 26 lists the distribution of all residential, cottage, and converted cottage properties for the six Rideau Lakes townships. Bastard and South Burgess contains the largest share of residential properties, followed by South Crosby and then South Elmsley. This is a much different ranking of townships than for population, where South Elmsley ranked first and Bastard and South Burgess third. North Elmsley, ranked second in population, ranks fourth in terms of its share of residential properties.

An explanation for these differences in ranking emerges from a township-level distribution of cottage-area properties. Across the Rideau Lakes area just over 40 per cent of all residential properties are found in the small-lot cottage-property areas. In the fastest growing townships of North Elmsley and South Elmsley, cottage-area properties account for less than 36 per cent of the residential property stock. In the slower growing townships of South Crosby and North Burgess, more than one-half of all residential properties are within the cottaging areas.

South Elmsley has 26 per cent of all converted cottage properties along the Rideau Lakes, while North Elmsley has approximately

Table 26
Residential Property Distributions

Jurisdiction	Total residential properties[1]		Cottage-area properties[2]		Converters' identified		Cottage-area properties converting[3]
	#	%	#	%	#	%	%
RIDEAU LAKES							
S. Elmsley[4]	2,493	18.4	896	16.2	78	25.6	8.7
N. Elmsley	2,004	14.8	471	8.5	60	19.7	12.7
Bast. & Burg.	2,990	22.1	1,057	19.2	47	15.4	4.5
N. Burgess	1,756	12.9	983	17.8	42	13.8	4.3
S. Crosby	2,580	19.0	1,300	23.6	48	15.7	3.7
N. Crosby	1,736	12.8	809	14.7	30	9.8	3.7
Total	13,559	100	5,516	100	305	100	5.5
CULTUS LAKE							
"Southern" section[5]	288	35.3	166	26.9	28	23.3	16.9
"Northern" section[6]	528	64.7	450	73.1	92	76.7	20.4
Total	816	100	616	100	120	100	19.5

Source: Property-assessment-roll records, 1992.

[1] Includes all farm, seasonal, and permanent residences as defined and identified by property-assessment records.

[2] Includes all small-lot residential properties located in the recreational amenity areas. In the Rideau Lakes area this includes properties along all lakeshores; in the Cultus Lake area this includes the Lindell Beach and Cultus Lake Park settlement clusters.

[3] Calculation of the proportion of recreational properties converted from seasonal to permanent occupancy between 1981 and 1991.

[4] South Elmsley sample of converters is composed of 10 households in the pre-test and 68 households in the final questionnaire mailing.

[5] The "southern" section of the Cultus Lake study area includes the Columbia Valley and Lindell Beach settlement areas. It does not include recreational-vehicle sites in the campground-holiday parks adjacent to Lindell Beach.

[6] The "northern" section of the Cultus Lake study area includes the Parkview and Cultus Lake Park settlement areas. It does not include the mobile-home parks adjacent to the Parkview subdivision.

20 per cent. A more striking illustration of the importance of conversion in local residential change is the proportion of cottage properties converted between 1980 and 1990. While the average around the Rideau Lakes was 6 per cent, in North Elmsley 13 per cent of cottage properties were converted in that ten-year period alone. These findings suggest that conversion plays an important role in local population growth, as the two fastest-growing townships contained the largest shares of conversion activity. The slower growth of the remaining townships reflects the large share of residential properties devoted to cottaging and the associated lower rates of conversion.

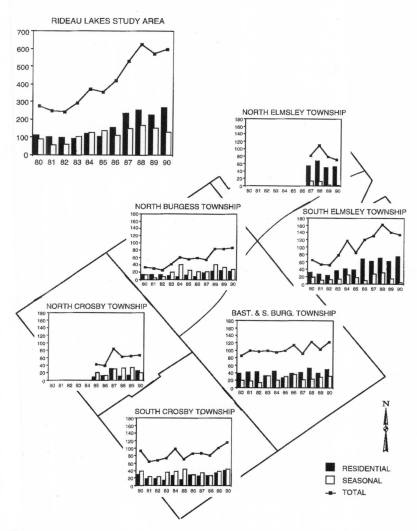

Figure 19
Issued building-permit activity, Rideau Lakes.

Figure 19 summarizes building-permit data across the study area. The peak in 1984 is associated with an equally strong performance by both permanent-use and seasonal-use permit activity. Two residential categories are used to classify building-permit information. The basic classes of use that underlie the mapping are "Seasonal Use," which the applicant identifies as either cottage or seasonal use, and "Permanent Residential Use," which the applicant identifies as a permanent residence. Through the late 1980s the permanent-housing sector out-performs seasonal housing two to one in terms of permits issued. These figures must be considered in light of an expected underreporting of building-permit activity, especially for weekend-cottage improvement projects. While local building inspectors have invested in public liaison and education to increase public awareness of local regulations and the types of construction requiring permits, there are no significant reasons why motivations for underreporting should have changed for the period under examination. In general, though, this pattern of increasing activity to 1988 follows the regional housing-starts trends described earlier.

At the township level there is wide variability in both the volume and types of permits issued. South Elmsley records some of the highest volumes and greatest variability in building-permit activity. Bastard and South Burgess, together with South Crosby, also record high-volume periods of permit activity, while the two other north-shore townships of North Burgess and North Crosby consistently record the lowest volumes.

When type of building-permit activity is examined, differences between townships emerge in the relative importance of permanent compared to seasonal-use housing. In both South Elmsley and North Elmsley far more permits for permanent residences are issued, with the seasonal component shrinking to near insignificant levels by 1988–90. In Bastard and South Burgess the shares are more balanced; for most years seasonal-use permits average between one-third and two-thirds the volume for permanent housing, with approximately equal numbers of permits issued through the mid-1980s. In the remaining townships it is not uncommon for seasonal-residence permits to exceed the number of permanent-housing permits issued in any given year.

In Figure 20 the building-permit data include only those permits issued for new permanent or new seasonal-use residences.[6] Along the Rideau Lakes a general downturn in new home construction around 1982 is replaced by steady growth into the late 1980s. This growth is composed of more seasonal-residence activity from 1983 to 1985, followed by stronger activity in the permanent-residence market. Compared to the regional housing-starts trend, the Rideau Lakes area recovery appears to have been manifest first in the cottage sub-market and later in the permanent-home sub-market.

At the township level, the growing divergence between North Elmsley and South Elmsley on the one hand and the remaining area townships on the other finds further support. In both North and

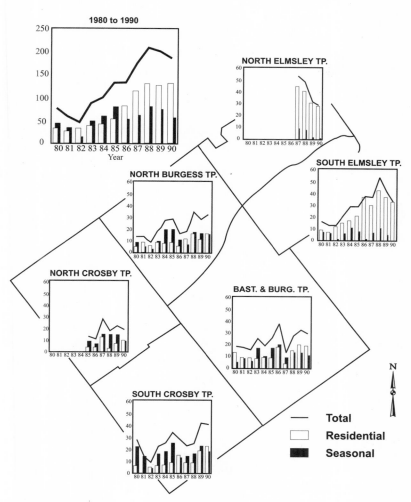

Figure 20
New-residence-permit activity, Rideau Lakes.

South Elmsley, permits for new permanent residences far outnumber permits for new seasonal residences. This is especially notable in South Elmsley, as more new permanent-residence permits have been issued there since 1986 than elsewhere along the Rideau Lakes.

In Bastard and South Burgess new housing permits show tremendous fluctuation from year to year. This is not a surprising result given the influence of such highly local factors as the number of new lots coming on-stream for development at any given time. In South

Crosby, North Burgess, and North Crosby, new seasonal-use housing continues to be an important element of local construction activity.

This review of building-permit activity highlights tremendous variability between townships. While the general patterns of activity follow regional trends for housing starts, the individual townships experience different kinds of activity. The emerging profiles for North Elmsley and South Elmsley regarding the overspill of residential development from Perth and Smiths Falls is supported here by building-permit activity for permanent residences and strong conversion pressures on existing cottage properties. In Bastard and South Burgess and in South Crosby the recent pattern of slow population growth has great potential for change, as a continuing large share of the local housing stock remains only seasonally occupied.

Cultus Lake

Table 26 shows the distribution of all residential, cottage, and converted cottage properties around Cultus Lake. For the purposes of this table the area is divided into two sections, with the southern half including Columbia Valley and Lindell Beach while the northern half includes the Parkview area and Cultus Lake Park. The three mobile-home parks adjacent to Parkview are not included due to the wide variability in the number of units they contain at any given time. As described earlier, all cottage properties are located at either Lindell Beach or Cultus Lake Park.

The northern half of the Cultus Lake area is clearly the more intensively developed, with 528 properties accounting for 65 per cent of all residential properties in the study area. The 450 cottage properties at Cultus Lake Park account for 85 per cent of all residential properties in the northern half of the study area and 73 per cent of all cottage properties within the entire study area.

Cottage properties make up approximately 75 per cent of the residential-property stock around Cultus Lake. The distribution of converted cottage properties closely approximates the distribution of all cottage properties. Approximately 17 per cent of cottage properties at Lindell Beach were converted from seasonal to permanent occupancy between 1980 and 1990; within Cultus Lake Park, approximately 20 per cent of all cottage properties were converted over this same period.

Figure 21 summarizes building-permit data for the Cultus Lake area. The most striking item of note is the relative lack of seasonal-residence building-permit activity. The zoning by-law covering Lindell Beach does not distinguish between permanent and seasonal

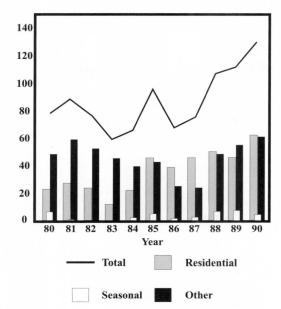

Figure 21
Issued building-permit activity, Cultus Lake.

occupancy of residential dwellings;[7] thus nearly all permits for residential work are classified by the building department staff as "residential," without distinction of occupancy. In Cultus Lake Park occupancy status is more clearly differentiated, depending on whether the lease is designated for six-month (seasonal) or twelve-month (permanent) entitlement. However, in this case there are simply very few permits issued for seasonal-use properties. One result is that relatively few seasonal-residence permits can be delineated within local records.

In the Columbia Valley, permits for general residential work follow the trend described by the area summary, with low periods of activity in 1982–83 and 1986. With one exception there is no building-permit activity for seasonal-residential purposes. Most of the other permits are for agricultural and associated structures.

At Lindell Beach, building-permit activity has generally increased since the early 1980s. The increase in "other" permits after 1987 mainly involves the attachment of cabanas and similar shelters to recreational travel-trailers at two seasonal recreational-vehicle parks near the cottaging area and does not represent a significant shift in Lindell Beach construction activity.

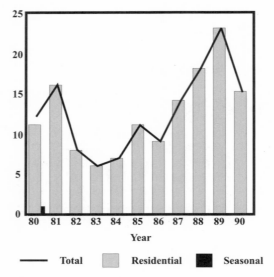

Figure 22
New-residence-permit activity, Cultus Lake.

The Parkview area adjacent to Cultus Lake Park shows little permit activity through to 1987, as this rural-residential subdivision remained until then largely undeveloped. From 1987 to 1989 the number of permits increases, as many of the remaining vacant lots were developed with permanent homes. This surge in activity is associated with a period of strong housing-start activity both in Chilliwack and across the province. The decline in permit activity in 1990 reflects the end of the supply of undeveloped lots.

Building-permit data for Cultus Lake Park are available only from 1985 through to 1990. Most activity is focused on permanent residences, as a large number of new homes have been built in recent years to replace older, usually much smaller cottages. The low level of seasonal-residence permit activity reflects what local residents suggest is a generally low level of reinvestment in the upgrading of older cottages. The only significant maintenance that can be noted for these seasonal-use cottages is attention to re-roofing.

Figure 22 shows building-permit data for new permanent and new seasonal-use residences. Most new residence building permits were for permanent homes rather than seasonal cottages. At both Lindell Beach and Cultus Lake Park there has been a recent increase in new permanent-residence permits. At Lindell Beach this follows a long period over which little new home construction occurred. While the data for Cultus Lake Park are limited, local officials similarly acknowledge limited construction activity during the early 1980s. At both Lindell Beach and Cultus Lake Park these new residence permits are associated with conversion activity. Nearly all properties have been fully developed for many years, and the replacement of older cottages by new residences is occurring either coincident with or shortly before a conversion move. In the case of construction prefacing a retirement move to the lake, a number of residents commented that they approve of this early rebuilding, as the property owner is less likely to rent out a new home for those few years prior to retirement.

In summary, building-permit activity for each sub-area around Cultus Lake reflects particular local characteristics. Within the cottaging areas two important issues emerge. First, nearly all significant investments are occurring in conjunction with conversion activity. Second, after generally stable activity levels through the 1980s, recent increases in new construction coincide with increasing local and regional pressures on housing. The community plan in place for most of the study area suggests that "future investment in seasonal homes is expected to grow considerably."[8] While investment indeed appears to be increasing, it is focused instead upon the transformation of a seasonal-use housing stock to a permanent residential community.

Patterns of change in local housing highlight an important internal difference in conversion pressures in both study areas. Cultus Lake has far fewer residential properties than does the Rideau Lakes area; however, cottage-area properties make up a substantial segment of the Cultus Lake property stock, approximately 75 per cent, compared to approximately 41 per cent along the Rideau Lakes. Thus, residential change within the cottage-property areas will have a greater proportional impact within the local community at Cultus Lake.

The conversion of seasonal-use cottages to permanent residences is occurring at a higher rate at Cultus Lake than along the Rideau Lakes. For the Cultus Lake area as a whole, 20 per cent of cottage properties were converted over the study period, compared to 6 per cent for the entire Rideau Lakes area. These results contribute to earlier suggestions that development pressures around Cultus Lake are greater than those along the Rideau Lakes.

From the review of local building-permit data it is clear that differences in local government land-use regulations and area population pressures have an impact on the types of permits issued. The downswing in the number of issued permits associated with the

Table 27
Location of Respondents' Previous Residence

	Rideau Lakes		Cultus Lake .	
Previous	Rural	Converter	Rural	Converter
residence	%	%	%	%
Local[1]	63.2	34.4	54.8	30.2
Adj. rural[2]	12.6	9.3	0	4.7
Adj. metro.[3]	7.4	36.4	19.4	58.1
Other	16.8	19.9	25.8	7.0
(n =)	(95)	(151)	(31)	(43)

Source: Resident survey, 1991.

[1] In the Rideau Lakes area "local" includes the study area and the incoporated places of Smiths Falls, Perth, Westport, and Newboro. In the Cultus Lake area "local" includes the study area and the District of Chilliwack.

[2] In the Rideau Lakes area "adjacent rural" includes all rural and small-town areas of Eastern Ontario, excluding the study area, between Ottawa and Kingston, and Westport and the Quebec-Ontario border. In the Cultus Lake area "adjacent rural" includes all rural and small-town areas of the lower mainland of British Columbia from the Vancouver CMA to the Town of Hope (excluding the Cultus Lake–Columbia Valley study area).

[3] In the Rideau Lakes area "adjacent metropolitan" includes all of the Ottawa-Hull CMA together with the Kingston CA. In the Cultus Lake area "adjacent metropolitan" includes all of the Vancouver CMA.

recession period at the beginning of the 1980s occurs later (1983–84) at Cultus Lake than along the Rideau Lakes. As well, the recovery at Cultus Lake is consistent with the slower recovery experienced in British Columbia into the late 1980s.

CONVERTERS AND CONVERSION

This section ties the residential behaviour of Converter households directly to cottage-area housing through three specific issues: location of former residence, the timing of residential moves, and the need to upgrade seasonal-use cottages to accommodate conversion to year-round living.

Rideau Lakes

Comparisons of the place of previous residence for Rural Residents and Converters suggests some important differences (see Table 27). While 63 per cent of Rural Residents report moving to their current residence from another location within the local area, 36 per cent of Converters report moving from the adjacent metropolitan areas of

Table 28
How Long Have You Owned/Leased Property? Converters Only

Resident Group	Rideau Lakes years					Cultus Lake years				
	1–5 %	6–10 %	11–15 %	16+ %	(n =)	1–5 %	6–10 %	11–15 %	16+ %	(n =)
Converter	27.0	25.8	19.0	28.2	(163)	33.3	8.9	20.0	37.8	(45)
Urban converters	14.6	12.7	29.1	43.6	(55)	20.0	8.0	24.0	48.0	(25)
Local converters	36.5	38.5	9.6	15.4	(52)	46.1	7.7	15.4	30.8	(13)
Urban elderly converters	3.7	11.1	33.3	51.9	(27)	17.6	5.9	11.7	64.7	(17)
Local elderly converters	33.3	16.7	33.3	16.7	(6)			33.3	66.7	(3)

Source: Resident survey, 1991.

Ottawa or Kingston. When Toronto and Montreal are included, approximately 45 per cent of Converters report relocating from an urban residence.

There is a complexity to this pattern, however, suggested by the approximately one-third of Converters who made their last residential move within the local area. In part this local mobility reflects earlier discussions regarding the separation of Rideau Lakes Converters into older professional families and retirees coming from urban areas, and younger families making a local-area housing choice to move to a converted cottage property. In other cases it represents Converters relocating from one lakeside property to another.

For Converters, I probed the relationship between place of former residence and the move to the lake by incorporating data on previous local experience or local familiarity. Comparative information on local familiarity derives in this analysis from the length of time over which respondents have owned/leased their property and from the age and former residential location of respondents (see Table 28). When we compare Converters according to whether they relocated from an adjacent metropolitan area or from within the local area, it is clear that former urban residents have planned for a conversion move, whereas those relocating within the local area have made a relatively recent property purchase. Approximately 44 per cent of exurban Converters have held their current property for more than fifteen years, while nearly 75 per cent of local-area Converters purchased

Table 29
How Long Has Your Family Owned/Leased Property? Converters Only

| | Respondent Owned the Property | | | | | | | |
| | Rideau Lakes years | | | | Cultus Lake years | | | |
	1–5 %	6–10 %	11–15 %	16+ %	1–5 %	6–10 %	11–15 %	16+ %
RESPONDENT'S FAMILY OWNED THE PROPERTY (years)								
1–5	16				5			
6–10	1	21				1		
11–15			11		2		4	
16+	4	3	6	20		1	2	11
(n =)	(21)	(24)	(17)	(20)	(7)	(2)	(6)	(11)

Source: Resident survey, 1991.

their current property within the last ten years – coincident with the period in which the property was converted.

To examine the question of planned conversion activity further, elderly Converters from either urban or local-area residences are also compared. Just over half of all exurban Converters were also elderly, while less than 12 per cent of local Converters were. While the pattern of property-ownership duration does not change for local elderly Converters, the urban elderly Converters are even more strongly skewed towards longer property ownership, suggesting a well-developed familiarity with the area and that the retirement move to the lake was a long-planned event.

The final length-of-ownership issue probed compares the length of property ownership by respondent with the length of time the respondent's family has owned the property (see Table 29). This introduces the issue of long-held family properties that have passed through generations of ownership. In the Rideau Lakes area most respondents report owning their property for the same length of time that the property has been in their family. Out of a total of 82 Converters, only 14 are readily identifiable as inheritors of the cottage property (that is, where the property has been in the family longer than it has been owned by the individual). Given this, recent concern among cottagers' associations[9] over capital-gains tax changes may have more to do with the simple issue of wealth transfer than with a heritage of family-cottage ownership.

Table 30
Property Use Prior To and Following Conversion, Converters Only

Months of use over year	Rideau Lakes %	Cultus Lake %
PRIOR TO CONVERSION		
1–3	52.2	48.4
4–6	13.9	3.2
7–9	1.7	0
10–12	32.2	48.4
(n =)	(115)	(31)
FOLLOWING CONVERSION		
1–3	2.6	0
4–6	7.7	2.2
7–9	12.3	8.9
10–12	77.4	88.9
(n =)	(155)	(45)

Source: Resident survey, 1991.

Table 31
Recent Major Renovations, Converters Only

	Rideau Lakes %	Cultus Lake %
TO USE ALL YEAR		
Yes	48.2	43.2
No	51.8	56.8
(n =)	(162)	(44)

Source: Resident survey, 1991.

One impact of conversion is that it results in an intensification of annual property use within the cottaging areas (see Table 30). Half of all Converters had used their cottage for only one to three months of the year prior to conversion. After conversion, over three-quarters of Converters use their property for ten to twelve months of the year. Interviews suggest that a large proportion of Converters also follow an annual snowbird migration to warmer climates for one or more months each year. This intensification of property use has important implications for lake water quality. The near universal use of septic tanks has been the focus of a heated public debate over pollution of the Rideau Lakes system.[10] A 1991 study reported that up to 40 per cent of the septic disposal systems along Upper Rideau Lake may not be functioning correctly and may be polluting the lake.[11]

A second impact of conversion concerns physical changes to the cottage. As shown in Table 31, about half of all Converters report that they had to undertake major renovation activity in order to live year-round at the property. Approximately 24 per cent of Converters identified work associated with general interior renovations such as the creation of new or separate rooms out of older configurations. A further 23 per cent identified the construction of additional living space. About 13 per cent of work was specifically identified as winterizing the structure, and 11 per cent involved upgrading of water/septic services on the property.

Cultus Lake

At Cultus Lake the majority of Rural Residents made their last residential move within the local area. The majority of Converters, however, relocated from metropolitan Vancouver, thus completing an urban-to-rural move (see Table 27). The cost of properties and house-price differentials between Vancouver and Cultus Lake are cited by former urban residents as important considerations in attracting them to the lake for at least their early retirement years. There are significant qualifications to these generalizations, however: 19 per cent of Rural Residents relocated from metropolitan Vancouver and 30 per cent of Converters made their last move from within the local area. Interviews suggest that exurban settlement into rural Columbia Valley is mainly accounted for by residents who had temporarily left, for reasons such as employment in the Vancouver area, and have now returned to their former rural community.[12] Among Converters, 39 per cent of those whose last residential move was from within the local area relocated between cottaging-area properties.

When we incorporate previous local experience into a probe of the relationship between former place of residence and timing of a conversion move, we find that approximately one-third of Converters had controlled their property for either less than five years or more than fifteen (see Table 28). Differences in behaviour are noted depending upon the location of previous residence. Converters moving from a former urban residence tend to have controlled their current property longer than Converters moving from another local-area residence. Although there is some support for the notion of local knowledge prior to a decision to move, the relationship is likely even stronger, as interviews with several Converters suggest a much longer attachment to place, including summer visits in youth and/

or the renting of cottages for a number of years prior to purchasing one's own.

Within the Converter group there is also a distinction between elderly and non-elderly respondents that suggests a strategy of planning for a retirement move to the lake. This is reflected in a longer duration of ownership: 65 per cent of elderly converters who moved from an urban residence had controlled their cottage property for more than fifteen years. When we extend our inquiry into length of ownership by incorporating the length of time that the cottage property may have been owned by other family members, we find that long-term family ownership is not common at Cultus Lake (see Table 29): just less than one-fifth of respondents report a legacy of family ownership.

In a comparison of the duration of annual cottage use prior to conversion, approximately half of Converters report using their Cultus Lake property for one to three months of the year, while the other half report ten to twelve months' use (see Table 30). Following conversion, the Cultus Lake properties are used ten to twelve months of the year by 89 per cent of Converters.

A second impact of conversion is the possible need to renovate the cottage for year-round occupancy. Less than half of Converters stated that they undertook major renovations in order to use their property year-round (see Table 31). The work described was principally concerned with upgrading the livability and winterability of homes. Approximately 35 per cent of the work identified constituted general interior changes such as room design or relocation. An additional 14 per cent was for the construction of additional living space. In terms of winterizing, 20 per cent of the identified work was for general exterior renovations such as window and door replacement, and an additional 18 per cent was for insulation and heating work.

Comparison of Converters in the Cultus Lake and Rideau Lakes areas highlights important differences in residential mobility. Along the Rideau Lakes there are two general patterns of residential moves. The first coincides with an exurban move, usually a planned retirement move, while the second is a housing choice made by local residents involving property purchases at time of conversion. In the Cultus Lake area, the much clearer predominance of retired households coincides with a higher degree of planning for a retirement move to the lake. As well, better winter access in the Cultus Lake area more easily accommodates year-round residential activity for these older residents than in the Rideau Lakes area. Comments from local residents in both areas confirm that winter accessibility is an important consideration in deciding whether to winter over at the lake.

Property turnover to purchasers from local rural, local small town, and adjacent urban areas was also noted by Davies and Yeates in their study of household movements associated with exurbanization pressures in southern Ontario.[13] This complexity of purchaser origin also reflects the mixing of resident pathways into the countryside. Beesley and Walker have tracked these pathways into the countryside and found that they usually involve a set of intermediate steps (ie, urban – suburban – small town – farm property). The result is an unevenness of exurban purchasers in the countryside.[14]

HOUSING PROFILES OF QUESTIONNAIRE RESPONDENTS

Rideau Lakes

A profile of the housing occupied by Rural Residents and Converters along the Rideau Lakes shows little difference between these groups in terms of property and house sizes (see Table 32). More than three-quarters of both Rural Residents and Converters report that their property is larger than 10,000 square feet.[15] As well, approximately 61 per cent of Rural Residents and 52 per cent of Converters report that their homes are larger than 1,500 square feet in size. The similarity in house sizes is also reflected in similarities in terms of the number of bathrooms and number of rooms within the residence. For both Rural Residents and Converters most homes contain two or more bathrooms and seven or more rooms.

The only real contrast in the housing of Rural Residents and Converters is in house type (see Table 33). Approximately half of Rural Residents report living in a two-storey house (with and without basement combined), while nearly two-thirds of Converters report living in a one-storey house (with or without basement). This difference somewhat reflects the genesis of converters' homes as cottages. As well, given the age and employment profiles of Converters, a one-storey layout with no stairs makes sense for an older resident population.

The final housing issue concerns the number of people living in the home. In a comparison of Rural Residents to Converters, it is clear that more people on average are living in the Rural Resident households. About half of Rural Residents report three or more people living in the house, while nearly three-quarters of Converters reported two or fewer. These findings confirm earlier studies of the

Table 32
House and Lot Size Comparison

	Rideau Lakes		Cultus Lake	
	Rural %	Converter %	Rural %	Converter %
LOT SIZE (sq. ft)				
<2,500	5.0	1.3	10.8	47.5
2,500–10,000	19.2	18.2	13.5	47.5
+10,000	75.8	80.5	75.7	5.0
(n =)	(120)	(154)	(37)	(40)
HOUSE SIZE (sq. ft)				
<500	2.4	0.6	0	0
500–1,500	36.6	47.8	45.9	81.8
1,501–3,000	53.7	45.3	48.7	18.2
+3,000	7.3	6.3	5.4	0
(n =)	(123)	(159)	(37)	(44)

Source: Resident survey, 1991.

differences in family structure between Rural Resident and Converter households.

Cultus Lake

The housing profile of Rural Residents and Converters at Cultus
Lake is marked by differences in property sizes. Approximately 48
per cent of Converters report their property to be less than 2,500
square feet in size (see Table 32). The very smallest of these lots can
be found in the older sections of Cultus Lake Park and Lindell Beach,
and it is many of these that have been subject to conversion. In terms
of dwelling size, Rural Residents at Cultus Lake tend to have larger
homes, with nearly all Converters reporting homes between 500 and
1,500 square feet in size. Rural Residents report more bathrooms and
more rooms on average within the residence than do Converters.
These results confirm a differentiation of housing between groups
that is consistent with the property-size differences. As well, comparison of the number of people living in the house complements earlier
discussions concerning family status and household size, with Rural
Residents reporting more people living in the residence.

The dominant house type for both Rural Residents and Converters
is the one-storey (with and without basement) (see Table 33). The
Lindell Beach area traditionally developed as a one-storey housing
landscape, although at times these may sprawl over nearly the entire

Table 33
House Descriptions

	Rideau Lakes		Cultus Lake	
	Rural %	Converter %	Rural %	Converter %
HOUSE TYPE				
One st./no basem.	11.3	20.3	28.9	51.1
One st./w. basem.	28.2	42.3	28.9	11.1
Two st./no basem.	7.3	20.9	10.6	26.7
Two st./w. basem.	44.4	11.0	18.4	8.9
Other	8.8	5.5	13.2	2.2
(n =)	(124)	(163)	(38)	(45)
NUMBER OF BATHS				
0	0.8	0	0	0
1	47.2	36.8	36.8	55.6
2	42.4	47.9	36.8	37.8
3+	9.6	15.3	26.3	6.7
(n =)	(125)	(163)	(38)	(45)
NUMBER OF ROOMS				
up to 3	2.4	10.5	10.5	22.2
4	18.4	16.1	21.1	35.6
5	20.8	24.1	21.1	22.2
6	18.4	19.1	15.8	11.1
7	20.0	16.1	7.9	8.9
+7	20.0	14.2	23.7	0
(n =)	(125)	(162)	(38)	(45)

Source: Resident survey, 1991.

property (quite an accomplishment considering septic-tank requirements). Redevelopment of some residences, usually at time of conversion, into two-storey dwellings has raised local comments of disapproval and objection. This disapproval has manifested itself in recent land-use policy debate, with the RDFC introducing a zoning amendment by-law to restrict "monster homes" in response to pressure from Lindell Beach residents over a proposed three-storey house.[16] While some Rural Residents report having basements, most Converters do not, since Lindell Beach and parts of Cultus Lake Park are composed of gravel soils with very shallow water tables unsuited to basement-style construction.

The very small lot sizes, the resultant smaller house sizes, and the lack of basements clearly differentiate the housing environment for Converters at Cultus Lake from those along the Rideau Lakes.

Among Rural Residents there is a much greater similarity in terms of lot size, house size, and house amenity in the study areas. In both areas Rural Residents report more people living in the dwelling compared to Converters, a reflection of the relatively smaller size of Converter households.

SUMMARY

Building-permit activity within both the Rideau Lakes and Cultus Lake areas generally follows the particular regional pattern of housing-development pressure as sketched by the housing-starts data. While the regional pattern in British Columbia appears to lag by approximately two years that seen in Ontario, both follow generally similar national economic trends. In each study area there is an unevenness in the distribution of both cottage properties and conversion activity. In the Rideau Lakes area, proximity to adjacent small towns creates a localized increase in conversion pressure through residential spillover; however, the important difference between the two areas is that greater development and conversion pressures are apparent at Cultus Lake. The larger general-area population (including Chilliwack), the smaller number of residential properties within the study area, and the larger proportion of the residential properties found in the cottaging areas account for the differences in conversion pressures.

The review of conversion activity within the local housing stock highlights a complexity of cottage-property turnover to purchasers from local rural, local small-town, and adjacent urban areas. While there is clear evidence that a large proportion of the Converter population completes an urban-to-rural residential move, there is also a mixing of resident pathways into the countryside. As well, the role of retirement, and of planning for a retirement move to a cottage property, is again emphasized as an important characteristic of Converters and a marker of the conversion process, reflecting both planning and motivational similarities to those found in earlier research by Clout.[17] These factors are of critical importance in trying to interpret and plan for change, as ownership patterns by age group, especially the pre-retirement 55–64-year group, may form an important indicator of latent conversion pressure.

In the Rideau Lakes area there is little difference between Rural Residents and Converters in terms of housing, with the exception of the distinction between one and two-storey homes. The cottage-area housing described by Converters at Cultus Lake not only differs from that occupied by local Rural Residents but also differs from that of their counterparts along the Rideau. In part, the small lot size and compact nature of the developments explain most of these differences. For both areas it is clear, however, that location is the fundamental characteristic distinguishing the housing of Rural Residents and Converters. The distinct lakeside focus of cottage properties marks the geographic separation evident within the rural-recreational countryside.

PART THREE

Change and Contention

7 Community Groups

To extend the argument that residential change via cottage conversion results in community change, our examination of the local population now moves from the individual to the group level to portray broader forms of interactions that together create community institutions. This study of community groups emphasizes themes of membership, participation, and an evaluation of the degree to which community groups act as a collective voice for their members. We examine two forms of community groups in the Rideau Lakes and Cultus Lake areas. The first are characterized as property-based organizations, such as resident/ratepayer or cottagers' associations. The second are characterized as interest-based organizations, such as local social groups for elderly residents. Particular attention is given to contention between the distinct social spaces represented by cottaging areas and the rural milieu within which they are set.

In the evaluation of local debates over residential change, it is important to identify whether local governments and property-based community groups represent similar or different sets of interests and residents. The literature on locality-based conflict identifies property-based groups as important actors in the control and ordering of geographic space. Early in this research, Wolpert, Mumphrey and Seley highlighted the differential ability of local residents to organize and act as an effective lobbying force in neighbourhood redevelopment debates.[1] Cox has greatly expanded upon ideas connected with conflict at the local level, conflicts he refers to as "turf politics." Among the research findings are that while property-based groups function as actors in local development debates, home-ownership and socio-economic status are important variables in determining levels of activism and relative resources brought to the debates.[2] I would argue that these characteristics intercede in the recognition of collective interests among rural and cottage-property owners. If the argument is that the separation of rural and cottage areas is important in the organization of property-based groups, then such organizational influence would be expected to overlap into interest-based community-group activity as well. To investigate this issue, two interest-based groups in each study area are examined to see how this separation of residential areas affects membership.

Commensurate with the change in scale from the individual to the collective level, there is also a change in the source of data used. While the previous chapter was developed from questionnaire responses by individuals, this chapter relies more on interviews with community-group leaders, newsletters and other publications of community groups, as well as local newspapers. This change in data source raises the problem of reliability. I used a number of checks to determine whether these evaluations portray valid images. First, issues of fact were cross-checked through alternate sources to determine accuracy. Second, I used expectations derived from the community-conflict literature to see if some interpretations needed closer scrutiny. Finally, interpretations were checked with other local residents or community-group members to see if essential issues in their minds had been captured.

RIDEAU LAKES

Property-Based Groups in the Rural Countryside

In the Rideau Lakes area, property-based community organizations do not play an important role in the organization of rural residents' activities or involvement. In fact, within the study area only one association for property owners outside of the cottaging areas could be identified. This association has only recently been organized, in conjunction with development of a new, high-status rural housing subdivision.

A principal reason for this lack of property-based groups in rural areas is that social or interest-based organizations, as well as those centred on important institutions such as local churches, have a long-established tradition of operation and involvement (see Table 34). Such groups have a legacy of providing necessary support and information networks to complement those of local government or

Table 34
Interest-Based Community Groups,[1] Rideau Lakes

Women's Institutes	*Service Clubs*	*Seniors Clubs*
Athens	Delta Legion (207)	Beverly Seniors
Chaffeys Lock	Elgin Lioness	Chaffeys Lock Seniors
Lombardy	Elgin Lions	Delta Seniors Club
Otty Lake	Lombardy Agricultural	Elgin Seniors
Phillipsville	Society	"Hands Across the Years,"
Port Elmsley	Portland Legion (231)	Westport
Rideau	Rideau Lakes Kinsmen	Perth Seniors Support
	Westport Legion	Portland Seniors Choir
	Westport Lions	Rideau Friendship Circle,
		Newboro
		Rideau Welcome Club (693),
		Portland
		South Crosby Friendship
		Club
		Westport Senior Citizens
		Club
"Church Women"	*Environmental*	*Miscellaneous*
Delta Anglican Church	Rideau Environmental	Chaffeys Lock and Area
Women	Action League	Heritage Society
Delta United Church	Rideau Lakes	Delta Mill Society
Women	Environmental Alliance	Delta Recreation Society
Elgin Anglican Church	Rideau Lakes Horticultural	National Farmer's Union
Women	Society	Local (318), North Leeds
Elgin United Church	Rideau Valley Field	Phillipsville Outreach
Women	Naturalists	Portland Bridge Club
Harlem-Chantry United		Westport Community Choir
Church Women		
Knox Presbyterian Ladies		
Guild		
Portland Anglican Church		
Women		
Portland United Church		
Women		

[1] This list represents groups that were locally based and clearly identified but not necessarily all such groups that may be active in the study area.

normal business activities. The extensive array of social or interest groups also places a considerable demand on the time and energy of local residents. Additional local groups are likely to be created only if a need is widely recognized.[3]

A second reason for the underdevelopment of property-based organizations is the common assumption that this is the role of local township councils. Many residents openly wondered in interviews why additional organizations would be needed when the township council manages property issues for the rural community. Indeed, for the six Rideau Lakes townships, all council members come from the rural or farm constituency. The rural-sociology literature warns of the over-organized rural community; in the Rideau Lakes area property-based organizations simply have not been needed in the already well-organized local community.

Local recognition of which set of interests, and which local constituency, township councils represent thus begins to emerge as an important element in understanding the current land-use planning debates. The view that the township council represents the rural community fits well with the description of a locally constructed separation between the cottage and rural areas. In the past the relatively low level of political activity on the part of cottage-property owners left this one-sided representation intact. However, the increasing political activity of cottagers' associations and of cottage-property owners moving to live year-round at converted cottages are placing considerable stress on this old formulation.

Cottagers' Associations

In contrast to rural property-owners' groups, cottagers' associations are an important part of the institutional and jurisdictional landscape of the Rideau Lakes (see Table 35). The cottagers' associations vary tremendously in size, ranging from the Opinicon Property Owner's Community (OPOC) of approximately 24 cottage owners to the Otty Lake Association (OLA), which numbers approximately 400 members. For the smaller associations such as the OPOC and the Newboro–Loon Lake Cottage Owner's Association there are usually no annual membership fees, and about half of members could be characterized as active. A number of the larger cottage associations charge an annual membership fee, usually in the order of ten to twenty-five dollars per property. Such fees are generally used to help offset operating and newsletter expenses. In the case of OLA, over 80 per cent of cottage-property owners at the lake are fully paid-up members.

While differences in membership size affect the formal level of organization, they do not seem to have an impact on the fundamental role the cottagers' associations undertake for their members. To begin with, there is clear recognition of a common or collective interest among cottage-property owners in these lake-centred organizations. Recently, a number of the cottagers' associations contacted have become formally incorporated bodies. The rationale is that incorporation simplifies an association's ability to obtain property and liability

Table 35
Cottagers' Associations, Rideau Lakes[1]

Beveridges Bay/Lower Rideau Lakes Association
Big Rideau Lake Association
Black Lake Cottagers' Association
Crosby Lake Association
Newboro-Loon Lake Cottage Owners' Association
Opinicon Property Owners Community
Otty Lake Association
Pike Lake Association
Sand Lake Estates Cottagers Incorporated
Upper Rideau Lake Association

[1] This list represents all cottagers' associations that could be identified by news-paper, local government, Parks Service, or FOCA sources and may not necessarily include all such groups active in the study area.

insurance on collectively owned property and to enter into contracts for the maintenance or management of property. In several cases this includes communal boat-launch and dock facilities, and in at least one case the negotiation of road-maintenance and snow-clearing contracts on private roads leading to cottage properties.

All the cottagers' associations contacted except the very smallest publish some form of regular newsletter. Given the wide geographic distribution of summer-cottage owners, the newsletter forms the basic communication link between the association's executive and the membership. These newsletters routinely contain statements on important current issues, including reports from the executive and the association's various committees on recent discussions or negotiations with local and senior government agencies, notices of upcoming township council meetings of interest, notices of the associations' upcoming events, reports on changes in local and provincial legislation or regulations affecting cottage owners, and tips or suggestions on issues ranging from property taxation to property security.

Two issues that recur in recent newsletters concern environmental protection and the representation of cottage-owner interests in interactions with local and senior government agencies. Environmental issues are cited by all cottagers' association members contacted as their principal area of activity. The OLA, the Upper Rideau Lake Association (URLA), and the Big Rideau Lake Association (BRLA) all promote participation in the Mutual Association for the Protection of Lake Environments in Ontario (MAPLE), the Provincial Ministry of Natural Resources' program of shoreline restoration and maintenance. The URLA and the BRLA have each participated in extensive water-quality surveys and septic-tank monitoring projects.[4] In fact, in 1991 the BRLA received an award from the Ministry of Environment in conjunction with their cottagers' self-help program, in recognition of ten years of contributing to the protection of the lake through water-quality sampling.[5]

Interaction between cottagers' associations and local township councils along the Rideau Lakes has not been uniform. Three of the six township clerks point to a relatively formalized system of information exchange with cottagers' associations within their jurisdiction. The relationships were reciprocally noted by the respective cottagers' associations.

The cottagers' associations contacted all express reservations about cottage-conversion activity. For some there are issues of concern, such as the need to maintain road access through the winter. At least one interviewee feels that year-round access has contributed to an increase in theft and vandalism through the winter months, occurrences that had previously been rare. For most, cottage conversion is seen in terms of its environmental impacts on lake water quality. Conversion is considered an issue to be managed by technical regulations developed from lake carrying capacity and environmentally sound development standards, directed at on-site sewage waste-disposal practices.

The activism of cottagers' associations around environmental issues and legislation is, however, difficult to interpret. Cross offers a sentimentalized account of this concern, suggesting that for cottage owners, "feelings go beyond ownership, [they] become custodians and protectors of the place. Any developer who has tried to build – either big or small – in summer territory learns the ferocious protectiveness of summer residents who band together as [self-appointed] legal guardians."[6] For example, the letterhead of the Big Rideau Lake Association reads "Serving the Rideau since 1911 – From Poonamalie to Narrows Lock." It is certainly true that along the Rideau Lakes system there is a concern over lake water quality and environmental degradation from recreational uses on the lakes.[7] However, it is clear that environmental protection is also being used as a euphemism within the cottaging areas for protection of a lifestyle and an increasingly exclusive control of access to cottage-property ownership. This observation is pursued in more detail in chapter 9.

Interest-Based Groups

Within the Rideau Lakes area there is a long-established tradition of interest-based community groups. Many of these groups are a legacy of the two organizing characteristics of early settlement: agriculture and religion.[8] The Phillipsville and Chaffeys Lock Women's Institutes have been chosen as two examples of interest-based groups. It should be noted that the generalizations offered with respect to the spatial organization of their membership mirrors that seen for other local groups such as the Elgin Seniors and the Chaffeys Lock Seniors.

The Women's Institute (WI) movement was founded in 1897 through the drive and vision of Mrs Adelaide Hunter Hoodless.[9] In its first ten years WI activity was extended across virtually all the agricultural and rural communities of Ontario. In 1919 the Federated Women's Institutes of Canada were founded to co-ordinate the national development of the movement, interest expanding to an international level with the organization in 1933 of the Associated Country Women of the World. Working "to fulfil the desires and needs for better home living of rural women," the WI movement has been involved in local community-service work and in making the voices of rural women heard in public-policy debate.[10]

The WI tradition of local activity and broader policy activism continues today.[11] The general mission statement for the organization is to encourage "personal growth and community action," with specific objectives addressing issues such as "promoting good family-life skills," "developing leadership skills," and the "identification and resolution of need in the community." In recent policy debates the Federated Women's Institutes of Ontario has been at the forefront of recycling, environmental, and waste-disposal issues as an advocate for the rural family.[12] Nearing its centennial, the WI movement in Ontario continues to address issues important to the contemporary farm and rural community.

The Phillipsville WI has been active in the Bastard and South Burgess/South Crosby area for more than seventy-five years. The current membership of approximately fifteen residents is drawn mainly from the farms and small villages of a very localized area. For many members, participation is an outgrowth of a life-long connection with the WI; several are following their mothers and even grandmothers in active service with the local WI. Most are empty-nesters, and many are retired. Most are also long-time area residents, although several new people have joined, new in this case generally referring to a first-generation resident lacking historic family ties to the area.

Service to the rural community has been a hallmark of the WI, and Phillipsville is no exception. Educational activities include annual field trips for members (offered at no cost to other area residents as well) to cultural events in the Ottawa and Kingston areas, as well as to the annual "ladies day" at the Kemptville College of Agricultural Technology. The Phillipsville WI also hosts invited speakers at its

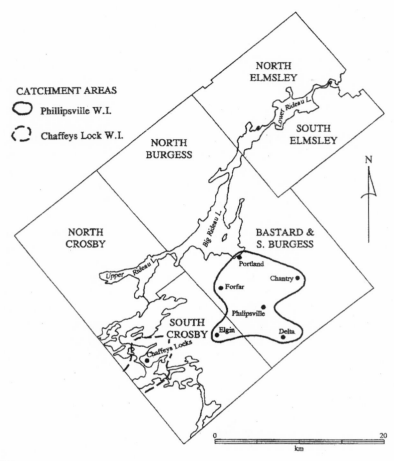

Figure 23
Catchment areas, Rideau Lakes Women's Institutes.

regular monthly meetings. Fund-raising activities focus on general contributions to the United Way, more directed efforts for the local food banks, and specific events such as for "burned-out families" – local families whose homes have been destroyed by fire. This is a sadly common occurrence; local newspapers report up to five such tragedies each winter across this study area alone. It is not uncommon to see advertisements in local newspapers notifying area residents of a Fire Benefit Dance to raise money and materials for the family in need.

The most ambitious undertaking of the Phillipsville WI is the operation of the WI hall, a former one-room schoolhouse in Phillipsville that the institute purchased for one dollar. The WI has upgraded the building and makes it available for community group functions. In 1987 the institute began preparing and hosting a monthly open-invitation dinner, called "Wheels to Meals," for area senior citizens. The WI charges a nominal fee to cover costs in this effort to get seniors out of the house, providing social contact and a special event as well as a meal. The first dinner served twenty-seven; current attendance is now between seventy-five and ninety.

Community activity is not taken lightly in the Phillipsville WI. Older WI concerns for efficiency in the home are still widely supported, as are new initiatives connected with recycling and protection of the rural environment. Members interviewed offered a harsh critique of other WIs, which have fallen into the comfortable routine of "old folks having cups of tea." In 1991 the Delta WI merged with Phillipsville. Although the Delta WI had nearly a dozen members prior to this merger, most were inactive and only a few remain active with the Phillipsville WI.

The problems of lagging membership and of a distinct aging of the membership represent difficult issues for WIs in general. While the mandate of community service is still viable, and even necessary in contemporary rural Canada, young women from the local area are not joining to revitalize the ranks.[13] Part of the reason is image, a perception of the institute's being out of style, but another is structure. The Phillipsville WI, indeed most WI in the Rideau Lakes area, hold their social and service events at weekday lunchtimes, and there is a hiatus of activities during July and August. This traditional pattern does not fit well with the schedules of the many working women in two-income farm and rural households. This problem of membership is similarly noted by representatives of several local-area church women's organizations.

The Chaffeys Lock WI represents the co-option of a rural/farm social organization by a very different group. As shown in Figure 24, the geographic distribution of membership is focused on Opinicon and Clear Lakes in South Crosby. Current membership in the Chaffeys Lock WI exceeds twenty, all of these members being seniors, all living within the general cottaging area, and most being exurban converters who moved to the lake at retirement. The membership composition makes the Chaffeys Lock WI unique among area WIs, as no members come from farm households.

As with the Phillipsville WI, the Chaffeys Lock WI puts considerable effort and energy into community service. Fund-raising for Guthrie House in Elgin, the local 4H clubs, and the Chaffeys Lock Heritage Society represent ongoing projects. Recovery of local heritage is another general WI concern, and the Chaffeys Lock WI is currently supporting restoration of the local cemetery. As well, for the past eighteen years the institute has hosted an open-invitation Christmas party for area residents. Interestingly, the Chaffeys Lock WI does not participate in hospital visits, a central activity for other area WI chapters. Members suggest that the relatively healthy status of the retired households living at the lake precludes the need for such visits. This self-acknowledgment of a healthy group status supports earlier suggestions about conversion involving retired households mainly during their relatively younger, fit years.

The Chaffeys Lock WI has adopted a much broader view of community service, extending it to include participation in policy debate concerning proposals by the local, provincial, or federal governments. The institute has been active in past debates over proposed automation of the lock doors at Chaffeys Lock and has participated in recent discussions over the Canadian Parks Service's new Rideau Canal Management Plan. It has also made submissions to the township council over recycling and waste-management proposals, and has recently become active on the managing boards of Family Focus and the North Leeds Abuse Task Force.

As an organization whose members are not drawn from a family tradition of WI activity, the Chaffeys Lock WI has approached the general issue of lagging membership very differently. Under the increasing flexibility offered by the WI organization, the Chaffeys Lock WI now operates year round and actively seeks the participation of women who only come to their cottages for the summer months. It is the opinion of the executive that this policy has reinvigorated the Chaffeys Lock WI, as many of these summer members are younger, are very active when they are in the area, and have introduced many new initiatives and ideas for the group to consider. This broader membership policy has allowed the institute to become an important part of integrating summer-only households into a cottage-area community.

Rural-community research has noted that in highly organized areas there tends to be a high degree of cross-over membership with other interest-based groups.[14] Many members of the Phillipsville WI are also active in the area's seniors' and church women's organizations. Such cross-over membership occurs among the Chaffeys Lock WI with the local seniors' and Heritage Society organizations.

CULTUS LAKE

Property-Based Groups in the Rural Countryside

Only one property-based community group outside of the cottaging areas has emerged at Cultus Lake as a stable organization with a long-standing period of operation. The Columbia Valley Ratepayers' Association has come to represent an important part of the activities and involvement of local residents. The locally developed sense of isolation and independence within Columbia Valley and, perhaps more importantly, the legacy of stress from property development or expropriation pressures exerted locally by external forces may explain this pattern.

The Columbia Valley Ratepayers' Association includes all property owners in the Columbia Valley benchlands above Cultus Lake. As described earlier, this group prides itself on direct community participation by residents. The self-conscious sense of isolation and self-sufficiency provides an impetus to this participation, as the association plays an important role in organizing a number of local services for persons and property, including the volunteer fire department and the associated women's auxiliary, as well as management of the community hall. The Ratepayers' Association also has a long-established tradition of organizing social activities within the community. Standing committees organize the annual parade, recreation, and the Christmas pageant. The response of local residents is a high degree of participation in activities organized through the association.

Residents of Columbia Valley have also experienced considerable stress in recent years from external initiatives to develop valley property. These external pressures have been instrumental in galvanizing local residents through a sense of "community under seige." Two specific examples of such external pressures are cited here to illustrate the form such pressures take and the collective response of residents.

The first of these pressures involved an attempt by the Department of National Defence (DND) to acquire much of the western side of the Columbia Valley for training grounds. In the early 1970s the DND had begun to evaluate possibilities for developing additional training areas for CFB Chilliwack as part of an expansion of the base's officer- and engineer-training role.[15] In 1974 the Columbia Valley, its relatively flat terrain isolated from areas of extensive residential development, was selected. Through negotiations with the provincial government, the DND began acquiring lease rights for Crown land along parts of Vedder Mountain to connect any future Columbia Valley training area with CFB Chilliwack at Vedder Crossing.

In March 1975 several Columbia Valley residents were contacted by DND property negotiators using what some residents described as high-pressure tactics. The "agents appeared on their doorsteps 'out of the blue' and asked them to set a price on their land and sign an agreement within three days."[16] The overwhelming of a local community by powerful external forces is clear in the voices of residents:

"We had no choice. There were no ifs, ands, or buts about it ... we were threatened with expropriation if we didn't sign the option now."[17] Only a few options were signed, however, as within a short time "the valley was buzzing with anger and rumour as the full scope of the military purchase plan became known. Neighbours exchanged views on land values and on the need to unify their opposition to being bought out."[18]

The community fight against the DND plan to purchase 700 acres in the valley was organized and conducted by the Ratepayers' Association. Certainly, the elected representative to the RDFC board, although not a Columbia Valley resident, raised the issue with the regional board and supported valley residents with strong statements to the media. Formal exchanges of letters between officials and institutions, including the area's MP, the DND, and the regional board, also followed. But it was the Ratepayers' Association that emerged as the voice of the Columbia Valley residents. They organized a petition drive against the proposal, and letter-writing campaigns.[19] D'Arcy Baldwin, president of the Ratepayers' Association in 1975, and Gordon Currie, president through 1976, became central media figures in newspaper coverage.[20] The Ratepayers' Association annual parade in 1975 became as much a protest march and show of solidarity against the DND proposal as it was the annual celebration of family life.

The success of community cohesion in the face of DND pressure is clear. In his review of the institutional planning process of the base expansion, Low argues that the "united public opposition to the property acquisition, the expressed desire of those who had signed options to somehow back out of the deal, and the escalating costs of the program led the Base staff to the conclusion that successful acquisition of the property by purchase was no longer feasible. Expropriation was an alternative, but was not politically advisable under the circumstances."[21]

In the face of a powerful external development force, whose land-use proposal would have effectively destroyed the existing Columbia Valley community, local residents were galvanized in opposition by their sense of community-under-siege. This unity of action mobilized the resources of the community through the organization and auspices of the Ratepayers' Association. The presence of a stable community-based organization, with a strong legacy of interest and participation among local residents, was critical in allowing the community to engage in a sustained and lengthy debate with the DND. The debate was between institutions, not individuals. An active public lobby and debate continued through the association even

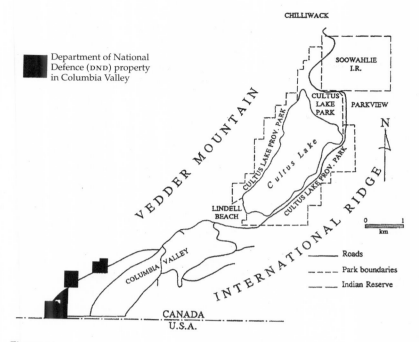

Figure 24
Department of National Defence (DND) lands, Columbia Valley.

when member officers changed, an example of the local community mobilization envisaged by Wolpert, Mumphrey and Seley, and later Cox.[22] Under pressure from the DND proposal and tactics, this community cohesion was also clearly grounded in a shared sense of place and history in the Columbia Valley, a legacy whose bond superseded local interpersonal disputes.

The handful of DND-purchased lands in the Columbia Valley remain highly visible reminders on the landscape of the attempt by an external force to destroy the lifestyle of local residents. The frequent appearance of soldiers on exercise in the valley continues to generate friction between local residents and CFB Chilliwack. The Ratepayers' Association records contain letters from the base commander responding at different times to the ongoing concerns of valley residents. These concerns include the discharge of weapons, the parking of DND vehicles and equipment on private and community property, and the spillover of military manœuvres from the DND lands. The threat to the local community, however, has not diminished. The January 1991 edition of the Columbia Valley Ratepayers'

Association newsletter quotes from a letter by the base commander to the president of the Chilliwack and District Real Estate Board that "the Base has a continuing interest in acquiring some additional land in the Columbia Valley for exercises and training. To that end, our Regional Property Officer has a mandate to survey the market on a continuing basis for any listings in that area."

The introduction of zoning regulations by the RDFC further contributes to a local distrust of outside initiatives and their impacts on valley life.[23] In fact, the legacy of the zoning by-law's introduction continues to colour relations between residents and the RDFC, and heightens local reactions to development proposals at public meetings.

In 1975 the RDFC conducted a series of public meetings concerning the introduction of land-use zoning regulations, developed by a consultant planner, into Electoral Area "E." While much of the recorded debate at these public meetings involves residents from nearby Chilliwack River Valley (the other half of the Regional District's Electoral Area "E"), the Columbia Valley meeting held on 1 December 1975 was attended by over 100 people. In the two public meetings held on this issue, nearly all who spoke were against all or portions of the proposed regulations. The public views expressed, however, were not intransigent, as 73 of the approximately 100 comments made for the record requested a postponement of the process for more public education and consultation, and so that local concerns could be considered in terms of possible amendments to the proposed regulations.[24] Residents requesting a postponement received their answer quickly: on 16 December 1975 the Regional Board voted to forward the proposed zoning by-law to the provincial Department of Municipal Affairs for approval.[25] The zoning by-law for Electoral Area "E" was adopted by the Regional Board at their meeting on 22 June 1976.[26]

Interviews with Columbia Valley residents highlight a continuing mistrust of local government initiatives and scepticism about the impact their comments at public meetings have on local decision-making.[27] This is disconcerting to local planning staff, who feel that considerable effort has been put into increased public consultation in Columbia Valley to counter perceptions forged years earlier during implementation of the zoning by-law. As well, the planning staff are quick to point out that recent Regional Board decisions do in fact reflect the community's views as expressed at public meetings.

Cottagers' Associations

As described earlier, there are two physically separate cottaging areas at Cultus Lake. Both Lindell Beach and Cultus Lake Park are intensively developed, small-lot cottaging areas that have experienced some degree of permanent occupancy since just after the Second World War. Each of these areas has also developed a separate property-based organization to act as a collective voice for its interests. However, the Lindell Beach Residents' Association and the Cultus Lake Community Association have very different histories of local activity and involvement.

The Lindell Beach Residents' Association was created at the same time as the original cottage lots. Since then, an active association has been responsible for most organizational and service-provision needs of the development. Property owners pay an annual fee to the association, which in turn operates and maintains a water system, a cable television system, and a collection of recreational facilities. The Residents' Association is also the registered owner of several large properties surrounding the cottage area and maintained as a privacy greenbelt.

As is common with forms of local government, a two-tiered set of jurisdictional relationships can be identified for the Residents' Association. The first tier is the internal relationship between property owners and the association. For the most part, this relationship is complementary. The executive of the association is charged with managing affairs for the benefit of all property owners. Not surprisingly, however, there are divisions between property owners over a range of issues that, interestingly, are closely marked by the seasonal or permanent occupancy of cottage property. Those living year-round at Lindell Beach often push for an increase in levels of services. A recent example has been the debate over street-lighting. In winter the Lindell Beach area is poorly lit, and concern with emergency-vehicle access on dark, narrow streets is a very real issue for year-round residents, most of whom are elderly. "Summer people," as one interviewee called them, have vigorously opposed more services, and these debates have been the focus of several lively annual meetings. The stated aim of the seasonal-only residents is simple: they wish to keep their association fees and property taxes as low as possible.

A second tier of relationships for the Lindell Beach Residents' Association is with external groups or agencies. In these relationships the association functions as the voice of a single, united collective of property owners. Negotiations with the provincial Ministry of Environment over the issue of flood protection from Frosst Creek along the western edge of Lindell Beach, and with the RDFC and provincial Ministry of Health on sewage-disposal monitoring and future planning, are two recent examples.[28] Periodic newsletters ensure the routine update of members on ongoing negotiations, and the annual meeting provides the forum for debate on future policy or strategy decisions.

The Residents' Association also maintains a continuous dialogue with the RDFC. Residents characterize the past relationship between the community and the RDFC as being very poor. In part this is a legacy of the zoning-by-law implementation process described earlier, but it also represents continuing resentment of a more general usurpation of local control and independence. This relationship has, however, significantly healed over the past five years, as the elected representative for Electoral Area "E" has, in fact, been a year-round resident of Lindell Beach. The importance of this voice on the Regional Board has not been lost on Lindell Beach property owners, and there is a strong commitment to voting in the municipal elections to maintain it. Local political participation in this respect is far more active than among cottagers in the Rideau Lakes area.

Interviews suggest that local concerns about the actions and initiatives of the RDFC have eased. This said, however, most are also quick to point out that there is a continuing degree of mistrust and an important need for the Residents' Association to stay vigilant for Lindell Beach interests. Even with a member resident on the Regional Board, the association's role has not diminished.

The Lindell Beach Residents' Association also supports and organizes social and recreational activities. The social event of the season is the regatta held on the August long weekend. First held in 1953, the regatta weekend includes activities ranging from swimming races and a local parade to the wind-up barbecue. This three-day event forms a kind of homecoming event for property owners. As many of the original families who purchased these lots have aged, the regatta now brings the grown children, and their children, back to Lindell Beach, reminiscent of both Wolfe's and Cross's commentaries that the cottage becomes a focal point of annual family renewal. It is during the regatta weekend that the annual meeting of the Residents' Association is held. The association's role in operating a number of important local services, controlling common greenbelt lands, and acting as the residents' voice in negotiations with other groups or governments are cited as important factors in the near 100 per cent attendance at this annual meeting.

The Cultus Lake Community Association, established in 1926,[29] has a similarly long-established existence; however, it has had a much less continuous history of local involvement. There are few community-wide activities or events that require the organization of volunteers, as in the Columbia Valley; and most local services are provided by the Park Board, so there are few money issues to debate, as at Lindell Beach. In the past the operation of the Community Association has relied upon energetic individuals or the emergence of issues broad enough to stimulate community-wide interest or stress in order to involve the membership.

Unlike at Lindell Beach, where sets of internal and external relationships can be discerned, the Cultus Lake Community Association has not sustained widespread participation by local leaseholders nor served as an effective collective voice. Several general issues raised in interviews with local residents combine to explain the disinterest. The first involves the large proportion of elderly residents living year-round within the park and their participation in non-property-based activity groups. The second concerns the very localized social spheres of Converters identified through the questionnaire. Third, there is the reduced interest in community affairs of seasonal-only residents, although this has curiously not been the case at Lindell Beach or along the Rideau Lakes.

The effectiveness of the Community Association in acting as a collective voice on behalf of the leaseholders in dealing with the Park Board has also been truncated. While this is partly a result of the discontinuity in interest levels expressed by leaseholders, it is also an outcome of the structuring of powers by the Cultus Lake Act and the leasehold nature of property tenure. The Cultus Lake Act confers broad powers on the Park Board,[30] confirmed by a 1965 court decision to allow the board to proceed with plans to ban year-round leases and remove lakefront cottages. This has reinforced a feeling of resignation among some long-term local residents. It is the expressed opinion of several locally active residents that their input is at best a delaying mechanism because the Park Board has the power to do what it wishes in the end anyway. They assert that the only reason the board did not proceed with its plans after the 1965 decision is the uncertainty that the affair generated for property investment in the park.

Despite this legacy there have been several widely attended local meetings over issues such as the installation of a commercial waterslide and the demolition of the historic park pavilion, episodes that suggest local resignation to Park Board powers is not yet complete. It is at these types of meetings that the leasehold nature of landholding becomes a critical issue in the local power structure. There is a certain amount of concern on the part of residents that the security of their leases could be placed in jeopardy. The Park Board approves all lease renewals, and property sales are actually sales of the "rights to apply" to the Park Board for a lease. Some residents fear that this

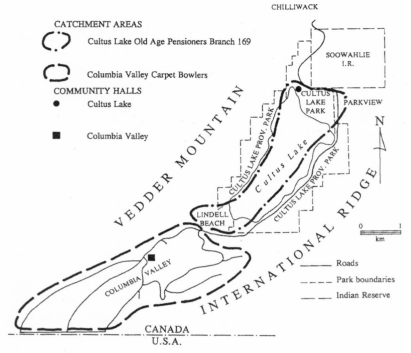

Figure 25
Catchment areas, elderly resident social groups at Cultus Lake.

power could be used as a bludgeon to cut short debate over Park
Board decisions.

Interest-Based Groups

Most notable of the few interest-based groups that are territorially
organized in the Cultus Lake area are those of elderly residents. This
section describes two such groups, the Cultus Lake Old Age Pensioners and the Columbia Valley Carpet-bowlers.

The Old Age Pensioners (OAP), Branch 169, Cultus Lake, was
formed in 1982 with 50 members, and now operates with about 150
active members. The group, which has a busy schedule of events and
activities, operates with its own organizing committee out of the
Cultus Lake Park community hall. It offers a range of bridge and
bingo games and organized lunches during the daytime, together
with a selection of card nights and dinner nights during the course

of each month. In fact, there are so many regular activities that the group seems to have almost exclusive use of the community hall.[31] It also publishes a regular newsletter and arranges for the transportation needs of some of its members.

Most Cultus Lake OAP members live in the Cultus Lake Park and Lindell Beach cottage areas. While a few additional members come up from the Chilliwack area, none is drawn from the Columbia Valley. For many of its members the group is a central focus of their energy and involvement. When new activities are suggested, they are often developed within the ongoing operations of the group. Finally, the group also serves to provide a common reference point for members by establishing a regular forum for social contact and information exchange.

In the Columbia Valley a carpet-bowling group has been active for several years, and this group forms the principal collective social activity for older residents. About 24 people regularly take part, meeting every Wednesday at noon in the Columbia Valley Community Hall for an afternoon of activity and refreshments. Most are from the valley, while a couple of former residents or friends of residents living in Chilliwack also participate. While not all participants are elderly, the group serves a function similar to that of the Cultus Lake OAP in terms of providing regular activity and social interaction for members.

As with most collective activities in the Columbia Valley, the carpet-bowlers are organized through the Ratepayers' Association. Unlike the Cultus Lake OAP, the carpet-bowling group is only one of a range of regular activities for older residents. The social institution that provides the common reference point remains the Ratepayers' Association, reflecting a continuing awareness of, and participation in, a broader social community compared to that described by elderly Converters in the cottaging areas.

DISCUSSION

Comparisons of group-level interactions highlight how important the socio-economic profiles of residents, their local activities, and the relative localization of social space is in the formation and maintenance of local community institutions. Levels of interest and involvement among residents in property-based organizations illustrate striking differences in the roles of these groups in the rural countryside surrounding the Rideau Lakes and Cultus Lake. These differences reflect the interactions between local residents and their recognition of community-wide issues and concerns.

In the Rideau Lakes area, property-based organizations are less important to Rural Residents, who feel that the township government most clearly represents their interests. In the Cultus Lake area, where residents are represented by only one seat on a wider regional board, there is less of an affiliation with local government and more emphasis on the Columbia Valley Ratepayers' Association as the local collective voice. Compared to the Rideau Lakes area, the association has developed into an important institution for residents, representing a focal point for many local activities, information networks, and investment of time in their community. Perhaps as a result of this interdependence, attendance at the annual general meeting is consistently reported at near 100 per cent of valley households. Impressive results of this community group's efforts include recent construction of community and fire halls, the publishing of a regular newsletter, and an extensive annual calendar of social events and activities.

In comparing cottagers' associations with rural property-owner groups, three important points need to be made. The first is that cottagers' associations are local resident groups different from those discussed for rural residents. Cottagers' associations in both study areas are well organized, have high rates of participation by members, are active in public debates over a range of local issues, and play an important role for their members in terms of managing collective property interests. Membership in a cottagers' association is based on the ownership of a cottage-area property. Second, these groups are at root instruments of property-value protection, although the issues of protection of property values and protection of an "image" of lifestyle and social activity are not so easily separable. Finally, cottagers' associations are emerging with many of the characteristics of a local government, operating for a specialized group of constituents within more formal political jurisdictions. These issues are an outcome of the locally constructed understanding that differences between rural and cottage-property areas mark a fundamental social and geographic division within the rural-recreational countryside.

At Cultus Lake the cottagers' associations are also recognized as the collective voice for local residents. This recognition is much more developed for the Lindell Beach Residents' Association, where the RDFC has established formal linkages for ongoing consultation that now extend even to the review of building-permit applications. At Lindell Beach there is a strong feeling of shared responsibility, and the Residents' Association is the means for both annually updating members and routinely managing their collective interests.

Within Cultus Lake Park, the effectiveness of the Cultus Lake Community Association has been truncated primarily by the leasehold nature of property tenure. When local residents have come together in the past, the Community Association has not been the focus; rather, an issue-based coalition has formed. This has proceeded in the past much as described in the politics-of-turf literature. This presents an awkward problem for residents of Cultus Lake Park; the local government is not regarded as interested in the fundamental well-being of residents, and the Community Association has not been a continuous or effective voice either. These findings modify Helleiner's[32] contention that recognition of collective interest is an important part of community building in cottage areas by introducing the issue of ownership tenure as an important element in mobilizing this interest.

Cottagers' associations appear to function much like a local government, with, of course, a very specialized constituency. Across the Rideau Lakes area these associations are sophisticated organizations formed around interest-based regions (the individual lakes), which allow them to avoid some of the difficulties of jurisdictional fragmentation that local townships must deal with in co-ordinating environmental or development policy. In some of the township council meetings the cottagers' associations are in fact called upon to assist the local government by attaching township notices to their newsletters. What is emerging is a dual system of government, with local rural residents represented by the township and cottage-property residents by the cottagers' association. In debates over new development or land-use regulations, it is clear that cottagers consider the associations legitimate collective voices for their interests.

Interest-based groups offer the possibility of transcending the spatial configurations of neighbourhood or settlement cluster to allow for study of the collective organization of residents. If there is a locally recognized separation of rural and cottage-area residents, then such a separation would be expected in the membership organization of local interest groups. In both study areas this is clearly the case. The interest-based groups examined are exclusive in their organization of members from either the rural or cottage-property areas.

The differences noted between the two study areas also involves the range of choices for residents. In the Rideau Lakes area there is a long tradition of interest-based community groups. One of these groups, the Women's Institute, can, however, exhibit very different spatial organization depending upon whether rural/farm women or cottage-area women are involved. Such long-standing rural community institutions may be withering, as few of the younger residents in these communities are joining them. This may be bound up in an image question (a matter of being "out of date" in both style and terminology), as the basic mandate or role of these institutions still appears relevant in the rural community. Comparison of the Phillips-ville and Chaffeys Lock WIS reveals how different residential constit-uencies use a similar social organization, with place of residence not only structuring membership but also influencing the range of activ-ities in which these groups feel it is legitimate to participate.

In the Cultus Lake area the distinction between the cottaging and rural-residential areas not only has an impact on the spatial organi-zation of elderly residents into activity groups but also acts to influ-ence the form and focus these social institutions take. In the Columbia Valley, activities are organized under the Ratepayers' Association, reinforcing its central role as a collective focus for valley residents. In the Cultus Lake Park and Lindell Beach areas, the Cultus Lake OAP forms the organizing body.

In the city's countryside, amenity landscapes located near the outer fringe of the urban field are developed as the domain of vacation-and recreation-seeking urban residents. Yet these recreational areas are also set within an existing rural landscape. The evolution of land uses and social patterns within the rural-recreational countryside represents an outcome of the interactions between these competing landscapes. It is clear that, within this socially and geographically divided landscape, distinct communities can be constructed within the wider community. Both the characteristics of the residents and the character of the settlement areas generate varying levels, and/or alternate forms, of collective expression. These communities-within-communities are one of the outcomes generated by the pressures of residential change in the rural-recreational countryside. As these pressures continue through processes such as cottage conversion, their outcomes in the local area will continue to have important con-sequences for the way relationships are structured.

8 Local Government Structure

The mandate of local governments to regulate land-use planning creates a unique forum in which debate and contention over residential development and resulting issues of community change can be resolved. As well, the activities of local governments in the land-use planning process also make them important institutional actors in the debates themselves. Elaboration of the structure and operation of local governments is, therefore, an essential building-block in the interpretation of community conflict over residential change. This chapter explores whether local government policies recognize recreational-development and cottage-conversion pressures, and describes the regulatory structures developed to respond to and cope with these pressures. Following this review, residents' perceptions of local government performance are probed to evaluate local satisfaction with land-use planning activity.

RIDEAU LAKES

Local government in the Rideau Lakes area is structured around the individual township. It is important to note from the outset that no grand plan or scheme governed the laying out of township boundaries. First surveyed between 1780 and 1820, the six Rideau Lakes townships functioned simply as a surveyor's baseline and an organizing unit for the identification of land for settlement along what had been until then an "unorganized frontier." In fact, it was not until the Baldwin Act of 1849 that the "township" was established as

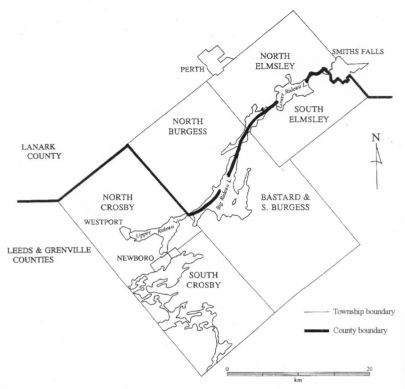

Figure 26
Township and county boundaries, Rideau Lakes.

a "rural unit of municipal government" throughout what is now Ontario.[1]

One of the first structural items of note in the organization of local government along the Rideau Lakes is the lack of any regional co-ordination mechanism for land-use planning. The townships have not been part of any regional municipality or restructured county program of local government reform. As a result, responsibility for management of local development and land-use planning policies continues to rest with the individual townships. Recreational-development pressures, however, are not necessarily limited to the boundaries of single townships; instead, they occur across the study area. The fragmentation of policy responses by individual town-ships, therefore, can have important ramifications for neighbouring townships.

The location of county boundaries further complicates jurisdictional fragmentation along the Rideau Lakes. North Burgess and North Elmsley are within Lanark County, while the remaining four townships are within the United County of Leeds and Grenville. Many county government activities, such as road construction and maintenance, have a direct impact on the management and planning of local land uses. With the study area divided between Lanark County and Leeds and Grenville County, co-ordination is made more difficult.[2]

The Sewell Commission on Planning and Development Reform in Ontario recognizes this issue of jurisdictional fragmentation as problematic for land-use planning at the township level. In fact, to illustrate its concern the commission cites a rural-recreational-countryside example from the Kawartha Lakes region, where four townships in two counties share the shoreline of a single lake. Using this example, the commission argues that "joint planning would help resolve environmental concerns and lead to consistency on policies concerning issues such as water quality and land use."[3] Studying the local impacts of cottaging and tourism in the Collingwood area of Ontario, Wilkinson and Murray found a similar jurisdictional situation, where co-ordination of local government land-use planning responses to these impacts occurs within a "regional planning vacuum."[4]

The six Rideau Lakes township governments demonstrate various stages of maturity in terms of administrative structure and range of services provided. The generally low level of municipal government development places considerable pressure on those governments to operate under legislation designed for larger, more urbanized jurisdictions. Leung argues that such rural local governments often "do not have the resources to perform all their planning functions" and must look to senior governments and consultants for assistance.[5]

The use of private consultants in the preparation of community plans, zoning by-laws, and evaluations of development proposals further complicates the local fragmentation of land-use policy and regulation, raising questions about accountability and introducing a range of other difficulties.[6] The first of these difficulties concerns the translation of local needs into documents designed to conform to legislative requirements and language. Again, Leung notes that many small local governments "have no capacity to evaluate (and sometimes even to understand) the policies and by-laws prepared by a far-away consultant before they are adopted and implemented."[7] The use of different planning consultants among area townships, or even within the same township at different times or for different types of work, introduces further discontinuity in the kinds of planning philosophies, tools, and options employed. As well, the use of consultants does not provide for the ongoing availability of a local resource person able to discuss with authority the questions or queries of local residents. Some residents suggest that responses from the township offices are often couched in terms of provisional answers that would need to be asked of the consultants formally in order to get a more reliable answer.

Along the Rideau Lakes the use of planning consultants has created some difficult situations. A recent public debate in North Crosby resulted in a considerable amount of ill feeling among residents attending the meeting over the consultant's chairing of the meeting.[8] The perception, described in interviews, is of an outside expert coming in and running roughshod over the residents' right to question their local council about issues that soon could become policy or regulation. Leung suggests that for small local governments where "the chains of command and responsibility are short and direct" the introduction of consultants can place those consultants in the difficult position of occupying the place formerly reserved for "big government" – that is, of a monolithic, dictating, extra-local force to be met with apprehension rather than trust.[9]

Local government recognition of the problems associated with cottage development has been slow. In 1977 Priddle and Kreutzwiser warned that the "tremendous increase in the number of cottages in [Ontario] and the changing patterns of use have ... created a pressure on cottage environments that has far outstripped managerial ability to cope with it."[10] While recognition of such pressures has been uneven among Rideau Lakes area townships, South Elmsley has been the most active in terms of introducing policies and regulations to manage cottage-conversion activity. This is perhaps not surprising, given that South Elmsley has also experienced the greatest population growth and conversion activity among area townships over the past fifteen years. South Elmsley's 1984 community plan identified cottage conversion as an important element of local growth and as an issue of concern for residential service provision.[11] The zoning by-law adopted as part of this planning process introduced the "Limited Services Residential" and "Limited Services Residential-Holding" zones advocated in the Ontario Ministry of Housing's discussion paper on cottage conversion.[12]

In a 1989 review of local governments, Bastard and South Burgess, and South Crosby, both with substantial numbers of lakeside properties, had not viewed conversion as a current pressure.[13] In the zoning by-laws currently in place for at least two Rideau Lakes townships, a "recreational" or "seasonal-residence" zone is the mechanism of cottage-development regulation. However, cottage-conversion activity along the Rideau Lakes is proceeding, and neither the limited-services zoning nor the exclusionary seasonal-residence zoning options are limiting or tracking this activity.[14] This represents an increasing challenge for local governments and one that several began to address through 1990 and 1991 (see chapter 9).

Resident Perceptions of Local Government

While there is some uniformity in structure among Rideau Lakes township governments, not all are as well developed in terms of in-house staffing, adoption of zoning and community-plan regulations, and recognition of cottage-conversion impacts in those regulatory documents. Despite these differences, it appears that Rural Residents and Converters have similar opinions of their local governments. Satisfaction with local government performance was probed as part of the questionnaire survey conducted in both the Rideau Lakes and Cultus Lake areas, and the results provide important background information for interpreting some of the recent debates chronicled in the following chapters, especially the views of different resident groups on important local land-use planning issues.

There is little difference between Rural Residents and Converters in their responses to three questions about satisfaction with local government. Approximately three-quarters of both groups report being satisfied with the time required to get building-permit approvals (see Table 36). On the questions of land-use planning and opportunities for public input into land-use planning decision-making, just less than half of respondents were satisfied with local government performance.

About one-third of each group answered none of the three questions concerning statisfaction with local government. As well, for the questions on satisfaction with land-use planning and public input, approximately one-third of those who responded in both groups are neutral. The high non-response rates and neutral expressions among those who did respond suggest that many individuals have little or no direct engagement with their local government. It is interesting that this appears to be a shared experience of both Rural Residents and Converters. While it is hardly surprising that many Rural Residents may have little regular contact with their local governments, some Converters reside in townships that require occupancy permits and/or zoning changes to permit year-round residency. Magnusson asserts that residential-service provision is an extremely divisive

Table 36
Satisfaction with Local Government

| | Rideau Lakes | | Cultus Lake | |
	Rural %	Converter %	Rural %	Converter %
TIME TO GET BUILDING-PERMIT APPROVALS				
Very satisfied	20.5	22.3	3.6	12.5
Satisfied	56.8	53.6	35.7	54.2
Neutral	13.6	13.4	28.6	20.8
Dissatisfied	6.8	8.0	21.4	12.5
Very dissatisfied	2.3	2.7	10.7	0
(n =)	(88)	(112)	(28)	(24)
LOCAL GOVERNMENT LAND-USE PLANNING ACTIVITY				
Very satisfied	8.1	5.4	3.6	4.0
Satisfied	33.7	43.2	17.9	40.0
Neutral	32.6	28.8	32.1	40.0
Dissatisfied	16.3	14.4	39.3	16.0
Very dissatisfied	9.3	8.1	7.1	0
(n =)	(86)	(111)	(28)	(25)
PUBLIC INPUT INTO LOCAL PLANNING DECISIONS				
Very satisfied	8.1	5.5	10.7	4.0
Satisfied	40.7	38.2	17.9	28.0
Neutral	31.4	31.8	25.0	24.0
Dissatisfied	14.0	18.2	28.6	44.0
Very dissatisfied	5.8	6.4	17.9	0
(n =)	(86)	(110)	(28)	(25)

Source: Resident survey, 1991.

local issue.[15] In reviewing resident perceptions of local government performance, respondents were also asked three open-ended questions about local government services (see Table 37). A slightly larger proportion of Converters than Rural Residents answered the questions calling for new or expanded services, while fewer of both groups identified services to be discontinued.

In the Rideau Lakes area, Rural Residents offer 97 suggestions on local services to be introduced or expanded. Most of these concern environmental services (33) such as recycling, sewage treatment, waste disposal, tree planting, and stream-bank rehabilitation. Calls for additional road maintenance (25) include grading, snow removal, and paving of rural roads. Further suggestions involve increased protective services such as the 911 emergency telephone service, ambulance, and fire protection (17), while 18 suggestions involve additional community services such as recreational facilities, child-care, seniors' housing, and drug/alcohol counselling.

Converters respond with many more individual suggestions (168) for new or expanded local services, although environmental services and road maintenance again predominate. Of the 71 comments offered on improved environmental services, most call for extension of township garbage collection to cottage properties. At present only South Elmsley provides this service. Of the 65 comments describing improvements to road maintenance, 26 call for townships to assume ownership and maintenance of the private roads accessing the cottaging areas. In terms of social services, 7 suggestions call for home support and other services for seniors, and 6 call for general community services such as libraries.

Few comments address reducing or discontinuing local services. Of the 28 such suggestions offered by Rural Residents, 13 address reductions in local social services, while 4 seek a reduction of local government bureaucracy. Only 7 Rural Residents call for a reduction in education/school taxes, an issue over which local governments have no control or input. Converters offered 28 suggestions for reduced services, nearly all (20) calling for a reduction in educational/school services and taxes.

Table 38 analyses the distribution of respondents who identified important local land-use planning issues. Concern for protecting the environment and the rural community are the central themes behind the 58 suggestions about important planning issues from Rural Residents. Of those, 17 address protection of the lake environment by limiting or better managing lakeside development and cottage conversion; 14 address the protection of agricultural areas from development, while 10 identify general environmental-protection issues such as septic-tank contamination of waterways. An additional 7 comments call for protection of the rural community by slowing the general pace of development.

Converters along the Rideau Lakes agree with Rural Residents that protection of the environment and existing lifestyles and landscapes are important local planning issues. Of the 101 suggestions made, 47 call for increased protection of lake environments by increasing regulation and management of shorefront development. A further 33 address general environmental protection such as monitoring of septic-tank contamination, and 10 involve a tightening of the land-use planning process to scrutinize development proposals more carefully and to ensure that the developer pays service costs, not the local taxpayer. Interestingly, only 3 comments spoke favourably of allowing more lakeside development.

Table 37
Local Services Provision

	Rideau Lakes % answering		Cultus Lake % answering	
	Rural	Converter	Rural	Converter
IDENTIFY SERVICES TO BE IMPROVED OR EXPANDED				
	44.8	57.7	57.5	48.9
(n =)	(125)	(163)	(40)	(45)
IDENTIFY SERVICES TO BE REDUCED OR STOPPED				
	22.4	15.3	22.5	8.9
(n =)	(125)	(163)	(40)	(45)
IDENTIFY NEW OR NEEDED SERVICES				
	32.0	35.6	40.0	35.6
(n =)	(125)	(163)	(40)	(45)

Source: Resident survey, 1991.

Table 38
Local Planning Issues

	Rideau Lakes % answering		Cultus Lake % answering	
	Rural	Converter	Rural	Converter
IDENTIFY IMPORTANT PLANNING ISSUES				
	44.8	55.2	57.5	46.7
(n =)	(125)	(163)	(40)	(45)

Source: Resident survey, 1991.

CULTUS LAKE

The structure of local government responsibility around Cultus Lake is complex. While the entire study area is officially unorganized – that is, not incorporated as a municipality under the British Columbia Municipal Act – there are local government responsibilities that make for a regulatory landscape not unlike any organized municipality. All of the study area is located within part of the RDFC's Electoral Area "E," and is subject to all regulatory functions developed for that area. The exception is Cultus Lake Park, which is managed as a separate jurisdictional area by the Cultus Lake Park Board under powers granted through the British Columbia Cultus Lake Act.

The RDFC was incorporated with letters patent on 29 September 1967.[16] As part of a provincial government program to introduce regional organization to local government, regional districts were imposed as an upper tier of local government. This was heralded as an important step in introducing some form of local government for unorganized rural areas and to assist in "co-ordination of municipal services, activities, and enterprises, and in the development of services."[17] There has been considerable debate about the ordering of these priorities, with some observers suggesting that the fundamental goal of the program was to introduce a mechanism to resolve perceived inefficiencies in the management of hard-services provision in metropolitan Vancouver.[18]

In the Cultus Lake area the RDFC acts as the local government for all areas except Cultus Lake Park. The context for current land-use policy and regulatory instruments develops from a three-tiered distribution of planning powers. Narrowing from the most general level, there is the regional planning function, the local or community planning function, and the local land-use regulations adopted under the zoning function.

The broadest attempt at providing a comprehensive statement of land-use planning objectives in either study area is contained within the Official Regional Plan (ORP). Developed by the four regional districts composing the Vancouver-centred Lower Mainland of British Columbia, the ORP "is not only a statement of the objectives of the four [regional districts] ... with respect to the development of the Lower Mainland; it is also a framework for joint planning in the Lower Mainland as a whole."[19] The need for a regional co-ordinating mechanism for policy recognizes that population/development pressure is "a dynamic process which shows little respect for municipal or regional district boundaries. Its management requires a plan and a planning process which is capable of addressing the requirements of the region as a whole as well as the particular needs and aspirations of the region's diverse local communities."[20]

Under the ORP both the Cultus Lake Park and Lindell Beach cottage areas were designated "Resort." Resort areas were broadly conceptualized "as integrated developments, with residential, commercial and recreational activities ... distinct from single purpose developments such as outdoor recreation facilities or isolated cottage subdivisions."[21] As an illustration, the resort designation around Cultus Lake Park included the commercial, country-residential, and mobile-home-park sections of the Parkview area.

Use policies of the ORP's resort designation identified a range of residential, recreational, and associated uses consistent with development

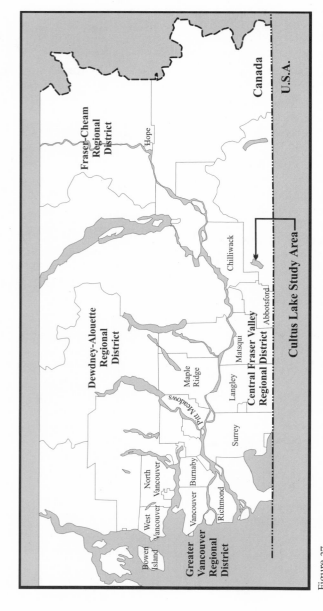

Figure 27

Area of application: Official Regional Plan (ORP) for Lower Mainland of British Columbia, Cultus Lake.

Source: Base map from Official Regional Plan for the Lower Mainland of British Columbia (1981).

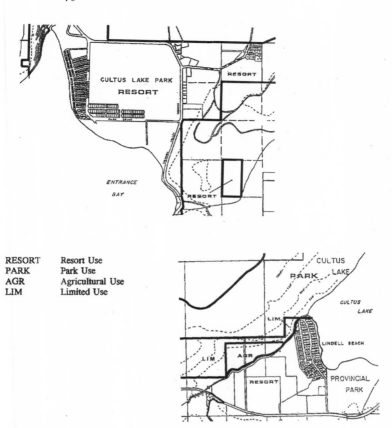

Figure 28
ORP Resort designation, Cultus Lake Park and Lindell Beach.
Source: Official Regional Plan (1981) mapping.

of integrated resort areas. Residential uses were not defined, or limited, in terms of occupancy status. In fact, stable resort areas were expected to contain a mix of both seasonal and permanent residents. The ORP also sought to ensure that public access to recreational/ natural amenities be maintained or enhanced, a policy that would preclude the linear form of cottage development seen along the Rideau Lakes. While the ORP established broad objectives and policy statements, it was to be an active component of local planning, as legislation required that lower-order plans and zoning by-laws should implement, not just conform to, provisions of the ORP.

The organization of issues and policies within the ORP is important for management of development at Cultus Lake. Recognition of

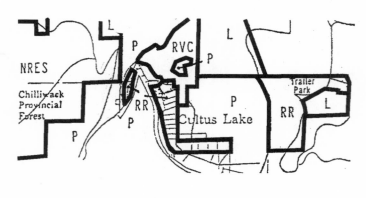

P   Park Areas
RR   Resort Residential Areas
RVC   Resort Village Centre
RTC   Resort Tourist Commercial
AG   Agricultural Areas
NRES   Natural Resource Areas
L   Limited Use Areas

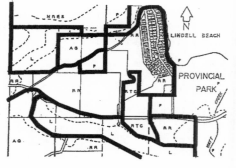

Figure 29
OSP Resort Area designations, Cultus Lake Park and Lindell Beach.
Source: Official Settlement Plan (1982) mapping.

regionally significant recreational values and of regionally generated development pressures coincides with the earlier discussion demonstrating that Cultus Lake Provincial Park is clearly of regional significance. The goal of maintaining broad public access to the lakeshore provides protection against the startling lack of public access along the Rideau Lakes. Policies concerning creation of more complete, serviced resort areas set the foundation for the transition to a year-round residential community. When the British Columbia Municipal Act was amended in 1983, however, all regional planning powers and responsibilities were deleted.

The second tier of planning policies below the regional level are the community land-use planning-policy statements embodied in the Official Settlement Plan for Electoral Area "E" (OSP).[22] While the policies and designations of the OSP include Cultus Lake Park, the adopting by-law exempted these lands, recognizing that "those portions of the plan concerning Cultus Lake Park, which is separately administered by the Cultus Lake Park Board ... are included only as an expression of the [Regional] Board's general objectives with respect to future planning and administration of Cultus Lake Park and do not form part of this Bylaw."[23]

Written to comply with and move towards implementation of ORP policies, the OSP's designation and use policies for Lindell Beach and Cultus Lake Park follow a similar thematic organization. A first concern is the maintenance of a regional perspective on local development pressures. Policy is clearly oriented towards a "regional public interest." Increasing use and development pressures require "that great emphasis be placed on the management of the remaining publicly owned lands."[24] Included in these publicly owned lands are Cultus Lake Provincial Park and Cultus Lake Park. The inclusion of policies and comments in the OSP regarding the future of Cultus Lake Park has been identified in local interviews as one of a continuing number of points of friction between the Cultus Lake Park Board and the RDFC.

A second concern of the OSP is the desire to maintain and enhance public access to local recreational features in the face of increasing pressures for private recreational developments. ORP policies with respect to public access to recreational amenities survive as an integral part of the OSP document.

A third concern is the maintenance of a broad conceptualization of resort areas. The OSP's resort-area policies seek to "encourage the development of well-planned, integrated resorts in the settlement plan area, and to ensure the most effective protection and use of the natural features on which the resorts are based."[25] This statement reflects the goals of the ORP and represents a more effective statement, by an agency with regulatory power to put policy into practice, than could be identified in the Rideau Lakes area. Discussing current pressures and challenges in managing resort-area development, the OSP notes that demand for recreational experiences continues to put pressure on the resource, while experience also "illustrates clearly the traditional role of resort residential development as a precursor to permanent settlement."[26]

The areas designated under the OSP resort policies coincide with those defined in the ORP. Use policies for the ORP "Resort Residential" areas, however, seem restrictive. While there is a range of more general uses listed, such as farming, forestry, and public utilities, specific residential-only uses are limited to "cottage residential" and "holiday park and recreational vehicle sites." Cottage residential is defined as "a residential use which is not intended to be used for permanent year-round residential occupancy."[27] This listing, which seems to limit permanent occupancy, was questioned by property owners during public meetings on the osp.[28] It is the position of the RDFC that existing residential areas enjoy the use rights conferred under the zoning by-law existing at the time of osp adoption, including the right of residential uses undifferentiated by patterns of occupancy. All new subdivisions of property, however, should be developed as holiday parks under the provisions of the Campground–Holiday Park regulatory by-law, which allows for development of permanent residences within strata-title subdivisions. The aim of this policy direction, the terminology used, and the development options it dictates are designed to remove responsibility for the considerable expense of providing residential services from the public tax-base. Specifically, where resort developments are proposed, "the costs of both water and sewer services will be borne by the developer, not the taxpayer."[29]

The day-to-day management of local planning and development is controlled through a zoning by-law that establishes current land-use regulations.[30] While the osp adopting by-law specifically excludes Cultus Lake Park from the area of application of plan policies, Zoning By-law No. 66 makes no such exclusion.[31] These regulations have, of course, never been enforced within the boundaries of Cultus Lake Park.

Zoning in the Lindell Beach area has been a contentious issue. The developed portion of Lindell Beach is currently zoned "Urban Residential"; in 1985 a proposal went forward to public hearing to rezone the area to "Campground–Holiday Park." In part this proposal was motivated by concerns over water- and sewer-service needs at Lindell Beach and who would be responsible for service upgrade costs. At the hearing, attended by 142 members of the public, the proposal was strongly opposed.[32] Arguments against were put forward by the president of the Lindell Beach Residents' Association, a lawyer retained to represent some Lindell Beach residents, and a number of property owners. While this specific proposal did not proceed after the public hearing, its legacy has been to increase local awareness of the seriousness of land-use and property-development issues in Lindell Beach, especially in the face of increased cottage-conversion activity. In fact, in his summary of the debate the planner noted "that he has every conviction that within the course of the next few months the [Lindell Beach] community itself will begin to address [these] problems."[33]

The Lindell Beach Campground–Holiday Park rezoning debate can be evaluated by focusing on two issues. The first concerns management of the conversion of summer-only cottaging areas to the mixed year-round communities envisioned in both ORP and OSP policy statements. The current Urban Residential zoning designation does not differentiate residential uses on the basis of occupancy status, nor does the OSP or zoning by-law identify specific procedures through which a seasonal-to-permanent transition of local housing can proceed. The only current management is through the building-permits process. As property owners obtain permits either for the construction of new homes or for changes in occupancy (as required under the National Building Code), the on-site facilities and services can be upgraded. However, Halseth and Rosenberg have detailed how this form of conversion management fails to capture adequately most of the activity that occurs,[34] principally because, in practical terms, "change of occupancy" permits are never applied for. The second issue is that, even if on-site requirements can be managed, there is still no mechanism other than the general public tax base to provide for upgrading of collective services. Local governments in both the Rideau Lakes and Cultus Lake areas are seeking to shift these service costs to those property owners benefiting from conversion. At Cultus Lake such a position is entrenched as OSP policy. The proposed rezoning of Lindell Beach would have created a strata-title development out of the collection of privately owned properties. The strata-corporation could then assume responsibility for the management and upgrading of collective services. The RDFC position is that rezoning would have formalized a mechanism now partially fulfilled by the Residents' Association.

Cultus Lake Park

The Cultus Lake Park area exists as a separate jurisdictional entity within the study area and within the RDFC's Electoral Area "E." The local government in this case is manifest in the Cultus Lake Park Board. The establishment of a local government jurisdiction outside of the Municipal Act, together with the leasehold nature of property tenure for local stakeholders, combine for uneasy relations in the ongoing operation, planning, and management of Cultus Lake Park.

The Cultus Lake Park lands were assembled beginning in 1924. For the first several years of the park's operation, a joint management committee with representatives from the two Chilliwack municipal councils handled park administration. After a number of years in which these councils had to commit additional funds to cover the park's operating expenses, pressure from both council members and local taxpayers grew for the severance of direct economic responsibility.[35] It was this concern for economic viability that led to the introduction of the Cultus Lake Act in 1932 as a private member's bill in the provincial legislature.

There are three key elements to the original Cultus Lake Act. First, the taxpayers of both the City of Chilliwack and the Township of Chilliwhack (now combined as the District of Chilliwack) were to be divorced from economic responsibility for the park. The city and the township are noted simply as "joint owners in trust,"[36] with the budget of the Park Board "limited to the money received from operating the said park," together with any grants made from time to time by the municipalities.[37]

The second element concerns the organization of Cultus Lake Park management. The Cultus Lake Act confers tremendous latitude of action on the governing Park Board. The preamble mandates that "the power of the said [Park Board] be made greater than that provided for by the 'Municipal Act' and the 'Provincial Parks Act.'"[38] Because the Park Board is not subject to provisions of the Municipal Act, there are no requirements to open board meetings to the public. As well, when the Park Board decides to undertake new initiatives or make major changes in operating policy, not only are there no requirements to hold public hearings; there is also no requirement that board members consider the views of local residents and stakeholders in their decisions. This is far removed from the broad vision of representative local government embodied in Ontario and British Columbia legislation, where land-use planning issues must be discussed at public meetings open to residents, property owners, and all whose interest in property may be affected.

The third element involves the issue of representation and responsibility. From its inception the Cultus Lake Park Board was composed of five members selected by the electorate of Chilliwack, as they were the owners of the park lands. An amendment in 1980 increased the size of the Park Board to seven, introducing local representation through two new places to be elected by the leaseholders and residents of Cultus Lake Park.[39]

Questions of economic viability and park management have been the subject of a number of reports by governments and private consultants. The OSP prepared by the RDFC argues for negotiations towards a new organization of the park and its operations. Subsequent to the OSP, a consultant's report sought to address issues of economic viability by examining alternative local-government frameworks for the park. The consultant failed, however, to recommend any preferred option, and no subsequent actions were taken.[40]

Prior to both the OSP and the 1986 management report, Cultus Lake Park had been the subject of other reviews. In 1961 the provincial Ministry of Municipal Affairs prepared an evaluation of the park and its operations.[41] More importantly, the Park Board commissioned a park development plan in 1963. Conducted by Joseph B. Ward and Associates Consulting Economists and Engineers, the scope of this development plan was narrow. Arguing that "Cultus Lake Park can expect to become a major recreational area, a source of both recreation and revenue to the residents of Chilliwack,"[42] the Ward Report examined all park operations in terms of costs, generated revenue, and potential revenue, and presented the Park Board with a set of nine long-term capital-improvement projects designed specifically to improve economic viability.

The importance of the Ward Report to recent development within the park, and to the debates surrounding these developments, cannot be underestimated. A former chair of the Park Board stated publicly that the Ward Report challenged the Park Board and that, in his opinion, the board had attempted or achieved a considerable number of the report's recommendations "at no cost to the taxpayer of the District of Chilliwack."[43]

It is clear that the Ward Report is being used as a plan or blueprint by the Park Board. Most leaseholders, however, are scarcely aware of the Ward Report or its continuing importance. Interviews with local residents inevitably turned to one of the many recent development controversies within the park, including construction of a shopping plaza, relocation of the administrative offices, and realignment of the entrance to Sunnyside Campground. In each case those interviewed suggested that the Park Board had "dreamed up" these projects in a vacuum, announcing final decisions long after they were too committed to reverse them. In each case the projects have, however, proceeded much as detailed in the Ward Report. Most recently the Park Board authorized development of an eighteen-hole golf course and driving range. Again, several leaseholders stated that this proposal seemed to come from "out of nowhere." The golf course has also proceeded much as outlined in the Ward Report.

Neither the Ward Report nor the various other consultants' reports pay particular attention to the issue of cottage conversion. The only Park Board policy in place at present is that leases must be amended to reflect year-round occupancy and be accompanied by a higher annual lease fee. Within the park the levels of residential services continue to be upgraded slowly and in some cases approximate those found in many urban areas. Currently services include garbage collection and a neighbourhood recycling bin. The water system is expected to undergo upgrading in the near future, while a sewage-disposal system was installed in the late 1970s.

The ongoing management of Cultus Lake Park remains a contentious issue between the Park Board and the leaseholder population. The preamble of the Cultus Lake Act demands only that the lands be used "for park purposes."[44] Beyond this, the legislation offers no guidance to the types of developments that would or would not be considered to enhance this "park" function. Central to recent debates are the three elements of the Cultus Lake Act. Management and planning by the Park Board have been preoccupied with economic viability, with the result that park-improvement projects are considered primarily in terms of revenue-generating capacity. The powers of the Park Board to make decisions in private alienates and angers some of the leaseholder population, many of whom have made substantial investments in their leased properties. The lack of representation has magnified these grievances, to construct a chasm of misunderstanding and lack of trust between the Park Board and some of the leaseholders.

Resident Perceptions of Local Government

Unlike the Rideau Lakes area, there are at Cultus Lake some notable differences between Rural Residents and Converters in their responses to three questions concerning satisfaction with local government (see Table 36). At Cultus Lake, 39 per cent of Rural Residents compared to 67 per cent of Converters are satisfied with the amount of time required to obtain building-permit approvals. On the question of satisfaction with land-use planning activity, most Rural Residents responded in a neutral or negative fashion, whereas most Converters responded in a neutral or positive fashion. However, when asked about the opportunity for public input into local land-use planning decision-making, both groups appear to be more dissatisfied than satisfied.

In evaluating these responses, two issues must be recognized. The first is that approximately one-third of Rural Residents and two-fifths of Converters did not answer the satisfaction questions. These high levels of non-response suggest either a lack of interaction with these aspects of local government or a lack of developed opinion on local government performance. Given these non-response levels it might, however, be expected that those responding would be motivated by some strong opinion; yet such a result is not evident.

Table 39
Satisfaction with Local Government: Cultus Lake Study Area, Converters Only

	Lindell Beach[1] %	Cultus Lake Park[2] %
TIME TO GET BUILDING-PERMIT APPROVALS		
Very satisfied	25.0	6.3
Satisfied	37.5	62.5
Neutral	25.0	18.7
Dissatisfied	12.5	12.5
Very dissatisfied	0	0
(n =)	(8)	(16)
LOCAL GOVERNMENT LAND-USE PLANNING ACTIVITY		
Very satisfied	11.1	0
Satisfied	44.4	37.5
Neutral	33.3	43.8
Dissatisfied	11.1	18.7
Very dissatisfied	0	0
(n =)	(9)	(16)
PUBLIC INPUT INTO LOCAL PLANNING DECISIONS		
Very satisfied	11.1	0
Satisfied	44.4	18.8
Neutral	11.1	31.2
Dissatisfied	33.3	50.0
Very dissatisfied	0	0
(n =)	(9)	(16)

Source: Resident survey, 1991.
[1] Lindell Beach under jurisdiction of Regional District of Fraser-Cheam (n = 15).
[2] Cultus Lake Park under jurisdiction of Cultus lake Park Board (n = 30).

The second issue is that at Cultus Lake, Rural Residents all live in areas under RDFC jurisdiction, while for Converters the jurisdictional responsibility is divided between the RDFC (Lindell Beach) and the Cultus Lake Park Board (Cultus Lake Park). While there is a community plan in place for Lindell Beach, many residents at Cultus Lake Park feel that the Park Board operates too independently of input from local stakeholders (in this case, the leasehold population). To pursue possible differences in opinion between jurisdictions, questions about satisfaction with local government can be further broken down for Converters by individual jurisdiction.[45]

When we compare Converters' satisfaction with the amount of time required to get building-permit approvals, we find that approximately 63 per cent of those at Lindell Beach compared to 69 per cent in Cultus Lake Park report being satisfied (see Table 39). Converters at Lindell Beach appear to be more satisfied with land-use planning activity or performance (57 per cent compared to 38 per cent) than those in Cultus Lake Park. Over half (56 per cent) of Converters at Lindell Beach who answered the question concerning public input in decision-making are satisfied, compared to only 19 per cent of those in Cultus Lake Park. In fact, one-half of those responding from Cultus Lake Park state they are dissatisfied.

These results must be interpreted cautiously, as the number of respondents involved is quite small. Given this warning, however, there seems to be support in both the Lindell Beach and Cultus Lake Park areas for the existing building-permit process. There is perhaps stronger support for current land-use planning activity expressed at Lindell Beach, sentiments that become much clearer when the focus shifts to public input. Again, although the numbers of respondents is small, suggestions of a chasm in communication between the Cultus Lake Park Board and local stakeholders are supported.

When asked about services the local government should expand, discontinue, or provide, respondents offer many more suggestions for new or expanded services than for services to be discontinued (see Table 37). Of the 53 suggestions by Rural Residents for new or expanded services, 15 focus on infrastructure such as road maintenance and street-lighting. Environmental services such as recycling and garbage collection, and protective services such as ambulance and 911,[46] are each suggested 10 times. A further 5 suggestions call for additional community services such as bus connections with Chilliwack. Finally, 5 suggestions focus on the local planning process and call for the extension of long-range planning policies.

Fewer suggestions (40) are offered by Converters. Of these, 11 address environmental services, primarily recycling, and 7 address infrastructure, principally street-lighting and road maintenance. Assorted other suggestions call for increased protection services (4) and more stringent local planning regulations (4). Finally, 5 suggestions also address the issue of a bus connection to Chilliwack. As a result of pressure from local residents a referendum on bus service was held on 14 November 1992.[47] A regular (three times daily) bus service between Cultus Lake and Chilliwack during the summer months was approved in that referendum. A paratransit transportation service was also approved in the same referendum for the Chilliwack River Valley, Cultus Lake, and Columbia Valley areas.

There are few suggestions for local services to be reduced or discontinued. Of the 10 suggestions by Rural Residents and all 4 of the suggestions by Converters, 8 call for a reduction in the size of local government (something that would be difficult to accomplish if all the desired new/expanded services were put into place).

About half of the Cultus Lake respondents in both groups comment on important local land-use planning issues. Of the 27 suggestions offered by Rural Residents, 11 address agricultural issues, although 4 of these call for a relaxation of development restrictions on farmland. An additional 5 comments call for more direct consultation with, and input from, local residents in planning decisions. Finally, 4 comments address protection of the rural lifestyle by limiting development.

Important local-planning issues for Converters at Cultus Lake centre upon protection of the cottage communities and the lake. Of the 22 comments offered, 13 focus on restrictions of development to preserve the lifestyle and character of the cottage areas. Likely influenced by recent public debate, 4 comments specifically suggest that no golf course on recreational housing be approved in the agricultural areas of the Columbia Valley (see chapter 10 for details of this debate).

DISCUSSION

This study of local government as it is manifest in the management of land-use planning for issues such as cottage conversion highlights three differences between the Rideau Lakes and Cultus Lake areas. The first involves the broad issue of jurisdictional fragmentation. Along the Rideau Lakes local government is achieved through individual townships. It is clear to both local governments and the Sewell Commission, however, that waterfront-development pressures and planning issues must be addressed on a scale larger than that of the individual township. Until recently the recognition of waterfront-development and cottage-conversion pressures was very uneven among individual townships along the Rideau Lakes. The recent round of community-plan and zoning-by-law amendments appears to involve a more co-ordinated implementation of planning-policy options and management tools across the study area. The foundation for this co-ordination has been the planning exercises of Parks Canada and the Rideau Valley Conservation Authority, two "supra-local" government agencies. Local reaction to these planning exercises is the subject of the next chapter on change and contention.

At Cultus Lake the RDFC provides a possible basis for broader co-ordination of responses to residential change and has attempted to achieve this through regional- and community-plan policies. In this case recognition of the complexities of managing growth within integrated resort areas has been a cornerstone of local planning policy since 1981. The jurisdictional status of Cultus Lake Park has, however, limited the effectiveness of even this co-ordination.

A second local-government difference concerns the representation of residents on local government councils. Along the Rideau Lakes all elected representatives come from within the townships. As described earlier, this representation has in the past been very clearly limited to the rural/farm constituency, without extensive participation by cottage-property owners. In part this explains some of the historical lack of attention to lakefront land-use planning issues. In recent debates, however, it is precisely concern over which constituencies in the rural-recreational countryside are represented in the land-use planning process that has been the subject of contention and negotiation.

At Cultus Lake both the areas under RDFC jurisdiction and those under the Cultus Lake Park Board have local governments with relatively little elected representation from local residents on decision-making bodies. For the RDFC, all of Electoral Area "E" elect just one representative to sit on the larger Regional Board,[48] while at Cultus Lake Park only two representatives are voted in by leaseholders to sit on the seven-member Park Board. Within the RDFC jurisdiction, this pattern of representation is a fundamental reason why property-owner groups in both rural and cottage areas have remained viable voices for the interests of local residents. This is very different from the pattern along the Rideau Lakes, where only cottagers' associations are notable as property-based organizations of local residents.

A third difference concerns accountability, specifically the level of professional and staff development and their importance in providing a continuity of reference for residents. In the Rideau Lakes area the individual townships engage in a joint-services agreement with respect to building inspection, with three building inspectors servicing six townships. In terms of planning expertise, no township has a planning staff, and all such work is contracted out. Combined with earlier comments regarding jurisdictional fragmentation, this situation has resulted in a legacy of uneven policy responses to lakefront-development planning and cottage-conversion pressures. At Cultus Lake the RDFC has a planning and building department staff. While the staff have responsibilities beyond the study area, local residents have, since about 1978, had a consistent point of reference to which questions or inquiries could be directed.

On questions of satisfaction with the performance of their local governments, it is interesting to note that in both study areas a large proportion of respondents in each resident group did not answer or offer a definite opinion. Rural Residents' satisfaction with the time required to get building permits is much lower at Cultus Lake than along the Rideau Lakes, and satisfaction with land-use planning is greater for Rural Residents along the Rideau Lakes. Satisfaction with public input into the land-use planning process is also greater for Rural Residents along the Rideau Lakes than it is at Cultus Lake.

The general satisfaction of Converters with local-government activity presents some intriguing contradictions. In terms of the more common type of personal interaction with local government (through the building-permits process), Converters in both study areas are strongly satisfied. A more general question on land-use planning performance results in somewhat less strong satisfaction among Converters, although in both study areas Converters are more satisfied than Rural Residents. Along the Rideau Lakes this may be an outcome of the lack of attention local governments have paid to the cottaging areas, a laissez-faire approach that fits well with the perception of cottaging areas as self-contained and separate from the surrounding rural community.

Converter satisfaction with public input into the land-use planning process is very different in the two study areas. In the Rideau Lakes area over 40 per cent report being satisfied, while at Cultus Lake 44 per cent report being dissatisfied. The Rideau Lakes response pattern follows from the earlier question on satisfaction with local government planning activity. At Cultus Lake the peculiar nature of structural relations within Cultus Lake Park must be taken into account, as the level of satisfaction among Converters at Lindell Beach, where there are channels for public consultation, approximates that found for Converters along the Rideau Lakes. Again, the implications of a leasehold status of property tenure marks a different local outcome.

The review of suggestions for new/expanded/discontinued local government services suggests some similarity in terms of issues of interest to respondents at Cultus Lake and along the Rideau Lakes. In both areas suggestions for new or expanded services focus upon improvements to the physical infrastructure, including road maintenance and improvements to emergency services, including the 911 telephone service. Service-reduction suggestions focus only upon reducing local taxes. In the Rideau Lakes area, comments on reducing school/education taxation and services occur despite the fact that local governments exercise no control in this area. At Cultus Lake there is a call for reducing the size of local government, a not uncommon call in British Columbia.

The range of additional or expanded services requested by Converters, however, sketches some real differences between the two study areas. Along the Rideau Lakes the underlying theme is to maintain the rural and isolated aspects of the cottage environment. Services requested are limited to provision of garbage collection and assumption of care for private roads by the townships, both of which demands are also consistent with the desire of cottage-property owners to reduce expenditures. At Cultus Lake there is, however, a merging of the "natural" cottage environment with the convenience of an urban residence. Additional services requested include street-lighting and bus service, services that represent a very different vision of the cottage environment. Reasons for these different visions include the compact form of cottage areas at Cultus Lake compared to the linear pattern along the Rideau Lakes and the differences in the profiles of Converters. Converters at Cultus Lake are nearly all elderly and are able to maintain their lakeside residence for a longer period than are their counterparts along the Rideau Lakes. It is not surprising, therefore, to find differences in the range of additional services requested in the two areas.

When asked about local land-use planning issues, respondents in both study areas identify protection of the status quo. Rural Residents identify a need to protect agricultural areas and the rural community by slowing the pace of development, or by restricting it altogether. A similar desire to protect the cottaging areas is also an important local planning issue to Converters, who identify the limiting of additional local and lakeside development as the way to achieve this protection. For Converters, this concern needs to be interpreted in terms of the effects such limits or restrictions will have on both the lake environment and lakefront property values. Protection of lake water quality is protection of the principal amenity that makes these cottaging areas attractive. Lake environmental quality is also a principal component of the cottage-property value. Perhaps more importantly, the increasing segregation and upward pressure on existing waterfront cottage-property values that result from limiting additional development simply reinforce the exclusivity of the cottage.

The contrasts between the structure and operation of local government in the two study areas is clear. In the Rideau Lakes area, township councils are elected by the local residents, while at Cultus Lake, local residents elect only a small number of the representatives who sit on the RDFC board or the Cultus Lake Park Board. In the management of land-use planning, Rideau Lakes townships rely on outside consultants, while the RDFC has in-house expertise. Finally, across the Rideau Lakes area the fragmentation of local government jurisdictions has resulted in an uneven implementation of policies and regulations on important local planning issues. An opportunity to address this issue of regional co-ordination may come out of the Sewell Commission review of planning and development in Ontario. In the evaluation of resident satisfaction with local governments, the first item of note is a general lack of interaction or of well-developed opinion, among both resident groups in the two areas. Among those expressing an opinion, provision of building-permit services are relatively well received. In the Cultus Lake area there is notable concern among Converters in Cultus Lake Park over land-use planning and public input into that process. This reflects the unique status of the development and its local government, an issue central to understanding local debates.

9 Change and Contention along the Rideau Lakes

The movement of new individuals or groups into established communities has long been recognized as a potential flashpoint for local contention. One aspect of residential change around which contention and debate can emerge is the struggle for control of local land-use planning debates. In a very real sense this is a struggle among residential groups for control of the decision-making process. It rests on the ability to put forward and to carry through on alternative visions for the future of the community.

Contention over residential change through cottage conversion is evident in a number of recent land-use planning debates along the Rideau Lakes and at Cultus Lake. In both areas these debates focus on changes to the status quo, in terms either of proposed new recreational-housing development or of new regulations to manage lakeside development. The debates themselves provide the events through which the broader pressures of community change, and contention over that change, can be interpreted. In effect, these debates illustrate the ways in which the local population is reacting to choices over alternative community futures and whether residential change is affecting a reorganization of the political landscape. The review of specific debates in this and the following chapter, while maintaining a focus on residential change, is set in the context of the local government land-use planning process. From the outset it is clear that two very different styles of debate are encountered in the Rideau Lakes and Cultus Lake areas.

Along the Rideau Lakes the major players in land-use planning debates include such supra-local government agencies as the Parks Service and the Rideau Valley Conservation Authority (RVCA), the local governments, and local property-owner organizations. Given the relatively low level of municipal expertise along the Rideau Lakes, it is not surprising to find active intervention in land-use planning by senior government agencies. The property-owner organizations active in these debates are almost exclusively cottagers' associations. In part their participation is a result of the debates' focus on managing lakeside development, a critical issue to cottage-property owners. Their participation also marks a deliberate attempt by the cottagers' associations to situate themselves in the decision-making process of a local government structure that has not traditionally represented their interests. For the cottager's associations the debates offer the opportunity both to participate in decision-making and to continue a longer negotiation for recognition that the group speaks for a legitimate local constituency.

In the Cultus Lake area several local property-owner groups have already established themselves as part of the decision-making process as representatives of particular local constituencies. Recent debates over additional recreational-housing development have included relatively little public participation by organized property-owner groups; instead, the debate has evolved among individuals. In large part the groups had little stake in particular debates, as their position in local decision-making was not in jeopardy; as well, their position on the "inside" allows for direct negotiation of critical issues with the appropriate decision-making body.

Three sets of theoretical guidelines are used in the evaluation of land-use planning debates. These guidelines assist in sorting out the positions and rhetoric of the debate and bind the interpretation of isolated debates into a broader framework. The first of these guidelines concerns those factors important in the physical and social separation of space between rural and cottaging areas, including the physical geography of property development, the social geography of local residents, and the folklore of cottaging.

The second set of guidelines develops from the local-conflict literature. When urban-conflict literature characterizes development debates as a form of politics of turf, it identifies residential property as a commodity around which resident or property-owner groups will form to contest changes that may adversely affect property values. The language is phrased in terms of property values, but the issue under contention is the perceived threat of change, of the unknown consequences of change. In evaluating local debates in the Rideau Lakes and Cultus Lake areas, the concept of commodity has been extended to include social as well as economic evaluations. This means that protection of property-use values is as important an objective as protection of property values alone.

The third set of guidelines arises from the integration of a rural locality into the perspective of urban-based conflict research. This requires attention to the continuing importance of individuals as well as groups in small communities, and to the organizing of property-owner interests and groups according to the rural or cottage-area location of properties in the rural-recreational countryside.

Researchers interested in the problem of "who governs" have identified questions concerning the participation of local residents and their access to decision-making. A geography of community conflict in the rural-recreational countryside, therefore, is interested in the changing access of residential groups to local decision-making power.

RIDEAU LAKES PLANNING EXERCISES

To introduce this study of contention and debate over cottage conversion and waterfront development, I review two important planning exercises by senior government agencies in the Rideau Lakes area. The Parks Service of Environment Canada and the RVCA have both been active in terms of policies or operations directly connected with the lakes and waterways of the area. Both agencies have recently completed extensive planning exercises: the Park Service's Rideau Canal Management Plan and the RVCA's Conservation Strategy. The impacts and implications of these planning exercises, however, extend beyond the agency mandates and must be incorporated into our understanding of local debates over cottage-property development and conversion activity. It is important to recognize that local government across Canada is a creation of more senior levels of government. This status sets up an unresolved tension for local governments in terms of their structural and operational relationship with senior governments. Through the exercise of their mandates, senior government agencies intrude upon areas of local government responsibility, while many local government areas of responsibility still require the review or approval of decisions by senior government.

The Parks Service, to avoid some of the ineffectiveness that beset the CORTS agreement, expanded its Rideau Canal Management Plan review process to include participation from federal, provincial, and local government jurisdictions, as well as local resident groups, cottagers' associations, and a range of interest groups. A draft Rideau Canal Management Plan went forward for public review in the fall of 1992.[1] Policy statements in the draft Management Plan are directed at five general strategy areas: historical features, shoreland use, the natural environment, management of canal lands, and education and tourism.

To understand the role of the Parks Service it is important to note that its image far exceeds its authority. The effective authority of the Parks Service is limited to a relatively small amount of property found almost exclusively surrounding the canal's lock stations. To follow through on most policy proposals, the Parks Service must rely upon the co-operation of the RVCA, local governments, and individual property owners. In an effort to achieve this co-operation the Parks Service opened its planning exercise to a wide range of stakeholders. As well, the Parks Service has been an active participant in the planning exercises of other groups, most notably the RVCA. The intertwining of the Parks Service and RVCA planning studies is remarkable, with participation including the joint review of commissioned background studies and co-membership on steering committees. A series of regular reports published in local newspapers on these planning exercises was prefaced by the statement, "the RVCA and the Canadian Parks Service are now taking action in a coordinated effort to preserve a living Rideau Waterway for future generations."[2] In the fall of 1992, when the Parks Service's draft management plan went to public meetings, the RVCA co-hosted these meetings throughout the Rideau Lakes area by presenting its draft conservation strategy to the public as well.

While the Parks Service initiatives are fundamentally bound up with a landscape aesthetic of improving the view for the boating public, the RVCA initiative is clearly directed at pollution abatement and lake-habitat protection. This terminology of pollution and lake protection now dominates as the overt language of local development debate. The Rideau Valley Conservation Strategy contains policy statements on three broad program areas: watershed planning, resource management, and conservation awareness.[3] Background information and policy suggestions are developed in the Rideau Lakes Basin Carrying Capacities and Proposed Shoreland Development Policies.[4]

Reaction to suggestions for reducing environmental degradation has been mixed. As abstract ideals or goals, such commitments have wide support across the Rideau Lakes. There has been a strong negative reaction among members of the farming community, who object to their portrayal as poor environmental managers. This antipathy results from a perception that nitrogen fertilizer use, one of the principal pollution sources identified in the carrying-capacity report, is a farm issue alone. Conversely, the Parks Service has welcomed the science-based policy suggestions concerning non-disturbance of lakeside soils and vegetation, co-opting them as justification for a more natural aesthetic appearance along the canal's shoreline.

Pollution-abatement measures receive the strongest and most detailed attention in the carrying-capacity study. Two contributions of the consultant's report include an innovative ranking of building-lot attributes to determine site-specific development standards and a range of development scenarios to accommodate clustered lots with collective services. The critical contribution, however, is the RVCA's assertion that, in order to co-ordinate the management of future waterfront development, proposed policy action must be organized at a regional or basin-wide level.

As with the National Parks Service, the RVCA planning strategy is to include a wide range of local stakeholders. This strategy seeks to accomplish two outcomes: first, to overcome the hostility of some local governments in cases where policies or guidelines developed by external agencies are "dropped from above" for local implementation; and second, to try to increase the commitment to implementation by giving local government representatives a personal stake in the planning process.[5]

The RVCA differs from the Parks Service, however, in its view of its continuing role. To ensure that its strategy is not shelved, the RVCA "will take a leadership role ... [to] act as a catalyst encouraging, advising and cooperating with one or more of our environmental partners ... Because of its unique watershed jurisdiction and direct municipal-provincial connections, the Conservation Authority is a logical agency for watershed planning and is well situated to coordinate many environmental initiatives in the valley."[6] This broad vision and formulation would make the RVCA the closest approximation to a regional-level co-ordinating body found along the Rideau Lakes.

The Parks Service and RVCA planning exercises have generated a great many policy suggestions for lakeshore development. For both agencies, implementation of suggested policies and initiatives will fall mainly to local governments. To enhance the likelihood of implementation, both agencies have co-opted local government staff and political representatives into their planning exercises. The effectiveness of the Parks Service and RVCA lobby efforts in incorporating municipal representatives into their planning process is clear, with at least four of the six Rideau Lakes townships following through with

major amendments to their community-plan documents. The bring-
ing of RVCA and Parks Service recommendations by municipal representatives back to their local councils is solidifying a linkage never
achieved by CORTS.

Recognition of lakefront-development pressure has previously been
uneven among Rideau Lakes townships. In South Elmsley a new
community plan is currently in preparation. The policies and regulatory tools to control cottage conversion contained in the 1991 draft
are nearly identical to those in the 1984 plan.[7] With respect to the
Parks Service and RVCA planning exercises, the South Elmsley plan
is a model of co-operation and caution. In wording similar to that of
the Parks Service literature, South Elmsley is committing itself to
"consider ... policies to ensure that shoreline development occurs in
a manner which is sensitive to the natural, historic and recreational
character of the Rideau Canal."[8] Some of the proposed policies, such
as accessibility, trails and pathways, visual impacts, and others, can
be negotiated as part of subdivision applications. In South Elmsley,
however, most of the waterfront is already developed, and these
policies may have little meaning beyond the pages of the plan.

The South Elmsley plan also recognizes that a "Concept Plan for
the Rideau Canal has been prepared by the Canadian Parks Service.
The major components of the Concept Plan have been incorporated
into the Land Use Plan and land use policies of [the new community
plan]."[9] The policies go on to say that Council will "make reference
to" the Parks Service study in the evaluation of development proposals, and will "cooperate with" the Parks Service in promotion of the
Rideau Canal. It is interesting to note that after much local debate
both the reference and co-operation statements are likely to be
deleted from the final version of the new South Elmsley plan.

A likely source of controversy within the South Elmsley plan is the
call for a thirty-metre setback from any water bodies for all buildings
and septic systems. The senior government influence in this policy
is clear, as the provincial ministries of Health, Environment, and Natural Resources all have this as a standard setback policy, and the
Parks Service and the RVCA strongly lobbied for these setbacks in
their recent planning exercises. The setback requirement also appears
in the North Crosby,[10] Bastard and South Burgess,[11] and South
Crosby[12] proposed community-plan-amendment by-laws. When
pressed in public debate, both the Parks Service and the RVCA, however, refuse to commit to an actual setback requirement, stating that

any final decision is up to the local government. The two agencies betray their responsibility in this regard by first pressuring local government and local politicians to play along and then escaping through a back door when heated debate develops.

Other townships have also incorporated the general policies of senior agencies into their community plans. North Crosby introduced its current community plan in 1985, at which time the township committed itself to pursuing further policy matters arising out of the CORTS agreement. As in South Elmsley's 1991 draft plan, specific regulations regarding setbacks from water bodies were incorporated on "the advice of the Ministry of Environment, the Ministry of Natural Resources and the [local] conservation authority."[13]

An amendment to the North Crosby community plan and accompanying zoning regulations is currently under consideration.[14] This amendment, which would result in a substantial revision of the existing plan, is a direct outgrowth of the recent Parks Service and RVCA planning exercises and seeks to implement strict new development guidelines outlined in the RVCA's technical study of carrying-capacity. The linkage is clear, as the township proposes that plan amendments "will assist in implementing the ... report prepared for the Rideau Valley Conservation Authority entitled 'Rideau Lakes Basin Carrying Capacities and Proposed Shoreland Development Policies,'" and the background RVCA technical reports are actually appended to the amendment by-law.[15]

The proposed amendments to the Bastard and South Burgess community plan follow the North Crosby example.[16] In fact, Bastard and South Burgess follow almost word for word the proposed North Crosby changes (the "entitled" and "prepared for" statements cited in our last paragraph above are reversed). This is one result of hiring the same planning consultant to prepare both community-plan amendments.

In South Crosby much of the public debate over the township council's move to amend the community plan following the Parks Service and RVCA exercises has focused on the issue of revised lot sizes and the thirty-metre setback. The council's interpretation, again working through the expertise of a consultant planner, increased the minimum setback for waterfront lots from fifteen to thirty metres and revised the minimum lot size for newly created waterfront lots to one hectare.[17] This blanket option is being pressed forward despite some of the more flexible alternatives proposed in the RVCA study of carrying capacity. The proposed changes were praised by the RVCA;[18] however, considerable negative reaction from rural residents was also clear at public meetings.[19]

RURAL PROPERTY OWNERS' RESPONSE

The Parks Service and RVCA planning exercises, together with the actions of several local townships to implement suggested policies via amendments to their community plans, have brought debate over issues of waterfront development and residential change through cottage conversion into a public forum. Local debate over land-use planning issues provides the lens through which to view contention and conflict over pressures of residential change, and in this debate the response of property owners and property-owner groups is a critical part of the interpretation.

As noted earlier, property-owner groups have not developed in the rural/village areas around the Rideau Lakes, but this has not precluded participation in land-use planning debates by rural residents. An active debate has developed over proposed community-plan changes in South Crosby. In this case, an ad-hoc coalition of residents has formed to oppose specific elements of the proposed new regulations. This type of issue-specific coalition is generally similar to the types of residents' groups described in research on urban and inner-city "turf" conflicts.[20] The difficulties the coalition has encountered in debating its positions reflect the long-standing argument of community activists about the implications of a lack of resources with which to engage local decision-making bodies.[21]

South Crosby began the public consultation process on a proposed amendment to the community plan in July 1991, with a second public meeting in May 1992.[22] It was at this second meeting that rural residents began to state their objections to the larger lot-size and increased setback requirements. Council was scheduled to adopt this amendment at its 17 August 1992 meeting. Prior to this meeting a notice was published in the local newspaper by "a number of citizens [with] serious concerns about the proposed changes" inviting residents to attend the council meeting to "let South Crosby Council hear your voice."[23] The notice outlined a series of five objections to the proposed amendments, including the claims that the increased costs of regulations would reduce property development potential; that reduced development would shift the property-tax burden to existing property owners; that less development would reduce the economic viability of local businesses; that site-specific regulations were needed as opposed to blanket policies; and that the high levels of current waterfront development – not new development – were the main pollution threat.

Local interviews suggest that the context for these objections is the concern of rural residents that their access to the limited resource of waterfront property will be further eroded. The proposed policy changes were seen as excessive, allowing "only elite or cluster development, excluding people who had lived in the area most of their lives."[24] The locally constructed understanding of a social and geographic separation of cottage and rural areas is the fundamental motivation for these objections. Local residents are resisting change that they expect will result in an increase of this separation in the broader community.

Interviews with individuals involved in the debate make it plain that those organizing active opposition to the proposed South Crosby amendments were rural/village residents. Some had placed the notice in the local newspaper, while others were circulating petitions through the community. The fragmentation of efforts was a result of the lack of a formal mechanism for co-ordinating information exchange or preparing studies or reports that might assist the group in arguing their position.

It is clear that all of the principals in the South Crosby debate knew one another and their respective positions. Despite the formal setting of a public hearing, the debate was between individuals rather than groups or jurisdictions. The continuing prominence of individuals in these debates confirms a long-standing finding of rural sociology, that the local context is an intimate one, where the political is very often personal. For the ad hoc group, changes to leadership would introduce a critical discontinuity that could severely damage their efforts.

Despite the arguments of those opposed to the amendments and a petition of 160 signatures, South Crosby Council approved the community-plan amendments at its 17 August 1992 meeting. The rural property-owner ad hoc opposition group organized an appeal to the Ministry of Municipal Affairs for a hearing on the matter before the Ontario Municipal Board. In September 1992 an appeal to the Minister of Municipal Affairs was formally submitted.[25]

COTTAGERS' ASSOCIATION RESPONSE

In the Rideau Lakes area the cottagers' associations are the most well-developed property-owner group. These associations have become increasingly active in environmental-protection issues on particular lakes,[26] and have also become active in local political debate as their membership increasingly becomes part of the year-round population. The public debates generated by the Parks Service, RVCA, and local government planning exercises have provided a forum for the cottagers' associations to legitimize their role as the collective voice for an identifiable local constituency. This recent activism also represents a pre-emptive strike in an ongoing struggle to maintain control of the lake before decision-making authority is usurped by government intervention.

The relationship between shoreline development and water-quality degradation was a driving factor behind the background carrying-capacity studies completed for the RVCA's new conservation strategy. Partly in response to these initiatives and partly as a result of their own recognition of the value of environmental protection, a number of Rideau Lakes cottagers' associations have taken independent action in surveying their members, distributing information, and promoting remedial actions respecting the lake environment.[27]

As part of the recent Parks Service and RVCA planning exercises, several cottagers' associations have participated directly in the decision-making process. As debates have shifted to the local government level, these cottagers' associations have engaged in an intense interaction with local councils on behalf of their membership.

The Upper Rideau Lake Association (URLA) has recently begun hosting an annual open house at the beginning of the summer as a way of promoting communication on environmental issues. Representatives from Parks Canada, the Westport Harbour Committee, the Westport Chamber of Commerce, MAPLE, and other cottagers' associations have been attending.[28] The URLA was also a joint participant in a 1991 survey of septic-disposal systems on properties along Upper Rideau Lake, undertaken with North Crosby Township, the RVCA, and the Ontario Ministry of the Environment.[29]

The URLA has also been an active participant in a very public debate with the provincial Ministry of Environment and the Village of Westport regarding water quality in Upper Rideau Lake. The debate has focused on responsibility for pollution entering the lake, specifically the relative contributions of Westport's sewage lagoon compared to those of individual cottagers, and the costs of correcting the problem. The principal issue of contention is the upgrading of Westport's sewage-disposal system, with the URLA arguing for zero discharge.

Both the URLA and the Village of Westport agree that it is in their interests to improve the quality of the lake.[30] The language and posturing of the debate, however, clearly evokes the impression of a jurisdictional tug of war. Commenting on proposals to upgrade the sewage lagoon, the URLA has argued that "it will demand an environmental impact study if its demands are not met."[31] The village council in return "has just about had it with the [URLA] and its demands on the Westport sewage lagoon,"[32] as Westport "can't be at the mercy of URLA."[33] For Westport the issue is critical, as a current freeze on new development cannot be lifted until the situation is resolved.

An outline of the URLA demands on Westport's sewage system was published in a 1992 letter. These demands include limiting effluent discharge to between 0.03 and 0.05 mgs of phosphorus (no time-scale cross-reference given), connecting remaining septic systems in Westport to the sewer lines, purchasing additional buffer lands, and continuing monitoring of the system by the provincial Ministry of Environment. The reeve responded: "In my opinion, and I'm speaking for myself and not this council, everything in this letter needs the reply 'no.' If they want to bump it up (to a full environmental impact assessment) then they can bump it up. The residents of Westport will not be held hostage."[34]

The most recent incarnation of this debate surrounds a hastily announced proposed provincial grant of $3.5 million to upgrade the Westport sewage system. Both the URLA and the Big Rideau Lake Association (BRLA) had lobbied the provincial government for these monies. Worried at the potential long-term cost to Westport residents, the reeve wondered whether the grant came with strings attached; if so, then "in his opinion Westport does not need the money."[35] As part of a running public dialogue, the following week the URLA responded that it was "very pleased to hear about the [grant] announcement ... [but was] not so pleased with the reeve's comments."[36] Recognizing the potential costs to Westport residents and the potential benefit to all lake users, the URLA stated it would support a public fund-raising campaign "and join any committee established to run such a campaign." The Westport Chamber of Commerce supports taking the provincial grant money and upgrading the sewage system, but in debating the issue some members "were concerned that Westport appeared to be caving in to pressure groups who are not going to have to pay for it," clearly implying the URLA.[37]

This debate illustrates clearly how the URLA has used public dialogue to impose itself in the approval and decision-making process. Whether the provincial ministries of Health or the Environment or the Village of Westport like it, the URLA will continue to have a say or role in any changes to Westport's sewage-disposal system.

The BRLA has also been active in a public-information campaign on environmental protection. In 1991 the BRLA initiated a three-year "Rideau Recycling and Restoration" program.[38] Activities in the first year included planting of shoreline vegetation, an inventory of shoreline erosion, installation of loon nesting platforms, and distribution of recycling and water-quality-protection information to 1,300 property owners.[39] In the summer of 1992 the BRLA opened an office in the historic Scovil Store in Portland. The office's principal function is to serve as a communications centre for information on environmental-protection efforts along the lake. As another part of this program, students were hired in 1992 through the federal Environmental Project Fund to continue the distribution of environmental-protection information to summer cottagers.

The Otty Lake Association (OLA) is also currently proposing to participate in water-quality and septic-tank monitoring through the Environmental Youth Corps.[40] As well, the OLA has been an active partner with the provincial Ministry of Natural Resources in a fish-stocking program, including the egg-recovery and hatchery-operation stages. Through 1991 the OLA pursued one case involving excavation and dredging of approximately 200 feet of environmentally sensitive shoreline. Their efforts identified fault in Ministry of Natural Resources procedures for granting the alteration permit, in the local township council's failure to enforce subdivision agreements with a developer, and in the general enforcement of zoning and community-plan provisions designed to protect the lakeshore from substantial alteration. The OLA issued a general call to its members for continued vigilance, "support and help to protect our most valuable asset – THE LAKE – from both uninformed and unintentional damage to the surrounding areas which influence the overall ecology."[41]

Darroch argues that the OLA has, through its actions on environmental stewardship, established itself as a legitimate local-management body for protection of the lake.[42] This is the type of role in local decision-making that Ontario cottagers' associations have been actively seeking in discussions with the Sewell Commission over reform of local land-use and development planning.[43]

The extent of the participation of cottagers' associations in environmental-protection projects suggests a clear sense of stewardship. This is a useful characterization, for it captures a number of salient features of lakeside-property ownership. First is the economic imperative to protect property values, since the lake is the key attractive feature of the cottage properties and any damage to the habitat could adversely affect property values. Second is an inherent recognition that the cottage community is responsible for some of the environmental degradation of the lakes. The activism of cottagers' associations on environmental issues is, however, difficult to interpret. It is worthwhile to recall the warnings that issues being debated may not be the "real" issues at stake. In cottaging areas along the Rideau it is clear that the language of environmental protection is also being

Table 40
Township Government and Cottagers' Associations:
Structural Comparison, Rideau Lakes Study Area

Sample Township	Sample Cottager's Association
COUNCIL	EXECUTIVE
Reeve	President
Deputy Reeve	Past President
Councillors (3)	Vice-President
	Secretary
	Treasurer
	Newsletter Editor
	FOCA Directors at Large[2]
COMMITTEES	COMMITTEES
Building	Development
Fire Department	Emergency
LACAC[1]	Fishing
Library	Gypsy Moth
Recreation/Park	Land-use/legal
Roads	MAPLE[3]
Waste Management	Membership
	Recycling
	Road Signs/Buoys
	Township Monitor
	Water Level
	Water Quality/Science
	Wildlife/Lake Preservation
STAFF	
Building Inspector	
Clerk-Treasurer	
Park Superintendent	
Receptionist	
Road Superintendent	
Tax Collector	

[1] LACAC: Local Architectural Conservation Advisory Committee.
[2] FOCA: Federation of Ontario Cottagers' Associations.
[3] MAPLE: Mutual Association for the Protection of Lake Environments.

used as a metaphor for protection of a lifestyle. It is also being used as a metaphor for control – control of the lake as an asset belonging to the cottage lots that surround it and in terms of maintaining local decision-making before such decision-making is usurped by government intervention.

Several Rideau Lakes area cottagers' associations have a more sophisticated organizational structure than the local township administration. In Table 40 it is clear that the larger cottagers' associations rival even the most well-developed municipal jurisdiction in terms of organizational structure. Not apparent in this table is that, in several of the larger cottagers' associations, members and heads of the various committees often have considerable expertise or experience in the topic area. Two association presidents referred to this as a set of in-house consultants available to evaluate and respond to any proposal or report that developers or township councils might commission.

The legitimation of cottagers' associations as representatives of an identifiable local constituency has been further assisted by their formal participation in recent planning debates. Both the Parks Service and the RVCA planning exercises have actively sought involvement of area cottagers' associations.[44] While the decision to include cottagers' associations to this degree stems from a planning strategy of including all stakeholders, the process itself has contributed to a legitimation of the associations' role as representatives of a recognized local constituency. Their participation represents the critical hurdle in moving from outside to inside the decision-making forum.[45] It also represents a recognition of their de facto power as a political force in the community.

Environmental protection and representation of the interests of cottage-property owners are preoccupations that are evident in debates over new development proposals or land-use regulations to manage future development. All of the cottagers' associations contacted have been following with interest the RVCA conservation strategy and carrying-capacity exercises as well as the most recent round of community-plan amendments based on these exercises. As described earlier, a number of the larger cottagers' associations have engaged in active dialogue with their local township councils on proposed changes to the community plans. While the cottagers' associations support the general intention of more stringent development regulations directed at environmental protection, points of conflict have focused on specific details of the regulations, most importantly on amendments to minimum required setbacks to water bodies. New planning regulations regarding larger lot sizes and other concessions at time of property subdivision will work to increase the pressure on waterfront property values and reduce the numbers of additional lots to be created. Both outcomes are potential benefits to current cottage-property owners. Larger setback requirements, which apply to all existing as well as future lots, may, however, represent significant costs to cottage owners, especially those with small properties and/or with cottages very close to the shoreline.

While recognizing that there is considerable debate on the question of defining local government,[46] in a very real sense many of the cottagers' associations studied are emerging with the characteristics of a local government – with, of course, a very specialized constituency. Tindal's[47] interpretation of the general nature of local government in Canada involves two basic sets of responsibilities: administration and representation. Tindal argues for four prerequisites: that there be a clear delineation of responsibilities; that boundaries and financial resources be appropriate to assigned responsibilities; that internal organization should promote access and responsiveness; and that internal organization should contribute to leadership and decision-making. As is apparent in Table 40, some cottagers' associations have a well-developed hierarchy and division of responsibilities, an organizational format that facilitates opportunities for leadership. As is evident from the active debates in which some cottagers' associations have engaged, these groups are actively putting forward positions and statements based on their constituency's interests.

Hasson and Razin employ and expand upon the notion of boundaries and boundary criteria in an effort to interpret inter-municipal conflicts.[48] Generally, these boundary criteria are that the size and shape should promote efficiency in carrying out functions; that they should provide an adequate fiscal capacity; and that boundaries should correspond to patterns of community. Clearly, for cottagers' associations the lake boundaries define not only the associations' boundaries but also the spatial scope of their activities. As well, in a geographically and socially divided landscape it is membership in a cottagers' association that defines membership in a specific community.

SUMMARY

The rural-recreational countryside is a geographically and socially divided residential landscape. Change through cottage conversion is not only introducing a new group of permanent residents into the local area but is also creating a challenge to the established system of local government representation. Along the Rideau Lakes, land-use planning debates are clearly between groups, and the property-owner groups in these debates are almost exclusively cottagers' associations. While cottagers' associations have long represented the unique collective interests of the seasonal-use population, they are becoming increasingly active in local land-use planning debates.

One of the important findings in the Rideau Lakes area is, quite simply, that there is local debate. The recitation of studies and reports by senior government agencies and organizations, and their translation into local policies or regulations, has not deterred local property owners from challenging the findings and proposed solutions.

Through their participation in a discourse over community change, and their challenge of a local council's action, local residents are in effect "taking back" the debate. They are reclaiming the decision-making rights over the future of their local area and community. The language of these debates is increasingly cast in terms of "environmental protection" or "ecological management." These phrases, however, serve as metaphors for a more basic struggle for control of property and development rights.

10 Change and Contention at Cultus Lake

Contention and debate over community change in the Cultus Lake area has come into the public arena largely through the actions of local government land-use planning activity. As in the Rideau Lakes area, this public debate builds strongly upon the locally constructed geographic imagination of separate landscapes for the cottage- and rural-property areas. But there are also differences between the two study areas. The first concerns the particular status of leasehold properties in Cultus Lake Park; the second, a perception by debate participants about whether their voices will be heard and will be effective. Unlike the relatively strong collective voices that cottager's associations have along the Rideau Lakes, rural residents in the Columbia Valley and cottage leaseholders in Cultus Lake Park have entered debates with more of a sense of powerlessness. The goal of recounting some recent debates is not to accentuate these differences – the argument has been made earlier that "geography" is important – but rather to demonstrate that, while local geographies vary, there are strong similarities in public debates across the rural-recreational countryside.

THE RANCH PARK PROPOSALS

Two versions of a golf-course development proposal called "Ranch Park" have recently gone forward to public hearing. The first version involved approximately two hundred new accommodation units, a health club, and a golf course. The second version was scaled down to include only the golf course. There were very large

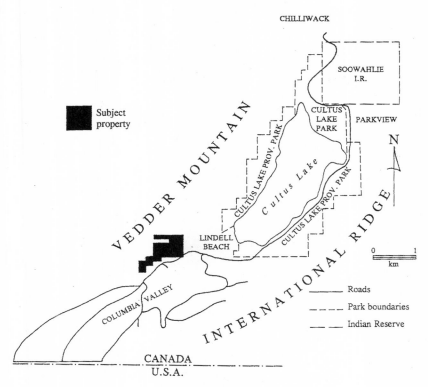

Figure 30
Ranch Park property, Columbia Valley and Cultus Lake.

turnouts at the public hearings for both versions, and while opinions about this contentious issue were mixed, the overall reaction was negative. In both cases the Regional District of Fraser-Cheam (RDFC) did not proceed with the amending by-laws required to allow development to proceed.

In these debates, residents relied upon locally constructed ideas of community and place, and quality of life, to bolster their arguments. Objections to change are based for many upon a desire that the Columbia Valley remain a small agricultural community, one where neighbours and government regulations are both kept at a distance. For others, namely the farming constituency, the sense of place and community is based on a desire to preserve an agricultural livelihood. Those who identify themselves as farmers have acted with considerable cohesion in resisting non-agricultural development proposals. In the Ranch Park debates, however, there was not the community cohesion evidenced in the DND debate (see chapter 7). Differences in

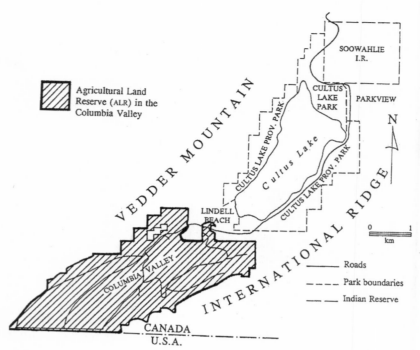

Figure 31
Agricultural Land Reserve (ALR), Columbia Valley and Cultus Lake.

the forms through which collective action was mobilized speak to an important issue regarding rural resistance to community change – that is, recognition of universal as opposed to incremental change.

The Ranch Park property is located at the divide between the Lindell Beach recreational area and the Columbia Valley agricultural area. The location along the edge of the benchlands affords a spectacular view northwards over Cultus Lake. The property is also located within the provincial Agricultural Land Reserve (ALR). Introduced in 1973, the ALR designation was intended to protect quality agricultural lands from subdivision or development activity that would degrade its agricultural potential.[1] An order-in-council of the provincial Cabinet in 1988 amended the Agricultural Land Reserve Act to allow golf courses as a permitted use with the ALR,[2] a move that prompted many applications, particularly in areas close to metropolitan Vancouver.

The ALR designation is critical to understanding some of the emotions expressed in the public debates. Columbia Valley residents

were largely opposed to the imposition of these provincially controlled land-use regulations, and indeed many continue to complain
– sometimes bitterly – about being overgoverned. However, there is
also an emerging opinion that the ALR provides a measure of protection against the urbanization of this rural and agricultural valley.
Some of this shift in opinion comes as the result of the RDFC community plan, where agricultural policies discourage the fragmentation of farmland, encourage the preservation and enhancement of
existing farming operations, and offer support and protection for the
variety of lifestyles in Columbia Valley. The first two of these policies
echo the fundamental ALR goals to maintain viable agricultural land
and farm units. As in the Rideau Lakes area, local government community-planning documents, and the policies they contain, require
the approval of the provincial government before they can be
adopted. Therefore, it is not a surprise to see provincial government
policy so transparent in local government regulation. Residents
interviewed hold the community plan as a commitment of their local
government to the status quo and protection against radical change.

The local impact of the ALR designation is also recognized through
the RDFC zoning by-law. For the Columbia Valley this recognition
has resulted in the introduction of a "green zone" Rural-Agricultural
(R-Ag) designation, designed to resolve locational conflicts between
intensive agricultural operations and surrounding land uses.[3] This
regulatory move is interpreted as the backbone of the currently thriving intensive swine-farm operations.

The first version of the development proposal, called "Ranch Park
Resort," involved a hundred-unit condominium complex, one hundred single-family "cluster homes," and a health club and eighteen-
hole golf course.[4] The proposal was put forward by a Vancouver-
based development company, West Georgia Enterprises, on behalf of
the current property owner and the prospective purchasers. The
introduction of non-local development interests added to the concerns of invasion already present in the Columbia Valley from earlier
conflicts over zoning or military land purchases. The arrival of the
West Georgia Enterprises representative at the public hearing in a
white limousine[5] certainly did not soothe concerns nor cool tempers
prior to the meeting.

An official public hearing on the Ranch Park Resort proposal was
held on 28 January 1991 in the Columbia Valley Community Hall.[6]
A verbatim transcript of statements made or submitted was com-
piled in a public-hearing report received at the 5 February meeting
of the RDFC Board, where it became part of the public record. More
than 190 members of the public were present, and the public-hearing

report includes 6 written statements submitted for the record as well as 31 verbal statements made during the hearing itself.

Of the 6 written statements, 2 were from Lindell Beach property owners. Of these, 1 was an outright rejection of the proposed development, while the other raised a series of difficult questions without specifying firm support or rejection. Of the 4 written statements from Columbia Valley residents, 3 rejected the proposal, while 1 raised a number of questions without specifying support or rejection.

Only 2 of the 31 verbal statements made for the record came from Lindell Beach property owners. One of these was against the proposal, while the other listed a series of questions on which it was felt more information was needed. The current Ranch Park property owner made a statement in support of the proposal.

Of the 28 statements made by Columbia Valley property owners, 6 spoke in favour of the development's proceeding; a further 5 raised issues and questions without confirming support or rejection of the proposal; and 17 spoke against the proposal. It is important to note that all 5 of the identifiable farm families speaking at the public hearing rejected the proposal. Three of these families are involved in the operation of large intensive swine farms. Reasons for their opposition centred upon issues of livelihood protection. The central theme of their argument was that "history [has shown] that wherever farms are encroached by residential housing there is nothing but heartache and strife for the farmer. Eventually the farms are forced to close and relocate."[7] This view was echoed in the observation that "golf courses and resort residential areas do not mix well with the present agricultural uses of our small valley."[8]

More general issues raised in opposition to the proposal involved concern about water supply and changes to existing road access. Among objections to additional development in the valley, 11 raised the issue of water licences and water-rights agreements. The question of water-supply rights has been a long-standing problem in the Columbia Valley, where a legacy of formal and informal water-rights agreements is extremely complicated and is one issue the RDFC's community plan specifically attempted to address.

At present there is only one road into the Columbia Valley, and 14 statements at the public hearing raised the issue of road access. Of these, 5 argued that additional access was needed whether the proposal was approved or rejected (2 actually spoke in favour of the proposal). All 9 of those who spoke against the need for additional access phrased their comments as part of a general rejection of the proposed development. Among these speakers there was general agreement with the comment that "another road into the [Columbia

Valley/Lindell Beach area] will mean easy access ..., not for us, for outsiders. You get increased vandalism, break-ins, pollution, rubbish scattered along the road. I don't want to live in a place like that."[9]

The most important issue, however, involved a concern for quality of life. More than a dozen specific objections to the proposal were based on concern for the rural community and the potential for its destruction by such a large development. Those raising objections did not see the proposal as a single isolated development but rather as the first of what could easily become an unstoppable series of speculative and development moves. Several agreed with the sentiment that it was the quiet isolation of Columbia Valley that drew them to the area: "I live here because I enjoy the rural nature of Columbia Valley. If I had wanted to be a 'Towny' I would have moved to Chilliwack."[10]

The quality of life in the Columbia Valley sketched at the public hearing emerges not only as a set of bucolic ideals but also from a sense of family and local history. One speaker offered a very personal expression of this sense of living history: "I have the great privilege also of being a great-great-granddaughter of the early pioneers, and I am so proud of that. I am proud of the way of life that was created here in Columbia Valley. I am proud to be a part of the people that worked so hard to take nothing and make it into something, and I know that the pioneer people when they moved here didn't move here to make big bucks, they moved here to make a life, and they did. And they made a life for us, for their children and their children's children, and I hope to do the same for my children."[11]

The feeling that there was something special in the sense of place and community in the Columbia Valley was central to rejection of the development proposal. One speaker argued, "What we have here is a way of life in Columbia Valley. I have been part of it on and off for thirty years and this proposal in no way is compatible with that way of life."[12] For another speaker that sense of a way of life, and the potential for its destruction, was more tangible: "Columbia Valley has always been a place that has been like a back eddy in the world where you can go and enjoy the tranquillity of peace and quiet of true country atmosphere. I don't believe that the social damage and the social costs of this development would be offset by the economic gain of a few people who own properties adjacent to the development."[13]

In the period immediately following the public hearing, local interest and participation in the debate remained high. At the 19 February 1991 meeting of the RDFC board additional views were entered into the public record, including 9 letters, containing 13 signatures, and a petition of general support with 62 attached signatures.[14] However, given the generally negative reaction at the public hearing, West Georgia Enterprises asked that their application for the Ranch Park Resort project be withdrawn. Subsequently, local newspapers reported that West Georgia Enterprises had come forward with an even larger resort-development proposal for another area of the Fraser Valley.[15] This withdrawal was not, however, the end of the attempt to develop the Ranch Park property. After September 1991 the Ranch Park property owner brought forward a second development proposal. This time the proposal focused on a golf course only and contained no plans for housing. A public hearing on the revised golf-course-only proposal was held on 4 February 1992, just over a year after the first public hearing.[16] The property owner may have felt the new plan was appropriate, as many of the objections to the first proposal had been prefaced by statements to the effect that "while we have no objection to a golf course …" In fact, three of the farm-property owners specifically conceded that a golf course "in our neighbourhood in itself, is not a threat to our existence"[17] and that they had "no objections to the golf course."[18]

If comments at the previous hearing suggested little objection to a golf course, those at the second vociferously dispelled that suggestion. In more than one respect the second hearing became a disaster and could easily be described as a showcase for the observation that local politics in rural communities is personal. Numbers of written and oral statements in the official report of the public hearing describe residents' anger at being called to repeat earlier objections to continued non-agricultural development in the Columbia Valley. Some of the statements include personal remarks directed at the applicant property owner, with the most pointed raising issues such as personal inconvenience, a lack of respect for the community, and greed as the sole motivation for the second proposal. One written submission summarized these opinions and suggested that the owner's action "has caused some heartache in this valley … has caused many to stand together to beat one of the most terrible trait[s] one can have and that is greed!!! This man is only concerned for himself not for the people of Columbia Valley!!! For every time something new, another idea, that Mr. ——— comes up with, we the people of Columbia Valley will be there to put him in his place!"[19] Given earlier suggestions that a golf course would be less problematic, these statements must have been stinging to the property owner.

The most concerted effort to organize opposition to the golf-course proposal came from the Columbia Valley farm community. While the arguments were generally similar to those voiced the previous year, there was a strong effort to increase the number of objections placed on the record. While the 1991 public-hearing report contains 6 written statements, the 1992 report contains 26. Many of the written statements were as simple and succinct as the comment that, "as a resident of Columbia Valley, I am tired of continued attempts to destroy a healthy agricultural area."[20] If the sheer volume of opposition could influence political decision-makers, the farming constituency would have carried the day.

Active opposition to the golf-course development by the swine-farm operators is notable. Participation included submission of written and oral statements, and in some cases, as the meeting broke down towards the end, a debate between individuals in the audience. In part this must be interpreted as an attempt to combat possible extinction of livelihood, a concern echoed in statements such as "the agricultural area of Columbia Valley should remain as it is, a prime agricultural area,"[21] and "as a young couple whose only chance at farming will be in Columbia Valley we feel that rezoning land will negatively affect our plans."[22] Non-agricultural development typically generates not only "nuisance" complaints over farm operations but also forces up local property values. Both outcomes will affect the viability of current and future agricultural activity.

The breakdown of the debate into disputes between individuals also suggests the surfacing of interpersonal disputes in the Columbia Valley community. In this case, the disputes between some swine farmers and particular neighbours simply built on tensions set in place at the first public hearing, at which time some residents speaking in favour of the development argued: "change is going to come to this valley ... I would rather see a golf course out my patio door than I would another pig farm";[23] and "I like to see progress [but] I don't like the smell of pig manure."[24] Such divisions have always been a part of this rural community, and their appearance in front of the RDFC board is evidence of the stress such a consultation process puts on local residents.

The tenuous links of goodwill built up over time between the RDFC and the Columbia Valley community were also strained. First, the public hearing was held in the Cultus Lake Community Hall, due to a comedy of errors that developed when the RDFC tried to book the Columbia Valley Community Hall. The RDFC was so concerned with criticism that the meeting was not held in the Columbia Valley that it entered into the public-hearing report a memorandum from the RDFC planning secretary to the effect that attempts to book the Columbia Valley hall had been thwarted by the hall booking agent's refusal to displace a community drop-in volleyball evening.

A second, and by far the more important dispute arose between the RDFC and the community Advisory Planning Commission (APC). Following the demise of the first development proposal, the RDFC board resolved at its 19 February meeting that an APC composed of local residents should be established to assist in a review of the OSP.[25] The APC had been established and meetings held over the intervening year. When originally adopted in 1985, the OSP was to undergo an update or review procedure at approximately five-year intervals; 1992 was four years late for a first review. There was a growing local perception that the RDFC was not taking the APC seriously, as evidenced by their cancelling at the last minute attendance at, or simply missing altogether, some APC meetings. Although these absences appear to have been more the outcome of a resource-allocation problem by a very busy planning-department staff, the local perception remains. In any event, the public hearing for the golf-course-only proposal was proceeding even though the APC had not yet completed its task of reviewing OSP policies. In a letter formally submitted at the public hearing, the chair of the APC argued that the Regional Board was aware of APC policy that community-plan amendment applications should be withheld until the APC completed its review. The letter expresses a more general tone of sadness and notes a sense of disappointment on the part of the APC membership at the lack of respect the Regional Board was showing the community. In the Columbia Valley the struggle for local control by residents is continuing even within the framework of its local government.

In neither of these debates did the Columbia Valley Ratepayers' Association or the Lindell Beach Residents' Association make a formal public statement. This is explained in large part by the wording of legislation and public notices that invite comments from property owners, wording that is interpreted by some residents interviewed as inviting participation by individuals, not groups. The Columbia Valley Ratepayers' Association encouraged attendance at the public hearings through its informal information network. It can also be suggested that the legacy of high participation in the volunteer-organized Ratepayers' Association has instilled a habit of participation in community affairs by local residents. When interviewed, members of the Ratepayers' executive reflected some of the divisions expressed at the public hearings. Concern over lifestyle and livelihood were dominant themes and proved to be the issues that generated strong support for protection.

For the Lindell Beach Residents' Association the question in these debates was whether additional development would result in more traffic congestion and increased competition for Cultus Lake beaches.

Interviews with members of the executive suggest that the Lindell Beach community is very concerned with the potential impacts of additional development. The concern with traffic congestion centres on problems with emergency-vehicle access in the summer months, an issue the Residents' Association is discussing directly with the RDFC, the provincial Ministry of Transportation, and the RCMP. The concern over increased competition for Cultus Lake beaches stems from the fact that the Lindell Beach community has essentially appropriated the public waterfront. This appropriation includes construction of some fences, many private boat docks and floats, and extensive signage noting "no public parking – anytime – anywhere." A self-contained golf-course resort was not considered a direct threat to the Lindell Beach community's use of their beach. In contrast to Columbia Valley residents, the muted response of Lindell Beach residents might also be due to differences in socio-economic status and the potential benefits Lindell Beach residents might enjoy through a golf course.

SALE OF INFILL LOTS AT CULTUS LAKE PARK

The second development debate in the Cultus Lake area involves the creation and sale of additional lease-lots in Cultus Lake Park. This debate is reviewed here to contrast the strength of public expressions by Columbia Valley/Lindell Beach property owners with the feelings of powerlessness of Cultus Lake Park leaseholders in their dealings with the Park Board. The nature of leasehold tenure is very different from that described in the Rideau Lakes area and at Lindell Beach, but in terms of cottage developments across Canada it is certainly not unique.

Much of the contentious debate within and over Cultus Lake Park has concerned its economic viability. In a recent attempt to generate revenue, the Park Board decided at its 16 October 1991 meeting to proceed with the sale of eight additional lease-lots. "Sale" in this case means the purchase of the "right to apply" to the Park Board for a lease. It is clear from local interviews that the Park Board, and especially those members elected from within Cultus Lake Park, did not embark on this course lightly but instead view it as one viable option within the restrictive framework of the Cultus Lake Park Act. The lots under consideration are shown in Figure 32 and are listed in Table 41, together with the expected upset prices for tenders.

Three themes that recur at Cultus Lake Park are reflected clearly in the debate over the sale of these additional lease-lots. The first

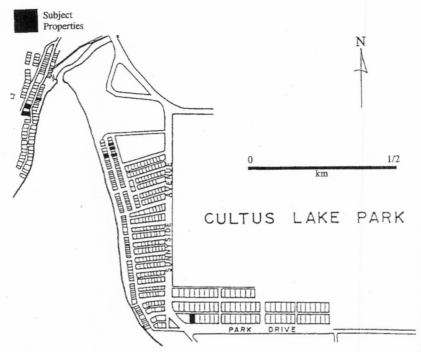

Figure 32
Proposed new lease lots, Cultus Lake Park.
Source: Base map from RDFC.

includes the lack of financial planning by the Park Board. The sale of the lots was originally expected to generate between $455,000 and $500,000 for the Park Board. This infusion of cash was considered necessary to fund infrastructure improvements, mostly associated with upgrades to the leased camping sites in Sunnyside Campground. Indeed, these improvements are recognized as necessary by a wide cross-section of people interviewed. Many of these interviewees, however, raised questions about the appropriate way to pay for such improvements.

Paying for capital improvements has been a difficult issue in Cultus Lake Park. The motivation behind the accounting of revenues by the 1963 Ward Report was also to generate funds for upgrading park infrastructure. Combined, the leased cottage lots and campground sites generate much of the Park Board's revenue. As far as current revenues go, the campground generates about 45 per cent of the operating budget, while the cottage lots generate about 20 per

Table 41
Cultus Lake Park: Proposed Additional Lease Lots

Lot number		Size (feet)	Expected upset price ($000)
22-W	Lakeshore Drive	45 × 86	55
216B-W	Lakeshore Drive	40 × 50	50
217A-W	Lakeshore Drive	35 × 78	55
208	First Avenue	30 × 60	50
209	First Avenue	30 × 60	50
212	First Avenue	24 × 60	45
112	First Avenue	24 × 60	85
504	Park Drive	60 × 125	65

Source: Cultus Lake Park Board.

cent.[26] These shares, however, have been subject to considerable shifts over time. In terms of operating costs, it is difficult to separate out the proportions consumed by either the campground operation or the cottage lots. It is argued by representatives on both sides of this debate that they should not be penalized for expensive capital improvements to benefit the other.

A central question in the debate for both the Park Board and leaseholders remains what to do when the next infusion of revenue is required. The potential annual lease-fee revenue from the proposed lots would not significantly increase current revenue levels. A solution to the question of financial viability in the framework of the Cultus Lake Park Act has not yet been determined. The stress that this places upon the Park Board, park management, and leaseholders begs for resolution. The separation of vested interests from collective benefit, however, makes this resolution seem as elusive as ever.

A second theme in the debate concerns the lack of interaction and information exchange between leaseholders and the Park Board. Dissemination among leaseholders of knowledge concerning the Park Board's 16 October 1991 decision to create eight additional lease-lots was spread only by word of mouth. At no point in the first weeks after the decision was made did the Park Board feel that any form of official notification to current leaseholders was necessary, including the leaseholders of property immediately adjacent to the proposed lots.

The lack of official notification of leaseholders by the Park Board following a decision that clearly marked a new direction in park planning is contrary to the principle of notification of affected property interests embodied in nearly all aspects of planning methodology and legislation. In the planning exercises they undertook in the Rideau Lakes area both the RVCA and Parks Canada made extensive efforts to contact stakeholders, broadly defined. Planning legislation in British Columbia requires that notices concerning land-use by-law changes or variances be sent to all owners or occupiers of real property, with the scope of contact being determined by the type of change or variance being considered,[27] and that "all persons who believe their interest in property" may be affected by proposed changes may be heard at a public meeting.[28] The Cultus Lake Act is silent on this issue, and the Park Board sought to continue its long-standing tradition of not undertaking consultation.

Not only did the Park Board fail to consult with the leaseholders prior to taking a decision, but when local residents first sought information on the decision, it was presented as "a done deed." Opposition in terms of letters and phone calls to the Park Board office was spurred by a letter published in Chilliwack-area newspapers.[29] The letter acted as a community notice calling attention to the issue and suggesting that concerned citizens should make their opinions heard. The distribution of proposed new lease-lots across the cottage area at Cultus Lake Park touched many properties, elevating participation in the debate from a couple of directly affected leaseholders to many.

The irritation this proposal, and the process surrounding it, seemed to cause among leaseholders, especially some of those living year-round at the lake, genuinely surprised members of the Park Board. Perhaps in response to the pressure by leaseholders, the Park Board, in their 7 November 1991 meeting, placed a moratorium on the project, although a letter from the park manager announcing the moratorium was apparently distributed to only one leaseholder.[30] The letter from the park manager specifically states that the Park Board resolved that "a moratorium be placed on the sale of all building lots until such time as the Board has had the opportunity to develop, and have in place, a complete development plan for the Park." This appeared to mark a significant change in the way the park was to be planned and managed, and perhaps to provide an opportunity to set in place a comprehensive community vision as well as procedures for amending that vision. Knowledge of the moratorium again became widely known among concerned leaseholders only by word of mouth.

Significant change, however, did not occur. On 28 February 1992 an advertisement appeared in the two Vancouver daily newspapers calling for sealed tenders for "the purchase of the Right to Lease"

Table 42
Cultus Lake Park: Additional Lease Lots Tendered

Lot number	Upset price ($000)
22-W Lakeshore Drive	55
217A-W Lakeshore Drive	50
504 Park Drive	75

Source: Vancouver Sun, 28 Feb. 1992, E9.

three new lease-lots at Cultus Lake Park.[31] Down from eight to three, the combined upset price of $180,000 for the new lots was considerably less than the Park Board had originally hoped to generate (see Table 42). No notification of the Park Board's abandonment of the moratorium was made to any of the leaseholders prior to these advertisements. A notice was mailed to leaseholders on 10 March 1992, informing them of the sale of the three lots. The closing date for tenders was 17 March 1992.

As part of its efforts to rebuild community rapport, the Cultus Lake Community Association invited the Park Manager and members of the Park Board to its general meeting on 5 April 1992. The minutes tersely record that "much concern was shown at the meeting [over] the handling of the sales." With regard to the promised moratorium until a comprehensive park-development plan was in place, the minutes record that, "after much discussion, it was finally agreed by the members of the Park Board that there was no such plan in place. [The Park Board Chair] accepted the crowd's disappointment and indicated this would not happen again. It was noted most forcibly that the Park Board must be very aware of the feelings of the leaseholders in matters relating to happenings in the Park."[32]

Despite the strong wording of the Community Association minutes, the issue of powerlessness in this debate was also made clear at that meeting. Interviews with participants suggest that, when the new lease-lots came up for discussion, the Park Board's unilateral power to approve leases and lease renewals was made clear, intimidating many in the audience fearful of the tenuous nature of their stake at Cultus Lake Park. The powerlessness of leaseholders to press for any normalization of planning practices within Cultus Lake Park is plain. In this discussion it must be recalled that the lands at Cultus Lake Park are owned by the District of Chilliwack. All cottage lots have always been leasehold in tenure. All those investing in property at Cultus Lake Park have always done so within the specific parameters of the park lease agreement. The Cultus Lake Park Board has long maintained that its fundamental responsibility is to the taxpayers of the District of Chilliwack and not to the current leaseholders in the park.

The powerlessness of the leaseholders at Cultus Lake Park results from tenure, lack of representation, and the political structure. In the first place a significant development decision was undertaken by the Park Board without consultation, or concern about consultation, with the leaseholders. Second, it was only by touching many leaseholders with a single proposal that noticeable pressure was exerted on the Park Board by the leaseholders and a suddenly reinvigorated Cultus Lake Community Association. Third, even after the Park Board became aware of their failure to consult leaseholders, and the objections of leaseholders to their actions, they chose to ignore the leaseholders again and carry on very much as usual.

SUMMARY

It is the opinion of some local planners and officials that the Cultus Lake area is at a crossroads, with the choice yet to be made between two very different futures for the community. One alternative would be to limit development at more or less the levels that exist today. Instead of growth, attention would be directed towards solving critical issues of access, safety, and personal and environmental protection. The second scenario would see the complete submergence of the Cultus Lake area into the recreational sphere of metropolitan Vancouver. This would include improving road access, accommodation of higher traffic and user volumes, and replacement of the area's current "quaint isolation" with the groomed maintenance of a park-like retreat for metropolitan day-trippers.

There is a third scenario, which is not being discussed locally but relates directly to local institutional change. It would respond to the need to integrate better the concerns of individual communities in a regional form of local government. It would also respond to the need to change the tenure, representation, and political structure of Cultus Lake Park to give the leaseholders ownership, effective representation, and orderly development planning. These clearly are important issues for the local community and must be dealt with before any co-operative progress on decisions between alternate community futures can be made. The debates reviewed here act as a window through which to probe local reaction to change within the community, a local reaction that, at this time, clearly favours the first scenario.

CONVERSION, CONTENTION, AND THE RURAL-RECREATIONAL COUNTRYSIDE

Residential growth and development in small places and rural communities is disruptive. As contention over residential change within a community becomes more acute, it can be expected that contending opinions will come to the surface in the form of public debates. One of the important findings is that there is indeed local debate over directions for future community development. The recitation of studies and reports by senior government agencies and organizations has not deterred local property owners from challenging official findings and proposed solutions. In the Rideau Lakes area some township councils have closely followed the recommendations of senior government bodies in drafting proposed community-plan amendments. Local residents, through participation in a discourse over community change, are challenging local government actions and, in effect, taking back the debate. They are reclaiming decision-making rights over the future of their local area and community.

The effectiveness of local residents in land-use planning debates depends to a large extent on the existence of organized property-owner groups and the degree of recognition of collective interests among group members. Where these groups do not exist, issue-specific coalitions must emerge; however, such coalitions often do not survive between debates. Pressures of organizing these groups, and criticism directed at individuals rather than a group's executive in the course of debate, act to discourage future organizational efforts. Where property-owner groups do exist, mechanisms for continued monitoring of local issues are clearly important if the group is to be effective in arguing for a legitimate constituency. As well, mechanisms for continuing information exchange or for the co-ordination of studies or reports will assist the group in arguing their position.

The argument that ability to organize an effective property-owners' group depends on socio-economic status may be correct, as the only such group identified in the rural areas along the Rideau Lakes is associated with a new development of rural estate properties – a development that differs from the residential mix of the local rural area. In both study areas it is the cottagers' associations that have been organized and active in local land-use policy debate. As described earlier, using resident-group profiles derived from survey data (see chapter 5), cottage-property owners can generally be distinguished by higher incomes and levels of education.

More consideration needs to be given in community-conflict theory to the role of unique interests. In this research, cottage-property owners clearly recognize a collective set of interests and issues, which they attempt to address. Through their associations the cottage owners also recognize that their collective interests are different from those of the rural and village property owners of the surrounding areas. Socio-economic characteristics play an important role in this recognition, but so too do the fundamental issues of property-value protection and the protection of a perceived lifestyle embodied in the folklore of cottaging. As cottage-property owners increasingly become rural residents living at the lake, both their stake and their interest in the affairs of local government increase. It is clear from the preceding descriptions of the characteristics of Converters and bases for a geographic and social separation of rural and cottage areas that cottage-property owners have a very different set of interests from those currently represented in local governments of the rural-recreational countryside.

In the individual planning debates reviewed, the issue of cottage conversion is not overtly raised as a contentious issue. Instead, it forms one of the two subtexts of local debate over additional waterfront development or new land-use regulations directed at managing such development. When the cottaging areas were essentially "summer-only" concerns, rural-based local governments had little interaction or interest in these areas. As well, the cottagers had little interest in the activities of the local government, since, "after all, we're only here for the summer." Cottage conversion has introduced a new set of rural residents into the area, and these people are now taking an active interest in municipal politics. The second subtext is the tension inherent in the separate social and physical spaces of the rural-recreational countryside. This separation provides a convenient "other" for both cottage- and rural-property owners, a geographic dynamic that affects who will speak for the collective of property owners and how effective that voice may be.

In the Rideau Lakes area environmental protection, broadly defined, is the reference-point in recent land-use planning debates. The parties central to these debates, the local government, cottagers' associations, and rural residents, all view environmental protection as a management issue to be resolved by revised development guidelines or enforcement of existing standards. To be sure, the degradation of the natural environment along sections of the Rideau Lakes area has reached alarming levels. Planning exercises of the Parks Service and the RVCA have established environmental protection as the language of land-use debate. In those debates, however, the language of environmental protection functions as a metaphor for a more basic struggle over who will effectively control property and development rights. The cottagers' associations have been proactive in taking control of environmental-management programs along the lakes and have been successful in legitimizing a place and role for themselves in government planning and management activities. The cottagers' associations have been active in establishing themselves as the jurisdictional body responsible for the individual lakes their members encircle.

In this context, it is the regulation of additional cottage development that is contested. To achieve environmental-protection goals, cottagers' associations have been favouring severe restrictions, which in turn also protect their property values by guaranteeing something akin to a monopoly on lakeside property. Rural residents are more mixed in their reactions. There are strong voices favouring tougher development controls, although prominent statements regarding the maintenance of local access and a feared loss of local control over lakeside properties mute this resolve.

Environmental issues are less prominent at Cultus Lake, in part due to the more extensive use of collective residential services such as the sewer system in Cultus Lake Park. Debates over the Ranch Park proposals highlighted the importance of livelihoods, property values, and lifestyles. In the Columbia Valley the importance of prominent persons cannot be ignored in evaluations of rural community organization, while at Lindell Beach the cottagers' association is actively seeking to maintain local control and participation in the decision-making process. The language of environmental protection does not dominate the debate, as it does along the Rideau Lakes; it is the hopes and fears of property owners about the future of their community and property values that are directly raised.

In summary, then, it is clear from both these case-studies that the rural-recreational countryside is a geographically and socially divided residential landscape. Residential change through cottage conversion is not only introducing a new group of rural residents into the local area but is also creating a challenge to the established system of local government representation. The particular land-use planning debates described in this chapter illustrate a range of responses by rural residents, cottage-property owners, and cottagers' associations. Participation in local planning or development debates by rural residents in both study areas is notable for being limited to individuals or, in some cases, to an issue-specific coalition. The legacy of rural-resident control of local government, the lack of property-based resident groups, and a fragmentation of opinion that limits collective responses all contribute to this pattern of participation.

Cottagers' associations in both study areas recognize the importance of effective participation in local debates and decision-making. At Lindell Beach the cottagers' association has established a mature working relationship with a number of local and senior government agencies. At Cultus Lake Park both individual cottagers and the collective association have been active and vocal in responding to recent development decisions by the Park Board; however, issues of tenure and political structure have greatly reduced the effectiveness of this participation. In the Rideau Lakes area cottagers' associations have participated effectively in a range of recent land-use planning debates to forge a legitimate claim to representing a separate local constituency. In some cases they have perhaps even moved from outside to inside the decision-making structure.

Cottagers' associations have long represented the unique collective interests of the seasonal-use population. As this population increasingly become permanent local residents, the cottagers' associations have increasingly become active in land-use planning debates in order to maintain control of cottage-property areas by cottage-property owners. Participation in land-use planning debates also marks a deliberate attempt by the cottagers' associations to situate themselves in the decision-making process of a local government structure that has not traditionally represented their interests. For the cottagers' associations, land-use planning debates are arenas that offer the opportunity both to participate in decision-making and to continue a longer process of negotiation for recognition that the group speaks for a legitimate local constituency.

11 Conclusions

This study has examined the implications of residential change within the local community by focusing upon a particular setting and type of residential change. The rural-recreational countryside is a geographically and socially divided landscape, with localized cottage and recreational areas juxtaposed within a broader rural and agricultural landscape. In the countryside, the conversion of cottages from seasonal to year-round homes is a dynamic responsible for the introduction of many new residents. The pressures and implications of this residential change have been explored through issues of individual and household characteristics, local organization and participation in community groups, and participation in debates over local land-use development and planning issues.

Through a comparative research methodology, two case-study areas were selected to examine residential change in the rural-recreational countryside. The Rideau Lakes area of eastern Ontario and the Cultus Lake area of the Lower Fraser Valley in British Columbia are both experiencing the pressures of cottage-conversion activity, yet important differences between these two areas may be recognized in the effort to separate general processes from place-specific outcomes. The history and geography of each place are critical variables affecting residential and community change. This said, there is considerable similarity of experience with cottage conversion and community change. This concluding chapter highlights the findings of the study around four themes – cottage conversion, separate spaces, collective interests, and contested turf – in order to integrate the results.

THEORIZING COMMUNITY CHANGE

It has been remarked that human geography, and indeed a good deal of social-scientific inquiry, currently validates a broad range of theoretical and methodological approaches. For studies such as the one described in this book this plurality is a strength, for it allows one to search broadly through current and past research for insights and evidence that help to explain and order the dynamics and processes under investigation. It also offers the freedom to explore alternative explanations in order, hopefully, to resolve some of the more puzzling questions confronted during the study. While no dogmatic straitjacket is imposed, this plurality also has potential weaknesses. Among these are the failure of some to acknowledge the theoretical basis(es) for their research choices, or even that their arguments are theoretically grounded at all, as well as the danger that coherent progress may be hampered by a reluctance to connect empirical research to broader debates over ideas and ways of conceptualizing.

The research problem of examining community change demands that a good deal of time be devoted to understanding, and making useful in a research sense, the central concept of "community," a very fluid concept, given that individuals within the same locality may each conceptualize multiple, alternate, and even overlapping collective memberships. The employment of "community" as some type of concrete entity has proved less than useful in past research and has hampered comparability. Instead, I argue for understanding community as a process. This emphasis allows the tracing of such memberships not as ends unto themselves but as part of both historical and contemporary processes of local participation and contention. As shown in chapters 9 and 10, this approach to community proved to be a useful tool for deconstructing local debates and for explaining what appear on the surface to be contradictions in the activism of specific community groups. The study of community change proved to be complex and multi-faceted, and as such required conceptual and theoretical tools that recognize this complexity.

This study adopts the theoretical perspective of political economy on the study of rural community change, an approach selected for two principal reasons. The first is the basic recognition of society as a complex and interactive entity. In order to probe a topic such as community change, and local contention over that change, it is not possible to legitimize purely economic, purely social, or purely political explanations. These elements all interact, and it is the research task to identify which components become important at which times. Second, political economy recognizes that all explanations are conditional – subject to change over time and in different places. This recognition is central to my geographic inquiry, both in the argument that the rural-recreational countryside is a distinct component of rural Canada and in the methodological decision to conduct comparative research in two different settings within which it is hypothesized that some general processes are occurring.

Bearing these thoughts in mind, this study drew upon a range of specific theoretical positions to inform the general political economy approach. These specific contributions, which are described in chapter 3, helped with both the development of the research and the interpretation of the results. I would now like to elaborate upon three key elements of theorizing community change in the rural-recreational countryside that have arisen from this study.

The first is that collective organization is indeed one of the key ways people differentiate one another in community settings. It also forms a crucial framework within which individuals understand and interpret local issues and events. In this study of community change in the rural-recreational countryside, property ownership is one of the central means of creating local collective membership(s). The economic issue of property ownership, and the increasing exclusivity of the cottage property sub-market, point to economic class as one foundation for local division and debate. Writers adopting a Marxist political economy perspective have done much in recent years to elucidate issues of contention and conflict, especially as they relate to property ownership and local political control at the rural-community level. In these respects, the concept of "commodification" has been an especially valuable addition. Yet other writers, notably Fitchen, have also remarked on the value of collective membership for ordering local peoples' understanding of both place and newcomers.

In the rural-recreational countryside, however, local debate over issues of community change cannot simply be construed as economically determined. The socially constructed images and folklore attached to the particular "cottage" landscapes of this book complicate the economic-class argument. Many cottage-property owners who gained access to their land by inheritance or other means readily adopt the cottage lifestyle when they are "at the lake," even though they may be at very different socio-economic levels from some of their lakeshore counterparts or may themselves be local rural-area residents the remainder of the year.

A second element in theorizing community change is that in rural areas and small towns individuals are still important. As the rural sociologists pointed out fifty years ago, community activism and protest often develop through key individuals and local leaders. This study confirms that local individuals can play significant roles in debate over community change. While the importance of such key local individuals has been downplayed in Marxist commodification research, debates in political science over local elites and struggles for community power have clearly linked individuals to the political dimension of contention over local change.

A third element to theorizing community change in the rural-recreational countryside is a reaffirmation of the importance of place. Each of the case-study areas examined in this book has a physical and human landscape. These landscapes are the products of past as well as current forces of change. In any interpretation of local contention and debate over community change, the place-specific geographic "memories" of these landscapes must not be excluded. This "respatialization of discourse" is critical both to interpreting contemporary debate and to developing a *geographic* study. Taken together, these issues point to the value of a political economy perspective in the study of local-community change. This is especially the case in the study of community change within the rural-recreational countryside, where places, people, property, pasts, politics, and power all combine and interact within a geographically and socially divided landscape.

COTTAGE CONVERSION

Cottage-conversion activity generates pressure for improvement of on-site facilities and the more general provision of collective residential services. Increasingly, as new seasonal-use cottages are built to National Building Code requirements, renovation activity at time of conversion will be directed more to issues of space and design preferences than to currently important requirements for winterizing. While the costs of these on-site upgrades are borne directly by the property owner, the expansion or extension of collective services is usually the responsibility of local government. Some of the local governments along the Rideau Lakes and at Cultus Lake have entrenched policy statements in their respective community-planning documents that, in effect, set limits or conditions on levels of available services. At Cultus Lake, for example, the RDFC specifically requires new cottage-property developers to assume responsibility for all collective residential-service needs.

As part of the residential life-course of households, participation in cottage-conversion activity occurs within some specific parameters. The most important issue identified in both study areas is the role of retirement and retirement planning. In this situation, households often have considerable local familiarity with the cottaging area, if not long-term ownership of the specific property being converted into a permanent home. Upgrading of the seasonal-use cottage usually begins in advance of the actual conversion move, with this move often coinciding with the retirement of the major income provider in the household.

In the case of a retirement decision to move to the lake, a very specific horizon is set on the expected length of the residential stay. In both study areas retirement living at the lake occurs during the younger, relatively fit period of the elderly years. Problems of home and property maintenance, access to emergency services, and the general isolation of cottage properties are exacerbated over the winter and become nearly impossible to cope with after individuals lose the ability to drive their own automobiles. Differences between winter climates and the morphology of settlement affect the ability to stay longer at converted properties in the respective study areas.

The conversion of cottage properties by retirement-age households, and the tendency of these households to leave their converted properties when they feel the need to be closer to family or needed services for their more frail elderly years, suggest that these properties may cycle through different stages of use. As seen at Cultus Lake, some converted properties have in fact reverted back to seasonal-use cottages following their sale by older converters moving into Chilliwack or back to metropolitan Vancouver. In the Rideau Lakes area, the increased difficulty of winter living reduces even further the period of time retirement-age households seem willing to commit to living at the lake. In this scenario it is not at all certain that cottage conversion will effectively change general seasonal-use cottaging areas into the stable, permanent communities some planners and researchers expect. At the outer bounds of the urban field a continuation of a mixed seasonal and permanent pattern of cottage-area occupancy is more likely.

The example of young families from within the surrounding rural countryside moving to convert a cottage property into a starter-home has received some attention in the popular press. Such conversions are more evident in the Rideau Lakes area, as cottage conversion at Cultus Lake occurs nearly exclusively among older and retired households. Along the Rideau Lakes, however, starter-home activity is limited more to the secondary lakes and less desirable locations than to the high-value properties along the major lakes. This is perhaps a leading edge of a separation of landscapes in the rural-recreational countryside. Easier year-round access to the clustered cottage developments at Cultus Lake appears to be an important reason for higher levels of retired households. In part, the participation of local-area families in the conversion process coincides with established patterns of local ownership of cottage properties.

SEPARATE SPACES

A second theme to emerge from this research is that there is a clear separation of both the physical and the social spaces of the rural and cottaging areas of these rural-recreational countrysides. Three constituent elements, the physical geography of property development, the social geography of local residents and local community institutions, and the folklore associated with cottaging activity, have been argued to be important elements in this separation.

While there is a mix of cottage and rural property through both the Rideau Lakes and Cultus Lake areas, there are important differences in their geographies that make the separation of rural and cottaging areas more straightforward at Cultus Lake. The common distinguishing feature of cottaging properties is location; in both study areas the key amenity feature is the recreational lakes, with the result that cottage-property developments compete for sites immediately adjacent to the lakefront. Along the Rideau Lakes the small-lot cottage properties form a single-tier necklace around most of the waterfront, a physical pattern of private property development that effectively limits public access to the lakeshore. At Cultus Lake limitations of topography and a public-policy commitment to maintain public access to the lake has resulted in dense clusters of cottage properties. Perhaps as a result of this clustering, cottage properties at Cultus Lake are much smaller than those of the surrounding rural areas, and are even smaller than the cottage lots found around the Rideau Lakes.

The structure of property ownership in cottaging areas adds to the issue of physical separation. In both the Rideau Lakes and Cultus Lake areas more than half of the seasonal-use cottage properties are owned by residents from adjacent metropolitan areas. This lends support to the argument that metropolitan areas dominate cottaging activity within their recreational hinterlands. It also supports the impressions recounted in the popular literature of a rural countryside seasonally invaded by an urban population seeking refuge at cottage properties set within, but not really part of, the rural landscape.

Ownership of seasonal-use cottage properties in both study areas is, however, not restricted to urban residents. In both cases up to one-fifth of the cottage properties are owned by residents living permanently in the immediately surrounding rural areas or adjacent small towns. This block of local ownership works to dispel part of the urban cottager myth and also acts to prevent complete non-local control of the cottage-property stock.

Another element important in the separation of rural and cottaging spaces in the rural-recreational countryside is the social geography of local residents. Based on results from a questionnaire survey, there are striking differences in education, occupation, and household income between Rural Resident and Seasonal Occupant respondents. As well, there are clear differences in terms of age, employment, and family status between the Rural Residents and Converters responding. While these generalizations hold true in both study areas, the difference between Rural Resident and Seasonal Occupant respondents is more acute along the Rideau Lakes, while the difference between Rural Residents and Converters is more acute at Cultus Lake. In terms of local social interactions, those living in the cottaging areas tend to have a more locally intense pattern of neighbouring. They also maintain a broader field of friendships that recognizes some continuation of ties to their former (often urban) place of residence.

To these generalizations at the individual level we must admit a range of exceptions as well. The most important of these is the use of cottage properties as starter-homes by young families from within the local area. Easier year-round access to the clustered cottage developments at Cultus Lake appears to be the reason behind higher levels of retired exurban households. As such cottage properties increase in value, younger households may, as a group, not be able to compete with older or retired households. This fact reinforces the finding that cottages as starter-homes tend to be restricted to the less-desired waterfront locations.

A second aspect of the social separation between rural and cottaging landscapes concerns the degree to which residential membership translates into community participation. In both study areas the organization of and participation in community social groups is strongly structured by place of residence. At Cultus Lake two clearly different organizations serve the needs of elderly residents either at the lake or in the Columbia Valley. Along the Rideau Lakes there appears a similar separation of social groups for older residents. The interesting anomaly in this case, however, is the use of a common organization, the Women's Institute, by very different memberships. Although fundamentally still an organization for rural women, its increased flexibility is reflected in the Chaffeys Lock Women's Institute, where no members come from farm households and nearly all are exurban residents living at converted cottage properties. In some respects this development can be seen as an appropriation of a rural icon by new residents eager to "act" rural.

The final element crucial to the separation of rural and cottaging areas is the folklore of cottaging. The legacy associated with cottaging activity is one that does not recognize the surrounding rural area, a place that is travelled through to get to the cottage and into which occasional forays are made for needed goods, services, or amusement. Whether characterized as an elite landscape or suburbia in the wilderness, the cottaging area is clearly organized as a self-contained community. The general surroundings are almost immaterial; it is the specific set of properties that constitute the cottage milieu that are the focus of activities and relationships. The late nineteenth-century restrictions of cottage and rural-resort visits to wealthy households may be taking a contemporary turn as costs of purchasing and maintaining these properties increase.

It is important to point out that this characterization of a physical and social separation between rural and cottaging areas does not represent a mean-spirited set of attitudes on the part of either set of actors, nor, I hope, on the part of the author. Nor is the separation a simple and clear-cut matter. It is, however, an important part of how residents organize their understanding of local geography and how they characterize and interpret collective relationships. This generalization also effectively captures the operation of cottage conversion as one form of residential change, a change that is perpetuating the foundations of separate social and geographic spaces and differences in views during public debate regarding choices between alternative local futures.

COLLECTIVE INTERESTS

The separate geographic and social spaces within the rural-recreational countryside affect the degree to which common or collective interests can be recognized, and action mobilized, by residents. Recognition of collective interests over issues of residential development and change was evaluated through analysis of property-based community groups and participation in local land-use planning debates. The physical layout of cottage properties, their costs, and their patterns of use have enhanced the recognition of collective interests and needs among property owners. Both study areas have established cottagers' associations and, with the exception of the leaseholders at Cultus Lake Park, these associations have acted vigorously to protect interests and provide solutions to needs. Also, again with the exception of Cultus Lake Park, the cottagers' associations have been recognized by local governments and some senior government agencies as the legitimate voice for a particular local constituency. These findings support and extend existing research on the recognition of collective interests among owners in cottage-property areas.

In contrast to the cottaging areas, there is less evidence of a recognition of collective interests among rural/village property owners. The exception to this observation is the Columbia Valley Ratepayers' Association at Cultus Lake, which has been active in local social and service-provision organization since 1968 and has been an important voice for local residents' concerns when dealing with governments and agencies. With the specific history of the Columbia Valley and the legacy of limited local political input through regional government, it can be expected that the Ratepayers' Association's role will not diminish in the near future.

To understand the lack of property-based community groups in the rural areas bordering the Rideau Lakes, we must examine the role of other local social groups. A wide range of interest-based community groups include church-based, agriculture-based, and other historically rural-based organizations. The mandates of many such groups remain important to the provision of social networks and an informal social safety-net in the countryside. While there has been, in recent years, a decline in participation noted by some of these groups, there remain a large number of rural residents, especially older women, who are busy several days a week with group activities. The high levels of activity leave little room for participation in other community groups. The cottaging areas do not share this established heritage of a wide range of community groups; in those areas the cottagers' association typically serves as the social convenor for property owners.

The lack of a property-based organization for rural residents is important in debates over issues of residential change. Property-based organizations act as formal channels for correspondence with planners and local governments, and as conduits of information to their membership. The property-based group also acts as an organizing platform from which to formulate and deliver the views, responses, and opinions of members. If no such organization exists, then one must be purpose-built for particular debates. The stresses of start-up and the specific public debate may strain relations between individuals to the point where the organization cannot be resurrected for the next issue that arises.

A second reason for the lack of property-based groups across the rural sections of the two study areas is participation in local government. In the Rideau Lakes area, as a result of long-standing participation in local government by rural residents, the township councils are perceived as the legitimate representatives of rural residents' interests. Until recently, in both the Rideau Lakes and Cultus Lake areas, there has been limited participation in local government by cottage-area residents. Cottage-property-owner participation in local elections has been more active at Cultus Lake, although calls for more active participation in the Rideau Lakes area may equalize participation levels in the two areas. As seen along the Rideau Lakes, historically low participation rates by cottage-property owners has resulted in the maintenance of local government control by the rural community. In this regard, the argument that the local government acts as the property-based organization for rural residents has some validity. The legacy of a near exclusion of cottage-property-owner interests by rural local government is reflected in calls by some local governments to cottagers' associations to act as the go-between with their members while the local government consults rural property owners directly. The result appears to be the emergence of dual local political representation, with the township councils continuing to represent their traditional rural constituencies and the cottagers' associations increasingly coming to serve a similar function for cottage-property owners. In this context the anomaly is the Columbia Valley Ratepayers' Association, which was organized at about the same time as the RDFC. Here it can be argued that the limited input of one rural community in a regionally elected board has strengthened the role of the Ratepayers' Association as a collective voice for property owners.

CONTESTED TURF

The separate geographic and social spaces within the rural-recreational countryside and the reflection of this separation in the organization of local collective-interest groups marks a flashpoint for contention and debate over local residential change. The location of their property largely decides the position of owners on the rural or cottage sides of these debates. The conversion of seasonal-use cottage properties to year-round homes introduces new residents into local areas, and as these new residents take an active part in public debates, the potential for conflict between rural and cottage communities increases. The debates over cottage-property development, or changes in planning regulations affecting cottage areas, identify cottage-property areas as contested turf.

The review of local debates over specific development or land-use planning initiatives highlights apparent agreement between cottage-

and rural-property owners in their overt public responses. In both study areas there appears to be a rejection of proposed changes to the status quo. When examined in detail, however, the motives of members of cottagers' associations and those of rural-area spokespeople differ considerably.

Along the Rideau Lakes, cottagers' associations opposed specific details of new planning regulations but generally supported the initiatives as part of an environmental-protection discourse, the lake after all being a principal determinant of cottage-property value. At Cultus Lake it was more clearly stated that additional development would destroy the isolated rural character important to the cottaging areas. In both areas cottagers clearly wish to protect their lifestyle and cottage landscape; however, in the Rideau Lakes area the language was couched in environmental terms. The impact of additional costs imposed through new regulations or the denial of additional lakefront development enhances the exclusivity of present cottage properties by maintaining their monopoly status. The debates have revolved around these issues and are set against a backdrop that includes resentment over increasing local government interference in cottaging areas and continuing irritation over property taxes imposed to pay for non-cottage-area services.

Rural opposition to more stringent cottaging-area planning regulations is based on a desire to protect local access to cottage-property ownership. Along the Rideau Lakes it is argued that changes that would increase the costs of cottage properties would further limit the range of local residents able to compete for these properties. At Cultus Lake, opposition to proposed additional cottage developments revolves around livelihood issues. The further incursion of cottage development into agricultural areas would put pressure on existing farming operations that, some fear, would destroy their livelihoods. All additional development would put upward pressure on property values near undeveloped waterfront areas, with market-value assessment raising very real concerns about ability to pay future property taxes.

In the Cultus Lake area there is also a noted rejection of any change and marked support for maintenance of the status quo. Objections to change at Cultus Lake, compared to those along the Rideau Lakes, are less cloaked in issues of environmental protection and more directly focused on lifestyle or livelihood issues. The cottagers' association at Lindell Beach did not take an active part in the Ranch Park debates, although several individual property owners spoke. The issue of further development was seen as exacerbating traffic and congestion, removing finally the last vestige of a valued isolation for the cottage areas at an intensively used recreational lake.

It is important to note that cottage-property owners in both study areas argue for a continued protection of their rural escape through maintenance of its current exclusivity. The striking part is that the cottage landscape along the Rideau Lakes is so very different from that found at Cultus Lake. The low-density pattern of isolated cottages along the waterfront found in the Rideau Lakes area is replaced at Cultus Lake with a high-density urban setting, with backstreets lacking any view of the lake. While the construction of the cottage image differs, the combination of this social concept together with a recognition of cottage properties as an economic commodity creates the foundations for community organization and political activism.

The comparison of cases illustrates the complexities of local-resident participation in contentious land-use debate. It especially highlights the powerlessness of some cottagers in such debates, a powerlessness that is rooted in property tenure. At Cultus Lake Park the effectiveness of cottager participation in planning and development debate is muted by cottagers' leasehold tenure and by the failure of the local government to recognize that the leaseholders also have a critical interest in local property issues and related debates. The extent of this powerlessness is strikingly highlighted by comparison to the effective participation of other cottagers' associations. Given this example, it is important to note that leasehold tenure is not an uncommon arrangement for cottage properties in Canada.

The differences in motivation between rural and cottage-area residents mark clearly the protection of property interests that characterize the politics of turf. The role that individuals play in particular debates cannot be underestimated. This is especially important in the public debates, where the suggestion that a more reserved rural audience will leave the floor to the more outspoken residents creates an interpretive problem for planners and elected officials trying to gauge public opinion. In contrast, effective participation by individual cottagers in the debates may be limited more by issues of tenure or government structure. Finally, the existence of property-based organizations in carrying out a more continuous dialogue on planning issues clearly gives an advantage to cottage-property owners, despite local elected officials' allegiances to their rural constituencies.

FUTURE CHALLENGES

Residential change in the rural-recreational countryside presents a series of difficult challenges for local residents and governments alike. In this study, pressures of accelerating cottage-property costs, continuing cottage-conversion activity, increasing supra-local participation in land-use planning by more senior government agencies, and a reorientation of local political control mark the immediate challenges. The themes of cottage conversion, separate spaces, collective interests, and contested turf suggest a range of issues and divisions of local opinion that complicate the formation and implementation of policies or actions to address these challenges.

One of the first challenges for rural-recreational countryside areas is the continuing upward pressure on cottage-property values. Restrictions on additional lakefront development, whether due to demands for protection of environments or of lifestyles, will only work to increase this upward pressure. One likely result may be that the ability of local residents to compete with metropolitan-area residents for cottage properties will diminish, and current socio-economic differences between rural residents and cottage property owners will be exacerbated. Given the current activism of many cottagers' associations in trying to increase their members' participation in cottage-country politics, increased non-local control of cottaging properties and increased differentiation of cottage owners from rural residents can only work to the detriment of those rural residents. If the elite landscapes of the late nineteenth century became more accessible to the general public by the mid-twentieth century, then this accessibility may be diminishing in the 1990s.

Differences in the relative value of cottage versus rural properties, and the costs associated with cottage-property ownership, have placed constraints on the ability of households to enter the cottage-property market. Some of these same costs, however, represent an important push factor in the decision to undertake conversion of a former cottage into an individual's permanent home. It is also clear that conversion activity is occurring regardless of the policy or regulatory options adopted by local governments to control or manage it. As property prices in cottaging areas increase, and as the folklore that cottaging areas are not really part of the surrounding rural area continues unabated, the cycling of cottage properties through seasonal and permanent occupancy will proceed. If pressures are so intense that permanent communities do emerge along lakeshores, then two very different communities can be expected. One community would be associated with cottaging properties in the high-prestige and high-cost locations, such as along Big Rideau Lake. A second community would likely develop around the less desirable, less expensive cottage properties. In this case, the communities would be marked by differing family and socio-economic characteristics.

The separation of cottage-area property interests between seasonal and permanent occupants, and perhaps even a future separation of interests between permanent occupants depending on the status of the site, suggests an increasingly complex rural-recreational country-side. At present this complexity is already manifest in rural areas. The bifurcation of the rural community between farm and non-farm households can be expected to continue. The challenge to rural social organizations will be to continue to attract members or to transform themselves. Along the Rideau Lakes most such groups still depend on older persons, usually women, and often from former farming households, for their continued operation. In part the perception that many of these are "farmers' groups" has discouraged participation by exurban households; however, the pattern of group activities organized for midday, weekday times also precludes participation by younger residents already committed to employment responsibilities.

The most important challenges in the rural-recreational country-side, however, concern local governance. Recent planning and development debates in both the Rideau Lakes and Cultus Lake areas suggest a reclaiming of the agenda by local residents. This has been a significant effort and, if it can be sustained, will be a considerable achievement under a structure of government and legislation not designed for these non-urban places. Unfortunately, it seems likely that such efforts will succeed only in those areas with strong and established property-owner organizations. Thus, where cottagers' associations are well developed, local government is likely to be increasingly dominated by the interests of converters and seasonal residents over those of the rural and farm-based population. The local reorganization of political representation and political power may occur swiftly in some areas, since cottage-area properties already outnumber rural properties, and calls for cottage-owner participation in local elections are becoming louder.

The activities and interactions fostered by the recent planning debates also generate opportunities for a better integration, and indeed represent a challenge to integration, of local interests in the governing of the rural-recreational countryside. While such co-ordination or integration might be possible within the Cultus Lake area, the RDFC is still viewed as a supra-local government body by many property owners. Along the Rideau Lakes, encouragement is found in the RVCA's recognition of the need for basin-wide co-ordination of policies and in the Sewell Commission's recognition of the policy-co-ordination needs of the rural-recreational countryside. In the near future such integration is not likely to happen through structural changes to local government but rather through formalization of channels of communication between different constituencies, and the recognition of the legitimacy of these different constituencies, in the formulation of visions and options for the future of these local areas.

Social geography remains fundamentally interested in the way individuals and groups define, construct, and interpret their local community. The collective understanding of local space continues to ground the interpretation of the pressures and processes of community change. In the rural-recreational countryside a fundamental separation of property into cottage and rural-residential areas sets the foundation for an enduring social and geographic separation of communities. In this study, recognition of a locally constructed separation has been central to the analysis of contention and debate over issues of residential and community change. It is critical that research in social geography remain sensitive to the need to integrate recognition of the wide array of pressures that continually put stress upon local-community formulations. The challenge of understanding the meanings and implications of locally constructed social geographies will continue to inform and motivate research interested in the broad question of community change.

Notes

1 I am also tempted to say that this is now an image commonly represented in television commercials advertising a range of Canadian beer products.

2 Beesley and Walker, "Residence Paths and Community Perception: A Case Study from the Toronto Urban Field," 1990; Coppack, Russwurm, and Bryant, *Essays on Canadian Urban Process and Form III – The Urban Field*, 1988; Davies and Yeates, "Exurbanization as a Component of Migration," 1991; Dykeman, *Integrated Rural Planning and Development*, 1988.

3 Clout, "The Growth of Second-Home Ownership: An Example of Seasonal Suburbanization," 1974, and "Résidences Secondaires in France," 1977; Dahms and Hoover, "The Evolution of Settlement Functions in the Southeastern Parry Sound District: 1971–1976," 1979; Keogh, "L'Impact social du tourisme," 1982.

4 Halseth and Rosenberg, "Conversion of Recreational Residences," 1990.

5 Coppock, "Issues and Conflicts," 1977d; Jordan, "The Summer People and the Natives," 1980; Wilkinson and Murray, "Centre and Periphery," 1991.

6 Gilg, *An Introduction to Rural Geography*, 1985; Krueger, "Urbanization of the Niagara Fruit Belt," 1978; Leckie, "Continuity and Change in the Farm Community," 1989; Smit, Joseph, Alexander, and McIlravey, *Non-Farm Residential Development, Service Provision, Taxes and Policy*, 1984; Troughton, "The Rural-Urban Fringe," 1981; "Modelling Change in the Canadian Rural System," 1984.

7 Barnes and Hayter, "'The Little Town That Did': Flexible Accumulation and Community Response in Chemainus, British Columbia," 1992; Bradbury and St Martin, "Winding Down in a Quebec Mining Town: A Case Study of Schefferville," 1983; Gill and Smith, "Residents' Evaluative Structures of Northern Manitoba Mining Communities," 1985.

8 Beesley and Walker, "Residence Paths and Community Perception: A Case Study From the Toronto Urban Field," 1990; Cloke, "Whither Rural Studies?" 1985; Coppock, "Social Implications of Second Homes in Mid-and North Wales," 1977c; Fitchen, *Endangered Spaces, Enduring Places*, 1991.

9 Fitchen, *Endangered Spaces, Enduring Places*, 1991; Hodge and Qadeer, *Towns and Villages in Canada*, 1983; Keddie and Joseph, "Reclassification and Rural-Versus-Urban Population Change in Canada, 1976–1981," 1991.

10 These terms have included cottage (Gordon, *At the Cottage*, 1989; Hodge, *Cottaging in the Toronto Urban Field*, 1970a; Wolfe, "Summer Cottagers in Ontario," 1951; "Summer Cottages in Ontario," 1977), chalet (Gardavsky, "Second Homes in Czechoslovakia," 1977; Godin, Boudreau, and LeBlanc, *Étude sur la villégiature dans le district d'aménagement Beaubassin*, 1988), second home (Coppock, *Second Homes: Curse or Blessing*, 1977a; Jaakson, "Second-home Domestic Tourism," 1986), vacation home (Lehr, Selwood, and Goatcher, "Wilderness Suburbias," 1984; Ragatz, "Vacation Homes in the Northeastern United States," 1970, "Vacation Homes in Rural Areas," 1977; Wolfe, "Discussion of Vacation Homes, Environmental Preferences and Spatial Behaviour," 1970), inessential house (Wolfe, "About Cottages and Cottagers," 1965), summer house (Cross, *The Summer House*, 1992), and recreational residence (Halseth and Rosenberg, "Conversion of Recreational Residences," 1990).

11 In popular literature the term "cottage country" is often used. In studying the rural-recreational countryside it becomes clear that this term has some particular limitations. While cottage country ostensibly includes all of the rural-recreational countryside, the rural element is all but invisible when the focus is exclusively upon the cottaging areas.

12 For examples of the farm/non-farm methodology, see Brunet, "L'Exode Urbain, Essai de Classification de la Population Exurbaine des Cantons de l'Est," 1980; Joseph and Smit, "Rural Residential Development and Municipal Service Provision," 1985; Russwurm and Bryant, "Changing Population Distribution and Rural-Urban Relationships in Canadian Urban Fields, 1941–1976," 1984.

CHAPTER TWO

1 Broad statements reflecting the current construction of this division between the cottaging and surrounding rural areas can be found in

articles and editorials in *Cottage Life* magazine, and in the cottage-area landscapes described by humorist Gordon (*At the Cottage*, 1989) and writers Cross (*The Summer House*, 1992) and Lampi ("Cottage Country from the Other Side of the Fence," 1992).

2 This comment is based on interviews and conversations with cottagers and local-area residents in a number of rural-recreational countryside areas in British Columbia, Ontario, and New Brunswick.

3 For recent exceptions see Jaakson, "Second-home Domestic Tourism," 1986; Jordan, "The Summer People and the Natives," 1980; and Wycoff, "Landscapes of Private Power and Wealth," 1990.

4 Bunce, *The Countryside Ideal*, 1994.

5 Osborne, "The Hinterland," 1988.

6 See also Butler, "The Impact of Informal Recreation on Rural Canada," 1984; Dilley, "Local Government, Public Expectations and Planning Policy in a Rural Recreational Area," 1985; or Lehr, Schultz, and Selwood, "An Investment in Health," 1983.

7 Wyckoff, "Landscapes of Private Power and Wealth," 1990, 335.

8 Cross, *The Summer House*, 1992, xiii.

9 Jaakson, "Second-home Domestic Tourism," 1986, 386.

10 Wolfe, "About Cottages and Cottagers," 1965, 7.

11 Cross, *The Summer House*, 1992, 14.

12 Wolfe, "Wasaga Beach," 1952, 62.

13 Clout, "The Growth of Second-Home Ownership: An Example of Seasonal Suburbanization," 1974, 102. Osborne, "The Hinterland," 1988, 278. Ragatz ("Vacation Homes in the Northeastern United States," 1970) conceptualizes this annual cycle as a form of "semi-permanent migration," something Jaakson ("Second-home Domestic Tourism," 1986) refers to as "second-home tourism."

14 RDFC, By-law No 66, 1976b.

15 Wolfe, "About Cottages and Cottagers," 1965, 6. Cross (*The Summer House*, 1992), Gordon (*At the Cottage*, 1989), and Jaakson ("Second-home Domestic Tourism," 1986) all describe in their own ways the physical separation of cottage-property areas from the surrounding rural landscape, and each extends this separation to include the social worlds of rural and cottage residents.

16 Gordon, *At the Cottage*, 1989.

17 Jordan, "The Summer People and the Natives," 1980, 50.

18 Cross, *The Summer House*, 1992, 81.

19 Wolfe, "About Cottages and Cottagers", 1965, 7.

20 Cross, *The Summer House*, 1992, 112.

21 Wolfe, "About Cottages and Cottagers," 1965, 7. While ownership remains an important variable in establishing collective membership in a cottaging community, as shown by Halseth's study of "Communities within communities" (1993), a wider range of "membership" qualifications is

evidenced in Lehr, Selwood, and Badiuk's 1991 study of "Ethnicity, Religion, and Class as Elements in the Evolution of Lake Winnipeg Resorts."

22 Helleiner, "Loon Lake," 1983, 35.
23 Wolfe, "About Cottages and Cottagers," 1965, 7.
24 Cross, *The Summer House*, 1992, xii.
25 Ibid., 141.
26 Shamas, "How I Spent My Summer Holidays," 1992, 90.
27 Clout, "Résidences Secondaires in France," 1977, 57.
28 Wyckoff, "Landscapes of Private Power and Wealth," 1990. ·
29 Wolfe, "About Cottages and Cottagers," 1965, 7.
30 Ibid., 8.
31 France (Clout, "Résidences Secondaires in France," 1977), Great Britain (Coppock, "Social Implications of Second Homes in Mid- and North Wales," 1977c; Rogers, "Second Homes in England and Wales," 1977), Czechoslovakia (Gardavsky, "Second Homes in Czechoslovakia," 1977), and Australia (Robertson, "Second-home Decisions," 1977; Selwood, Curry and Koczberski, "Structure and Change in a Coastal Vacation Village," 1995).
32 Wolfe, "Summer Cottagers in Ontario," 1951; "Recreational Travel," 1966.
33 The number of households sampled in the HFE survey has varied from about 30,000 in 1973 to over 44,000 in 1991. Statistics Canada estimates the standard error for the HFE data at the national level to be 2.6 to 5.0 per cent. For Ontario, the estimated error ranged from 2.6 to 5.0 per cent (1985) to 5.1 to 10.0 per cent (1980, 1990), while for British Columbia it was 10.1 to 16.5 per cent (Statistics Canada, HFE, 1973, 1990).
34 That neither source is an actual count of vacation homes is representative of a long-standing data-quality issue concerning an entity and pattern of occupancy, where the definition has proved too malleable to operationalize in a more consistent manner. Data-quality issues that limit more precise estimation of cottage impacts on rural communities is just one examplar of a continuing poor body of statistical data for studying the changing communities of rural Canada. See Coppock ("Second Homes in Perspective," 1977b), Hart ("Population Change in the Upper Lake States," 1984), Hinch ("A Spatial Analysis of Tourist Accommodation in Ontario," 1990), and Jaakson ("Second-home Domestic Tourism," 1986). In trying to explain population change in the Upper Great Lakes area of the United States, Hart ("Population Change in the Upper Lake States," 1984) expresses some dissatisfaction with his experiments in alternative methods of estimating the role of cottages within a regional housing-stock framework. A first attempt

was made through counts of unoccupied housing units, while a second used the percentage of inland water in each study-unit as a surrogate index for resort development.

35 Wolfe, "Summer Cottagers in Ontario," 1951.

36 Ibid.

37 The importance of adjacent metropolitan areas as a source of cottagers or cottage-owners is now a well-documented phenomena. Wolfe reports that, in the Lake of the Woods area of northwestern Ontario, cottagers from the nearest metropolitan area, Winnipeg, predominate ("Summer Cottagers in Ontario," 1951). The impact of metropolitan Winnipeg on the northwestern section of Ontario was confirmed in an historical study of Winnipeg's cottaging community by Lehr, Selwood, and Goatcher ("Wilderness Suburbias," 1984). As well, Wilkinson and Murray's ("Centre and Periphery," 1991) study of cottage owners in the rural Collingwood area highlights the importance of residents from metropolitan Toronto. See also Coppock (*Second Homes: Curse or Blessing*, 1977a) and Hallman ("Migration, Commuting and Economic Development in Toronto's Outer Urban Field," 1990).

38 The identification of cottaging properties within this region is relatively straighforward, as the small-lot cottage properties form a narrow band along the lakeshore. The depth of development usually does not exceed a single tier of lots, and these are easily distinguished from the surrounding extensive agricultural uses. Property-assessment data, including "use" and "taxation" codes and owners' mailing address, were used to classify cottage ownership. See, for example, Halseth's 1992 study of "Cottage Property Ownership" in eastern Ontario.

39 See also Halseth and Rosenberg ("Cottagers in an Urban Field," 1995), which reports on similar patterns of local- and urban-resident ownership of cottage properties along the Beaubassin coast of New Brunswick.

40 Comparison of property-assessment indexes for the cottaging areas at Cultus Lake with those of the adjacent rural Columbia Valley was not possible as a result of complications introduced by the calculation of farm uses and agricultural buildings as part of the reported assessed values.

41 Calculation of household incomes into 1986 constant dollars uses conversion factors from Statistics Canada's Consumer Price Index, and the formula [(Current Year $) * 100] / (Conversion Factor) = Constant 1986 $. Conversion factors are 1982 – 83.7; 1985 – 96.0; 1987 – 104.4; 1988 – 108.6; 1989 – 114.0; 1990 – 119.5; 1991 – 126.2.

42 See also Royal Trust, *The Cottage – Keeping It in the Family ... and away from the Taxman*, 1992.

43 Wolfe, "About Cottages and Cottagers," 1965, 6.

44 Dilley, "Local Government, Public Expectations and Planning Policy in a Rural Recreational Area," 1985; FOCA, Executive Director's Report – Subject: Proposed Market Value Re-assessment, 1991.
45 Rosenberg and Halseth, *Recreational Home Conversion in Canada*, 1993.
46 *Cottage Life*, "From the President: Thanks for Two Well-Organized Efforts," May/June 1991, 121–3; Westport Mirror, "N. Crosby Endorses Controversial Reassessment Plan," 10 Mar. 1993, 5.
47 An "entitlement" is supposed to refer to whether the property is being used seasonally or as a year-round residence.
48 *Cottage Life*, "From the President: Keep up the Pressure on Property Tax", July/August 1991, 93–94.
49 Royal Trust, *The Cottage: Keeping It in the Family ... and away from the Taxman*, 1992, 12. For further information on this issue see *Cottage Life*, "From the President: Lake Stewardship Programs Are a Promising First Step," June 1992, 89–92, and "Looking for Loopholes," Sept./Oct. 1993, 13–14, 16.

CHAPTER THREE

1 Halseth and Rosenberg, "Conversion of Recreational Residences," 1990.
2 Excellent examples from this large literature include Bryant, Russwurm, and McLellan, *The City's Countryside – Land and Its Management in the Rural-Urban Fringe*, 1982; Coppack, Russwurm, and Bryant, *Essays on Canadian Urban Process and Form III – The Urban Field*, 1988; Krueger, "The Geographer and Rural Southern Ontario," 1980, and "Urbanization of the Niagara Fruit Belt," 1978; Pond and Yeates, "Rural/Urban Land Conversion II," 1994; Russwurm, *The Urban Fringe in Canada*, 1974; Yeates, "The Extent of Urban Development in the Windsor-Quebec City Axis," 1987.
3 Dahms, "'Demetropolitanization' or the 'urbanization' of the countryside?" 1984, and *The Heart of the Country*, 1988; Everitt and Gill, "The Social Geography of Small Towns," 1993; Hodge and Qadeer, *Towns and Villages in Canada*, 1983.
4 Halseth, *The Conversion of Summer Homes to Permanent Residences and Its Impact on Local Government Provision of Services*, 1989; Helleiner, "Recreation and Leisure-time Patterns," 1980; Joseph, Keddie, and Smit, "Unravelling the Population Turnaround in Rural Canada," 1988; Joseph and Smit, "Rural Residential Development and Municipal Service Provision," 1985.
5 Davies and Yeates, "Exurbanization as a Component of Migration," 1991; Joseph, Keddie, and Smit, "Unravelling the Population Turnaround in Rural Canada," 1988; Russwurm and Bryant, "Changing Population

Distribution and Rural-Urban Relationships in Canadian Urban Fields, 1941–1976," 1984; Walker, *An Invaded Countryside*, 1987. In the case of Walker's *An Invaded Countryside*, readers have an opportunity to follow one researcher's evolving understanding of the countryside, as this work is a fuller treatment of processes earlier suggested in his 1976 article "Social Perspectives on the Countryside."

6 Simmons, "The Challenge of Rural Perspectives on the Rural-Urban Fringe," 1981.

7 Troughton, "The Rural-Urban Fringe," 1981, 219.

8 Coppack, "Book Review of *Conflict and Change in the Countryside*," 1991, 435.

9 Friedmann, "The Concept of a Planning Region," 1956.

10 Friedmann and Miller, "The Urban Field," 1965, 314.

11 Examples of research interested in the "ex-urban" movement of people include Beesley and Walker, "Residence Paths and Community Perception: A Case Study from the Toronto Urban Field," 1990; Coppack, "The Evolution and Modelling of the Urban Field," 1988; Davies and Yeates, "Exurbanization as a Component of Migration," 1991. Examples of research interested in the management of urban expansion include Gayler, "The Demise of the Niagara Fruit Belt," 1990 and "The Demise of the Niagara Fruit Belt," 1991; and Krueger, "Urbanization of the Niagara Fruit Belt," 1978.

12 Hayes, *The Dispersed City*, 1976.

13 Dahms, "The Evolving Spatial Organization of Small Settlements in the Countryside," 1980a, 297.

14 Walker, *An Invaded Countryside*, 1987. See Bowles and Beesley, "Quality of Life, Migration to the Countryside and Rural Community Growth," 1991, and Oppong and Ironside, "Growth Centre Policy and the Quality of Life," 1987, for a characteristic sample of perception research. For an interesting but rather different exploration of perceptions (in this case resident and tourist) of a rural and small-town place, see Tye's 1994 work on the "Multiple Meanings Called Cavendish" and the Prince Edward Island phenomena of beach resorts and L.M. Montgomery/ Anne of Green Gables tourism.

15 Fuller, *Farming and the Rural Community in Ontario*, 1985; Leckie, "Continuity and Change in the Farm Community," 1989; Mackenzie, "'The worse it got, the more we laughed,'" 1992.

16 Fitchen, *Endangered Spaces, Enduring Places*, 1991, 102. Similar processes of "creating" collective belief systems that categorize community members by length of residence or by location from which they moved are also examined in the work of Pierce Colfer and Colfer in their 1978 study "Inside Bushler Bay" and in Forsythe's 1980 work "Urban Incomers and Rural Change."

17 Cloke, "Whither Rural Studies?," 1985; Halfacree, "Locality and Social Representation," 1993.

18 Krueger, "The Geographer and Rural Southern Ontario," 1980; Russwurm, *The Urban Fringe in Canada*, 1974; Yeates, "The Extent of Urban Development in the Windsor-Quebec City Axis," 1987.

19 Joseph, Keddie and Smit, "Unravelling the Population Turnaround in Rural Canada," 1988; Keddie and Joseph, "Reclassification and Rural-Versus-Urban Population Change in Canada, 1976–1981," 1991; Parenteau, "Is Canada Going Back To The Land?" 1981; Taaffe, Gauthier and Maraffa, "Extended Commuting and the Intermetropolitan Periphery," 1980.

20 Bryant, Russwurm, and McLellan, *The City's Countryside – Land and Its Management in the Rural-Urban Fringe*, 1982; Friedmann and Miller, "The Urban Field," 1965; Friedmann, "The Urban Field as Human Habitat," 1978.

21 Cloke, "Whither Rural Studies?" 1985; Dahms, "Small Town and Village Ontario," 1980b; Lamb, *Metropolitan Impacts on Rural America*, 1975; Yeates, "The Extent of Urban Development in the Windsor-Quebec City Axis," 1987.

22 Wirth, "Rural-Urban Differences," 1964.

23 Hodge and Qadeer, *Towns and Villages in Canada*, 1983.

24 Lewis, *Rural Communities*, 1979; Leckie, "Continuity and Change in the Farm Community," 1989.

25 Cloke, "Rural Geography and Political Economy," 1989, 173.

26 Newby, *Country Life*, 1987.

27 Harper, "A Humanistic Approach to the Study of Rural Populations," 1987, 309.

28 Fuguitt, "The City and the Countryside," 1963; Hillery, "Selected Issues in Community Theory," 1972; Sanderson, "Criteria of Community Formation," 1938; Wilkinson, "In Search of the Community in the Changing Countryside," 1986.

29 Sanderson, "Criteria of Community Formation," 1938, 371.

30 Fitchen, *Endangered Spaces, Enduring Places*, 1991, 259.

31 Cloke and Goodwin, "Conceptualizing Countryside Change: From Post-Fordism to Rural Structured Coherence," 1992; Harper, "A Humanistic Approach to the Study of Rural Populations," 1987; Phillips, "Rural Gentrification," 1993; Whatmore *et al.*, *Rural Enterprise*, 1991.

32 Cloke and Goodwin, "Conceptualizing Countryside Change," 328; Marsden *et al.*, *Constructing the Countryside*, 1993; Phillips, "Rural Gentrification," 1993.

33 Cloke and Goodwin, "Regulation, Green Politics and the Rural," 1993, 27.

34 Cater and Jones, *Social Geography*, 1989; Everitt, "Community and Propinquity in a City," 1976; Hillery, "Definitions of Community," 1955.

35 Broom and Selznick, *Sociology*, 1968; Crysdale and Beattie, *Sociology Canada*, 1973; Hale, *Controversies in Sociology*, 1990.
36 Harper, "A Humanistic Approach to the Study of Rural Populations," 1987; Hillery, "Selected Issues in Community Theory," 1972.
37 See also Gans, *The Urban Villagers*, 1962; Suttles, *The Social Order of the Slum*, 1968; Craven and Wellman, *The Network City*, 1973; Wellman, *The Community Question Re-evaluated*, 1987.
38 McClenahan, "The Communality," 1946.
39 Webber, "Order in Diversity," 1963.
40 Lee, "The Value of the Local Area," 1982, 163.
41 Pahl, *Urbs in Rure*, 1965.
42 Lewis, *Rural Communities*, 1979; Leckie, "Continuity and Change in the Farm Community," 1989.
43 Helleiner, "Loon Lake," 1983.
44 Dilley, "Local Government, Public Expectations and Planning Policy in a Rural Recreational Area," 1985; Helleiner and McGrath, "Incipient Urban Centres in the Recreational Hinterland of Toronto," 1988.
45 Flynn *et al.*, "The Redistribution of America's Older Population," 1985; Golant, *Housing America's Elderly*, 1992; Longino and Biggar, "The Impact of Retirement Migration on the South," 1981; Meyer and Speare, "Distinctively Elderly Mobility," 1985.
46 Gober, McHugh, and Leclerc, "Job-Rich but Housing-Poor," 1993, 19.
47 Hallman, "Migration, Commuting and Economic Development in Toronto's Outer Urban Field," 1990.
48 Beck and Hussey, "Politics, Property Rights, and Cottage Development," 1989.
49 Sanderson and Polson, *Rural Community Organization*, 1939, 316.
50 Ibid., 323.
51 Dahl, "Who Governs?" 1968.
52 Bell and Newby, *Community Studies: An Introduction to the Sociology of the Local Community*, 1971, 231.
53 Bell and Newby, *Community Studies*; Hawley and Wirt, *The Search for Community Power*, 1968a.
54 Hunter, *Community Power Structures*, 1953.
55 Vidich and Bensman, "Small Town in Mass Society," 1968, 258.
56 Hawley and Wirt, "Community Power," 1968b, 90.
57 Bell and Newby, *Community Studies*, 234.
58 Cox, *Conflict, Power and Politics in the City*, 1973; "Social Change, Turf Politics, and Concepts of Turf Politics," 1984; and "Urban Social Movements and Neighborhood Conflicts," 1988. Cox and McCarthy, "Neighbourhood Activism as a Politics of Turf," 1982.
59 Clarke and Kirby, "In Search of the Corpse: The Mysterious Case of Local Politics," 1990.
60 Cloke and Goodwin, "Conceptualizing Countryside Change," 1992.

61 Cox, "Social Change, Turf Politics, and Concepts of Turf Politics," 1984, 289.
62 Orbell and Uno, "A Theory of Neighbourhood Problem Solving," 1972; Tiebout, "A Pure Theory of Local Expenditures," 1956.
63 Cox, *Conflict, Power and Politics in the City*, 1973, 4.
64 Clarke and Kirby, "In Search of the Corpse," 1990, 396.
65 Ibid., 402.
66 It is suggested that both the economic and social components of this argument form sufficiently robust "structures" as to have an effect upon human "agency." This formulation clearly links with Giddens' (*Studies in Social and Political Theory*, 1977) ideas about the connection between such structures and processes of power and contention. As detailed elsewhere in this book, Cottagers in the rural-recreational countryside can employ their economic advantage (either as power or to get power) to maintain the socially constructed differences that mark local landscapes. Both structures not only facilitate processes and patterns of relative advantage and disadvantage; they also facilitate conflict at a local level over these same processes and patterns.
67 Cloke and Goodwin, "Conceptualizing Countryside Change," 1992.
68 Ibid., 328.
69 Ibid., 329, 331.
70 Mikesell, "Comparative Studies in Frontier History," 1960; Bloch, "Toward a Comparative History of European Societies," 1953; Fredrickson, "Comparative History," 1980; Grew, "The Case for Comparing Histories," 1980; Riemersma, "Introduction to Marc Bloch," 1953; Sewell, "Marc Bloch and the Logic of Comparative History," 1967.
71 Riemersma, "Introduction to Marc Bloch," 1953.
72 Sewell, "Marc Bloch and the Logic of Comparative History," 1967, 211.
73 Ibid., 208; see also Tilly, Tilly, and Tilly, *The Rebellious Century, 1830– 1930*, 1975; Fredrickson, "Comparative History," 1980.
74 Bloch, "Toward a Comparative History of European Societies," 1953, 496.
75 Buttimer, *Society and Milieu in the French Geographic Tradition*, 1971; Sauer, "Foreword to Historical Geography," 1941; Hartshorne, *The Nature of Geography*, 1939, and *Perspective on the Nature of Geography*, 1959.
76 Massey, "Introduction: Geography Matters," 1984, 9. See also the introductory comments on this text by Allen, "Introduction, Synthesis: Interdependence and the Uniqueness of Place," 1984.
77 Moore, "Research Agendas and Statistics Canada Products," 1991.
78 Hodge and Qadeer, *Towns and Villages in Canada*, 1983, 5.
79 Barnes and Hayter, "'The Little Town That Did': Flexible Accumulation and Community Response in Chemainus, British Columbia," 1992, 468.
80 For examples of the farm/non-farm methodology, see Brunet, "L'Exode urbain, essai de classification de la population exurbaine des Cantons

de l'Est," 1980; Joseph and Smit, "Rural Residential Development and Municipal Service Provision," 1985; Russwurm and Bryant, "Changing Population Distribution and Rural-Urban Relationships in Canadian Urban Fields, 1941–1976," 1984.

81 Rosenberg and Halseth, *Recreational Home Conversion in Canada*, 1993.

82 Sosdian and Sharp, "Non response in mail surveys," 1980.

83 Feitelson, "The Potential of Mail Surveys in Geography," 1991.

84 Harper, "A Humanistic Approach to the Study of Rural Populations," 1987.

85 Schoenberger, "The Corporate Interview as a Research Method in Economic Geography," 1991, 188.

86 Ibid., and "Self-Criticism and Self-Awareness in Research," 1992; McDowell, "Valid Games?" 1992.

87 McDowell, "Valid Games?" 1992, 213. A second aspect of the interviewer-subject dynamic concerns social/cultural relations. McDowell invokes feminist research to suggest that gender relations are significant in affecting the differential exercise of power in the organization of interviewer-subject relations (see also Oakley, "Interviewing Women," 1981).

88 See Rowles, "Reflections on Experiential Field Work," 1978, for a wonderful example of interviewer-interviewee relations.

89 Hamilton, Capozza, and Helsley, *Government Involvement in Residential Renovation*, 1986.

90 Halseth, *The Conversion of Summer Homes to Permanent Residences and Its Impact on Local Government Provision of Services*, 1989.

91 Under a range of conditions, permits for certain types of building work may not be required. In the case of the Regional District of Fraser-Cheam (RDFC), the building by-law sets monetary limits such that certain general works below $2,000 do not require permits (RDFC, Building Bylaw No. 280, 1984, 1986). In such cases, work of this nature will not be recorded in the building-permit records.

92 The generic term "community plan" is used throughout this book to identify the long-range local-planning documents that set out the future land-use planning and development policies and objectives of local governments. Community-plan documents are differentiated from the current set of land-use regulations embodied in the local zoning by-laws. In each study area these community plans are technically referred to by the name designated in provincial legislation (ie, Settlement Plan or Official Plan).

93 British Columbia (1979), Municipal Act, 1979, RSBC, c. 290.

CHAPTER FOUR

1 For a description of the evolution of settlement and commercial activities along the Rideau Canal, see H. Brown, *Lanark Legacy: Nineteenth*

Century Glimpses of an Ontario County, 1984; Leggett, *Rideau Waterway*, 1985; Osborne and Swainson, *The Rideau Navigation, 1832–1972*, 1985; Kennedy, *South Elmsley in the Making 1783–1983*, 1984; Haskins, "My Own Four Walls," 1985; and Parson, "An Investigation of the Changing Rural Economy of Gatineau County, Quebec," 1977, and "An Overview of Landscape Assessment and Settlement Policy on the Southern Ontario Section of the Canadian Shield in the 19th Century," 1983.

2 Osborne and Swainson, *The Rideau Navigation, 1832–1972*, 1985.

3 Bennett and McCuaig, *In Search of Lanark*, 1980; Helleiner, "A History of Recreation on the Trent-Severn Waterway," 1982; Leggett, *Rideau Waterway*, 1985; and Wyckoff, "Landscapes of Private Power and Wealth," 1990.

4 Kennedy, *South Elmsley in the Making 1783–1983*, 1984, and H. Brown, *Lanark Legacy: Nineteenth Century Glimpses of an Ontario County*, 1984; see also Cross, *The Summer House*, 1992, and Wyckoff, "Landscapes of Private Power and Wealth," 1990.

5 Rideau Valley Conservation Authority, 1992b.

6 Bielckus, "Second Homes in Scandinavia," 1977.

7 Gober, McHugh, and Leclerc, "Job-Rich but Housing-Poor," 1993; Dahms, "'Demetropolitanization' or the 'Urbanization' of the Countryside?" 1984.

8 An introduction to such recreation-hinterland issues is found in Wall, "Recreational Land Use in Muskoka," 1977; Marsh and Wall, "Themes in the Investigation of the Evolution of Outdoor Recreation," 1982. A much more general and theoretical treatment of this issue can be found in Coppack's 1988 discussion of "The Role of Amenity" in the urban field.

9 Wall, "Recreational Land Use in Muskoka," 1977; "Environmental Impacts," 1989.

10 Triantis, "Economic Impact of Tourism and Recreation in Muskoka," 1979.

11 CORTS, CORTS, Canada-Ontario Rideau, Trent-Severn Policies, 1982.

12 RVCA, Rideau Lakes Basin Carrying Capacities, 1992b.

13 Ibid.

14 Canada, Draft – Rideau Canal Management Plan, 1992.

15 Joseph and Smit, "Rural Residential Development and Municipal Service Provision," 1985.

16 Township of South Elmsley, Official Plan for Township of South Elmsley, 1984a.

17 Ontario, Discussion Paper on Seasonal Residential Conversions, 1978.

18 Halseth and Rosenberg, "Conversion of Recreational Residences," 1990; Township of South Elmsley, Zoning By-law, 1984b; Township of Bastard and South Burgess, Zoning By-law, 1983; Township of North Crosby, Zoning By-law, 1988.

19 Canada, 1986 Rideau Canal Boater Survey, 1988; 1987 Rideau Canal Land-Based User Survey, 1989; Recreation and Tourism, 1990b; and Historical Environment, 1990d. CORTS, Canada-Ontario Rideau, Trent-Severn, Policies, 1982; RVCA, Rideau Valley Conservation Strategy, 1992a.

20 Hinch, "A Spatial Analysis of Tourist Accommodation in Ontario," 1990.

21 Ramsey, *Five Corners – The Story of Chilliwack*, 1975.

22 *Chilliwack Progress*, "Plan for Cultus Lake Park Revived by Stacey – Township and City Appoint Committees to Report on Feasibility of Purchase of Forty Acres of Lake Shore for Recreation Purposes," 10 Mar. 1921, 1.

23 *Chilliwack Progress*, "Parks Board Awards Concessions – Contract Entered Into With Mr. Baxendale for Term of Three Years – Will Spend $3000," 15 May 1924, 3; "Summer Campers are Enthusiastic – Cultus Lake Park Presents a Busy and Interesting Scene – Lots are Going Fast," 21 May 1924, 1.

24 British Columbia (1932), Cultus Lake Park Act, SBC, 1932, c.63.

25 British Columbia (1980), Cultus Lake Park Act Amendment Act, RSBC, 1980, c.61.

26 In a condominium or strata-title system of property ownership, each residential unit is owned separately in fee-simple. As well, each unit owner is a tenant-in-common, or has the right in common to use the common property and common facilities in shares proportional to his/her unit entitlement. The term strata-title is more commonly used in British Columbia as referenced in the Condominium Act, RSBC, 1979, c.61.

27 RDFC, Official Settlement Plan for Electoral Area "E," 1983a, 7.

28 Ibid.

29 RDFC, By-law No. 66, 1976b; Official Regional Plan, 1981; Official Settlement Plan for Electoral Area "E", 1983a.

30 RDFC, Official Settlement Plan for Electoral Area "E" – Adopting By-law, 1983b.

31 Pennier, Joseph, and Mohs, *How Secure Is Our Future?* 1984; Scott and DeLorme, *Historical Atlas of Washington*, 1988; Wells, *The Chilliwacks and Their Neighbours*, 1987.

32 Stanley, *Mapping the Frontier*, 1970.

33 McCombs and Chittenden, *The Fraser Valley Challenge*, 1990; RDFC, Official Settlement Plan for Electoral Area "E" – Adopting By-law, 1983b.

34 Knight, *Stump Ranch Chronicles*, 1977.

35 RDFC, Official Settlement Plan for Electoral Area "E" – Adopting By-law, 1983b, 5.

36 As of 1995 the Cultus Lake Park elementary school goes to grade 6. A junior secondary school is located at Vedder Crossing, a senior secondary school at Sardis. Vedder Crossing and Sardis are distinct

residential communities within the municipal jurisdiction of the District of Chilliwack.
37 British Columbia, Visitor Satisfaction Survey – Cultus Lake Provincial Park, 1990a.
38 Yeates, "The Extent of Urban Development in the Windsor-Quebec City Axis," 1987.

CHAPTER FIVE

1 Occupational Classifications

Condensed Categories	Standard Categories
Retired	Retired
Professional	Administration
	Medicine
	Teaching
	Natural Sciences
	Legal
Service	Clerical
	Sales
	Service
	Technological
	Self-Employed
	Government
Primary	Primary
Secondary	Processing
	Assembly
	Construction
	Transport
Other	Part-Time
	Housekeeping
	Student
	Disabled
	Unemployment

Source: Based on Census of Canada Occupational Index.

2 Meyer and Cromley, "Caregiving Environments and Elderly Residential Mobility," 1989; Rogers and Woodward, "The Sources of Regional Elderly Population Growth," 1988.
3 Hodge, Cottaging in the Toronto Urban Field, 1970a.
4 Gill and Clark, "Second-Home Development in the Resort Municipality of Whistler, British Columbia," 1992.

5 Hodge, *Cottaging in the Toronto Urban Field*, 1970a; Rogers, "Second Homes in England and Wales," 1977.
6 Davies and Yeates, "Exurbanization as a Component of Migration," 1991.
7 Fischer, *To Dwell among Friends*, 1982.
8 The tenuous nature of local newspapers in the Rideau Lakes area seems clear. The *Westport and Rideau Valley Mirror* published jointly with the *Athens Laker* for a number of years, then separated to publish independently again in 1991. The *Mirror* was then challenged by another Westport newspaper, the *Rideau Reporter,* and a rather tense dialogue occasionally reappears in both newspapers as a reflection of their local "turf war." The *North Leeds Lantern* was a non-profit community-run newspaper that, though well regarded locally, could not generate additional volunteer labour and ceased publication in January 1993.
9 Hodge, *A Probe of Living Areas in the Periphery of the Toronto Urban Field*, 1970b.
10 In an effort to increase response rates and to assist with respondents' comprehension of the scale involved in the best-local-friends question, the questionnaire listed distances to best local friend in imperial (mile) units. For consistency, these same units are used in the discussion.
11 Fischer, *To Dwell among Friends*, 1982; Cohen and Shinar, *Neighbourhoods and Friendship Networks*, 1985.
12 Hodge, *A Probe of Living Areas in the Periphery of the Toronto Urban Field*, 1970b.
13 Dahms, "The Evolving Spatial Organization of Small Settlements in the Countryside," 1980a; Hayes, *The Dispersed City*, 1976.
14 Dahms and Hoover, "The Evolution of Settlement Functions in the Southeastern Parry Sound District: 1971–1976," 1979; Keogh, "L'Impact social du tourisme," 1982.
15 Windley, "Community Services in Small Rural Towns," 1983.
16 Similar findings on the importance of local social groups to community sustainability can be found in Leckie, "Continuity and Change in the Farm Community," 1989, and Fitchen, *Endangered Spaces, Enduring Places*, 1991. The role of local social groups in community debate is highlighted in later chapters of this study and in Halseth, "'Community' and Landuse Planning Debate," 1996.
17 Walker, "Networks and Politics in the Fringe," 1984.
18 Clout, "The Growth of Second-Home Ownership: An Example of Seasonal Suburbanization," 1974, and "Résidences secondaires in France," 1977; Dilley, "Local Government, Public Expectations and Planning Policy in a Rural Recreational Area," 1985. For a more general treatment of issues connected with rural land-use planning policy, see Cloke and Little's 1990 book *The Rural State?*

CHAPTER SIX

1 Values for $year_x = (year_{x-1} + year_x + year_{x+1}) / 3$.
2 "SFR" is the number of new detached single-family residence permits issued. "Tot." refers to the total number of permits issued for new residential units. "URBAN" is defined as census or municipal areas with a population of more than 10,000. The "*" notation denotes changes in reporting-area boundaries from the previous year. The source for this table includes Statistics Canada's *Housing Starts and Completions*, cat. no. 64–022 (1973 to 1989 editions), and Canada Mortgage and Housing Corporation's *Canadian Housing Statistics*, cat. no. NH 12–1 (1990 and 1991 editions).
3 CMHC, "British Columbia Housing Data Special Tabulation," 1992.
4 Data from CMHC, Pacific Region office, special tabulations, 1992.
5 Municipal building-permit data were collected from the building-department records for the following jurisdictions: at the Rideau Lakes study area, for the Townships of South Elmsley, North Elmsley, South Crosby, North Crosby, North Burgess, and Bastard and South Burgess; and at Cultus Lake, for the Regional District of Fraser-Cheam and the Cultus Lake Park Board.
6 To clarify patterns of activity, the mapping of permit activity focuses on two aggregations of the type of proposed work: NEW and TOTAL. This was considered appropriate because the NEW category often constitutes a large share of the TOTAL number of permits issued, and it did not prove useful to pursue any further level of disaggregation.
7 RDFC, By-law No.66, 1976b.
8 RDFC, Official Settlement Plan for Electoral Area "E", 1983a, 12.
9 *Cottage Life*, "Looking for Loopholes," Sept./Oct. 1993, 13–14, 16; Royal Trust, *The Cottage – Keeping It in the Family ... and away from the Taxman*, 1992.
10 *Westport Mirror and Athens Laker*, "Westport's Lagoon Project in Jeopardy," 15 Jan. 1992, 5; *Westport Mirror*, "Upper Rideau Lake Building Freeze Extended by Township," 15 Apr. 1992, 3; *Westport Mirror*, "URLA Wants More Time To Respond to Changes," 29 Apr. 1992, 5. See also discussions in chaps. 7 and 9.
11 *Westport Mirror*, "40% of Upper Rideau Septic Systems Unsatisfactory," 9 Dec. 1992, 1, 3.
12 See, for example the descriptions of household migrations in Fitchen, *Endangered Spaces, Enduring Places*, 1991.
13 Davies and Yeates, "Exurbanization as a Component of Migration," 1991.
14 See also the graphic illustration of urbanization pressure presented by Beesley and Walker, "Residence Paths and Community Perception:

A Case Study from the Toronto Urban Field," 1990 and Fesenmaier, Goodchild, and Morrison, "The Spatial Structure of the Rural-Urban Fringe," 1979.

15 In an effort to increase response rates and assist residents in understanding these property- and house-size questions, the survey document used imperial measures to identify the size categories. In the survey document the metric equivalents were provided in parentheses. To maintain consistency in this discussion, the imperial measures are used in Table 32.

16 *Chilliwack Progress*, "Monster Homes," 29 July 1992, 5.

17 Clout, "Résidences Secondaires in France," 1977.

CHAPTER SEVEN

1 Wolpert, Mumphrey, and Seley, *Metropolitan Neighborhoods*, 1972.

2 Cox and McCarthy, "Neighbourhood Activism as a Politics of Turf," 1982.

3 For examples of research interested in "community" group organization, see Fitchen, *Endangered Spaces, Enduring Places*, 1991; MacKenzie, "'The worse it got, the more we laughed,'" 1992; Sanderson and Polson, *Rural Community Organization*, 1939.

4 *Westport Mirror and Athens Laker*, "Upper Rideau Septic Tanks To Be Checked Next Year," 4 July 1991, 2; *Westport Mirror*, "URLA To Hold Open House June 7th at Local Legion," *Mirror*, 3 June 1992, 15.

5 *Smiths Falls Record News*, "Lake Association Recognized for Water Quality Efforts," 19 June 1991, 2.

6 Cross, *The Summer House*, 1992, 50–1.

7 RVCA, Rideau Lakes Basin Carrying Capacities, 1992b.

8 Fuller, *Farming and the Rural Community in Ontario*, 1985; Haskins, "My Own Four Walls," 1985; Kennedy, *South Elmsley in the Making 1783–1983*, 1984; MacKenzie, "'The worse it got, the more we laughed,'" 1992.

9 Federated Women's Institutes of Ontario, *Ontario Women's Institute Story*, 1972.

10 Ibid., 24.

11 The structure of the WI movement in Ontario remains that of a department still attached to the provincial Ministry of Agriculture and Food.

12 *North Leeds Lantern*, "Federated Women's Institutes of Ontario," Jan/Feb 1992, 16.

13 See also MacKenzie, "'The worse it got, the more we laughed,'" 1992.

14 Leckie, "Continuity and Change in the Farm Community," 1989; Sanderson and Polson, *Rural Community Organization*, 1939.

15 Low, "Interorganizational Relations in Local Land-Use Planning," 1979.

16 *Chilliwack Progress*, "Halt Land Plan, Petition Urges," 2 Apr. 1975, 1.

17 *Chilliwack Progress*, "DND Wants Land in Columbia Valley," 26 Mar. 1975, 1.

18 Low, "Interorganizational Relations in Local Land-Use Planning,", 1979, 29.

19 *Chilliwack Progress*, "Halt Land Plan, Petition Urges," 2 Apr. 1975, 1; *Vancouver Sun*, "Tearful Valley Old-Timer Sells the Farm," 7 Apr. 1975, 1; "Army Base Growth Routs Valley Residents," 23 Apr. 1976, 33.

20 *Chilliwack Progress*, "Halt Land Plan, Petition Urges," 2 Apr. 1975, 1; "Answers from DND 'Nothing New' – Baldwin," 13 July 1975, 1; *Vancouver Sun*, "Columbia Valley Land Bid Abandoned by Military," 11 June 1976, 8; "Army Base Growth Routs Valley Residents," 23 Apr. 1976, 33.

21 Low, "Interorganizational Relations in Local Land-Use Planning," 1979, 31.

22 Wolpert, Mumphrey, and Seley, *Metropolitan Neighborhoods*, 1972; Cox, "Social Change, Turf Politics, and Concepts of Turf Politics," 1984.

23 The DND expropriation issue and the introduction of zoning regulations are not the only actions contributing to local residents' distrust. The closure of the border crossing and the provincial government's imposition of the Agricultural Land Reserve (ALR), which effectively froze development on farmland, are other examples often cited by local residents.

24 RDFC, Public Hearing Minutes, 1975a, 1975b.

25 RDFC, Minutes of the Regional Board Meeting, 1975c.

26 RDFC, Minutes of the Regional Board Meeting, 1976a; By-law No.66, 1976b.

27 In answer to the questionnaire survey, 47 per cent of Permanent Residents stated they were dissatisfied with opportunities for public input into the local land-use planning process.

28 British Columbia, Frosst Creek Flood Mitigation Study, 1988a, and RDFC, Pre-Feasibility Study for Community Sewage Disposal in Lindell Beach, 1988.

29 The Cultus Lake Community Association, which includes the leased lots within the Cultus Lake Park area, has also previously been known as the Cultus Lake Association and the Cultus Lake Lease Holders' Association (*Chilliwack Progress*, 28 July 1926).

30 This question of Park Board powers is developed further in chapter 8.

31 The extensive use of the community hall has also been noticed by the Cultus Lake Park Board. In March 1993 the Park Board increased the rents charged to the Cultus Lake OAPS from $40 to $200 per month. This decision has sparked a new controversy in Cultus Lake Park (*Chilliwack Progress*, "Pensioners Fight Back against Big Rate Hikes," 24 Feb. 1993, A8.)

32 Helleiner, "Loon Lake," 1983.

CHAPTER EIGHT

1 Tindal and Nobes Tindal, *Local Government in Canada*, 1990, 22.
2 For the social geography of the local area, county boundaries also structure public school-board jurisdictions. In this case the location of schools, the length and cost of bus trips, and school tax levels all will have an impact on local-development pressures and debates.
3 Commission on Planning and Development Reform in Ontario, *New Planning News*, 1992, 4.
4 Wilkinson and Murray, "Centre and Periphery," 1991.
5 Leung, "'Big Brother' and Small Town Planning," 1990, 14.
6 Benveniste, *Mastering the Politics of Planning*, 1989; R. Brown, "Bureaucratic Bathos or How To Be a Government Consultant without Really Trying," 1979.
7 Leung, "'Big Brother' and Small Town Planning," 1990, 17.
8 *Westport Mirror and Athens Laker*, "Would You Believe This in North Crosby Twp.?" 20 Nov. 1991, 5.
9 Leung, "'Big Brother' and Small Town Planning," 1990, 17.
10 Priddle and Kreutzwiser, "Evaluating Cottage Environments in Ontario," 1977, 165.
11 Township of South Elmsley, Official Plan for Township of South Elmsley, 1984a.
12 Township of South Elmsley, Zoning By-law, 1984b; Ontario, Discussion Paper on Seasonal Residential Conversions, 1978.
13 Halseth, *The Conversion of Summer Homes to Permanent Residences and Its Impact on Local Government Provision of Services*, 1989.
14 Ibid., and Halseth and Rosenberg, "Conversion of Recreational Residences," 1990.
15 Magnusson, "Introduction: The Development of Canadian Urban Government," 1983.
16 British Columbia, Statistics Relating to Regional and Municipal Governments, 1968.
17 British Columbia, Statistics Relating to Regional and Municipal Governments, 1967, 5.
18 Bish, *Local Government in British Columbia*, 1987; Tindal, *Structural Changes in Local Government*, 1977; Tindal and Nobes Tindal, *Local Government in Canada*, 1990.
19 RDFC, Official Regional Plan, 1981, 99.
20 Ibid., 89.
21 Ibid., 71.
22 RDFC, Official Settlement Plan for Electoral Area "E," 1983a.
23 Ibid., Adopting By-law, 1983b, 1.
24 RDFC, Official Settlement Plan for Electoral Area "E," 1983a, 47.
25 Ibid., 44.

26 Ibid., 17.

27 Ibid., 79.

28 RDFC, "Public Information Meeting Minutes," 1983c.

29 RDFC, Official Settlement Plan for Electoral Area "E," 1983a, 46.

30 Other regulatory bylaws enacted by the RDFC pertain to building permits, subdivision of lands, and development of campgrounds and holiday parks.

31 RDFC, By-law No.66, 1976b; Official Settlement Plan for Electoral Area "E" – Adopting By-law, 1983b.

32 RDFC, Public Hearing Minutes, 1985a.

33 RDFC, Minutes of the Regional Board Meeting, 1985b, 3.

34 Halseth and Rosenberg, "Conversion of Recreational Residences," 1990.

35 Chilliwack Progress, "Cultus Lake Park," 8 Jan. 1931, 1; "Officials Support Park Bylaw," 15 Jan. 1931, 1; "New City Council Holds First Session – Committees Appointed," 29 Jan. 1931, 1; "Important Announcement by Cultus Lake Park Board," 5 Feb. 1931, 1.

36 British Columbia, Cultus Lake Act, 1932, 295.

37 Ibid., 298.

38 Ibid., 295.

39 British Columbia, Cultus Lake Park Act Amendment Act, 1980.

40 Cultus Lake Park Board, Local Government Options, 1986.

41 British Columbia, Cultus Lake Park Development Plan, 1961.

42 Cultus Lake Park Board, Development Plan, 1963, 5.

43 Matthews, "Cultus Lake Park," 1983, 6.

44 British Columbia, Cultus Lake Act, 1932, 295.

45 Using the property-tenure variable, with owned indicating Lindell Beach and leased indicating Cultus Lake Park, we can re-examine the questions about perceptions of local government.

46 It can be noted that an enhanced 911 service for the Chilliwack-RDFC region was introduced in 1992.

47 Chilliwack Progress, "Cultus Lake Transit System Is Approved," 25 Nov. 1992, 3.

48 Debate over representation of rural-area interests on the Regional Board is not a new issue for the RDFC. Numbers of representatives on the board and the number of votes each has are determined by population. As a result of this formula, the District of Chilliwack can very nearly carry any board decision on its own.

CHAPTER NINE

1 Canada, Draft – Rideau Canal Management Plan, 1992.

2 North Leeds Lantern, "The Cataraqui Region Conservation Authority, the Rideau Valley Conservation Authority and the Canadian Parks Service

are now taking action in a coordinated effort to preserve a living Rideau Waterway for future generations," Sept. 1992, 10.

3 RVCA, Rideau Valley Conservation Strategy, 1992a.

4 RVCA, Rideau Lakes Basin Carrying Capacities, 1992b.

5 See Benveniste, *Mastering the Politics of Planning*, 1989, for examples of how "participation" increases the commitment to implementation.

6 RVCA, Rideau Valley Conservation Strategy, 1992a, 6.

7 Township of South Elmsley, Official Plan for Township of South Elmsley, 1984a; Draft Official Plan of the Township of South Elmsley, 1991.

8 Township of South Elmsley, Draft Official Plan of the Township of South Elmsley, 1991, 22.

9 Ibid., 23.

10 Township of North Crosby, Amendment No. 3 to the Official Plan of the Township of North Crosby, 1992a.

11 Township of Bastard and South Burgess, Amendment No. 5 to the Official Plan of the Township of Bastard and South Burgess, 1991.

12 Township of South Crosby, Draft Official Plan for Township of South Crosby, 1992.

13 Township of North Crosby, Official Plan for the Township of North Crosby, 1985, 17.

14 Township of North Crosby, Amendment No. 3 to the Official Plan of the Township of North Crosby, 1992a; Zoning By-law Amendment – Shoreland Development, 1992b.

15 Township of North Crosby, Amendment No. 3 to the Official Plan of the Township of North Crosby, 1992a, 4.

16 Township of Bastard and South Burgess, Official Plan of the Township of Bastard and South Burgess, 1986; Amendment No. 5 to the Official Plan of the Township of Bastard and South Burgess,1991.

17 Township of South Crosby, Official Plan for Township of South Crosby, 1986; Draft Official Plan for Township of South Crosby, 1992.

18 *Westport Mirror*, "RVCA Praises South Crosby's Official Plan," 16 Sept. 1992, 3.

19 *Rideau Review*, "S. Crosby Amendment To Be Fought by Residents at OMB," 2 Sept. 1992, 3; *Westport Mirror*, "South Crosby Should Rescind Zoning By-law Amendment," 26 Aug. 1992, 6.

20 Cox, "Social Change, Turf Politics, and Concepts of Turf Politics," 1984.

21 Piven, "Whom Does the Advocate Planner Serve?" 1970.

22 *North Leeds Lantern*, "Township of South Crosby – Notice of a Public Meeting To Review the Draft Official Plan," July/Aug. 1991, 7; *Westport Mirror*, "Township of South Crosby – Notice of a Public Meeting To Review the Revised Draft Official Plan," 29 Apr. 1992, 5.

23 *Westport Mirror*, "Notice to the Residents & Ratepayers of the Township of South Crosby," 12 Aug. 1992, 3.

24 *Westport Mirror*, "Residents Furious over Official Plan," 26 Aug. 1992, 6.
25 Ibid.; and personal communication, 1992.
26 Darroch, "An Assessment of the Otty Lake Association and a Recommendation for Future Provincial Policy on Lake Planning," 1992.
27 *Westport Mirror and Athens Laker*, "Action Needed Now," 27 Mar. 1991, 6; "Lake Association Focuses on Water Testing," 26 June 1991, 5; *Westport Mirror*, "Determined Students Working To Save a Lake," 8 July 1992, B8; *Perth Courier*, "Rideau Lake Water Survey Complete," 6 Feb. 1991, 3; "Rideau Lake Awareness Program," 3 July 1991, 5.
28 *Westport Mirror and Athens Laker*, "Upper Rideau Lake Association Open House Attracts 150 People," 29 May 1991, 1; *Westport Mirror*, "URLA To Hold Open House June 7th at Local Legion," 3 June 1992, 15.
29 *Westport Mirror*, "Employee Says MoE Largely Responsible for Westport's Sewage, Water Problems," 9 Dec. 1992, 1, 16.
30 *Westport Mirror and Athens Laker*, "Council, URLA To Work Together in Improving Lake," 15 May 1991, B12; *Westport Mirror*, "First Step Toward Restoration of Lake," 29 Jan. 1992, 5; *Westport Mirror and Athens Laker*, "URLA Worried about Progress," 17 Oct. 1991, 7; *Smiths Falls Record News*, "The Upper Rideau Lake Association," 17 July 1991, 3; *Westport Mirror*, "Time Running out for Lagoon Improvement Suggestions," 15 Jan. 1992, 1; *Westport Mirror*, "Building Freeze Could End – Thake Says Water Meters Help, But Conservation Essential," 1 Apr. 1992, 1, 3.
31 *Westport Mirror*, "Thake Doesn't Want $3.5M Grant," 17 Feb. 1993, 1, 2; "URLA Says All Avenues Should Be Examined in Sewage Problem," 3 Mar. 1993, 5.
32 *Westport Mirror and Athens Laker*, "No 'Enemy,' Says URLA, but Council's Had Enough," 27 Nov. 1991, 2.
33 *Westport Mirror*, "Thake Doesn't Want $3.5M Grant," 17 Feb. 1993, 1, 2.
34 *Westport Mirror and Athens Laker*, "Time Running out for Lagoon Improvement Suggestions," 15 Jan. 1992, 1; "Westport's Lagoon Project in Jeopardy," 15 Jan. 1992, 5.
35 *Westport Mirror*, "Thake Doesn't Want $3.5M Grant," 17 Feb. 1993, 1, 2.
36 *Westport Mirror*, "Lake Association Embraces Funding," 24 Feb. 1993, 3.
37 *Westport Mirror*, "Chamber of Commerce Wants Westport Lagoon Expansion To Proceed," 17 Mar. 1993, 1, 2.
38 *Westport Mirror and Athens Laker*, "BRLA's Lake Improvement Project off to a Good Start," 23 Dec. 1991, 9.
39 *North Leeds Lantern*, "Federated Women's Institutes of Ontario," Jan./Feb. 1992, 16.
40 In the summer of 1993 it is likely that the URLA, the BRLA, and the OLA will all have students hired through the Environmental Youth Corps working on projects around their respective lakes.

41 Otty Lake Newsletter, Apr. 1991, 1.
42 Darroch, "An Assessment of the Otty Lake Association and a Recommendation for Future Provincial Policy on Lake Planning," 1992.
43 *Cottage Life*, "John Sewell Cites Cottagers as Leaders for the Environment," Apr./May 1993, 107.
44 RVCA, Rideau Valley Conservation Strategy, 1992a; Canada, Draft – Rideau Canal Management Plan, 1992.
45 Piven, "Whom Does the Advocate Planner Serve?" 1970.
46 See Tindal and Nobes Tindal, *Local Government in Canada*, 1990.
47 Tindal, *Structural Changes in Local Government*, 1977.
48 Barlow, *Spatial Dimensions of Urban Government*, 1981; Hasson and Razin, "What Is Hidden behind a Municipal Boundary Conflict?" 1990.

CHAPTER TEN

1 British Columbia, A Guide to the Relationship between Agricultural Land Reserves and Local Government Plans and Bylaws, 1982.
2 British Columbia, Consolidated Regulation 238/88, 1988b
3 RDFC, By-law No.66, 1976b; Official Settlement Plan for Electoral Area "E," 1983a.
4 *Chilliwack Progress*, "Developers Propose Second Road to 120-hectare Columbia Valley Golf, Housing Development," 24 Dec. 1990, 4.
5 *Chilliwack Progress*, "New Lake Links Shunned," 23 Jan. 1991, 1.
6 RDFC, "Public Hearing Minutes," 1991a.
7 Ibid., 16.
8 Ibid., 11.
9 Ibid., 18.
10 Ibid., 6.
11 Ibid., 23.
12 Ibid., 17.
13 Ibid., 19–20.
14 Also, the RDFC had received about 87 responses to an ill-conceived questionnaire attempting to solicit public opinion. Most of these responses suggested general support for the proposal, although the origin of the questionnaire was not clear and its style clearly biased results.
15 *Chilliwack Progress*, "New Popkum Golf Course Proposal Similar to Columbia Valley Plan," 11 Sept. 1991, 4.
16 RDFC, "Public Hearing Minutes," 1992.
17 RDFC, "Public Hearing Minutes," 1991a, 13.
18 Ibid., 16.
19 RDFC, "Public Hearing Minutes," 1992, 9.
20 Ibid., 24.

21 Ibid., 25.

22 Ibid., 15.

23 RDFC, "Public Hearing Minutes," 1991a, 15.

24 Ibid., 23.

25 RDFC, "Minutes of the Regional Board Meeting," 1991b.

26 Cultus Lake Park Board, Local Government Options, 1986.

27 British Columbia, Municipal Act, s.727(3), s.720(3).

28 British Columbia, Municipal Act, s.720(5).

29 *Chilliwack Progress*, "Question New Lots," 13 Nov. 1991, 5; *Chilliwack Times*, "No Lane for Lots," 9 Nov. 1991, 5.

30 Private communication, 1992.

31 *Vancouver Sun*, "Cultus Lake Park Board – Purchase of Right To Lease at Cultus Lake, BC," 28 Feb. 1992, E9. This advertisement also appeared in the *Vancouver Province*.

32 Cultus Lake Community Association newsletter, 1992, 3.

Bibliography

NEWSPAPERS, NEWSLETTERS, AND MAGAZINES

Newspapers

Chilliwack Progress, 1921–31, 1975, 1989–93
Chilliwack Times, 1991
North Leeds Lantern, 1990–92
Perth Courier, 1989–92
Rideau Review, 1992–93
Smiths Falls Record News, 1989–92
Westport Mirror, 1992–93
Westport Mirror and Athens Laker, 1989–91
Vancouver Sun, 1976, 1992
Vancouver Province, 1992

Newsletters and Magazines

Columbia Valley Ratepayers' Association, 1979–91
Cottage Life, 1990–93
Cultus Lake Community Association, 1992
Greater Bob's Lake Landowner's Association Newsletter, 1989–90
Otty Lake Newsletter, 1991–92

BOOKS AND ARTICLES

American Automobile Association (1992). *AAA-CAA Tourbook: Ontario, 1993.*
  Heathrow, Fla.

Allen, J. (1984). "Introduction, Synthesis: Interdependence and the Uniqueness of place." In *Geography Matters! A Reader*, ed. D. Massey and J. Allen.
Cambridge: Cambridge University Press. 107–111.

Barlow, I.M. (1981). *Spatial Dimensions of Urban Government*. New York:
Research Studies Press.

Barnes, T.J., and R. Hayter (1992). "'The Little Town That Did': Flexible Accumulation and Community Response in Chemainus, British Columbia."
Regional Studies 26 (7), 647–63.

Beck, R.L., and D. Hussey (1989). "Politics, Property Rights, and Cottage
Development." *Canadian Public Policy* 15 (1), 25–33.

Beesley, K.B., and G.E. Walker (1990). "Residence Paths and Community
Perception: A Case Study From the Toronto Urban Field." *Canadian Geographer* 34 (4), 318–30.

Bell, C., and H. Newby (1971). *Community Studies: An Introduction to the
Sociology of the Local Community*. London: George Allen and Unwin Ltd.

Bennett, C., and D.W. McCuaig (1980). *In Search of Lanark*. Renfrew, Ont.:
Renfrew Advanced Ltd.

Benveniste, G. (1989). *Mastering the Politics of Planning*. San Francisco and
Oxford: Jossey-Bass Publishers.

Bielckus, C.L. (1977). "Second Homes in Scandinavia." In *Second Homes:
Curse or Blessing*, ed. J.T. Coppock. Oxford: Pergamon Press. 35–46.

Bish, R.L. (1987). *Local Government in British Columbia*. Vancouver: Union of
British Columbia Municipalities.

Bloch, M. (1953). "Toward a Comparative History of European Societies."
Trans. J.C. Riemersma. In *Enterprise and Secular Change: Readings in Eco-
nomic History*, ed. F.C. Lane and J.C. Riemersma. Homewood, Ill.: Richard
D. Irwin, Inc. 494–521.

Bowles, R.T., and K.B. Beesley (1991). "Quality of Life, Migration to the
Countryside and Rural Community Growth." In *Rural and Urban Fringe
Studies in Canada*, ed. K.B. Beesley. Toronto: York University, Geographical
Monograph no. 21. 45–66.

Bradbury, J., and I. St. Martin (1983). "Winding Down in a Quebec
Mining Town: A Case Study of Schefferville." *Canadian Geographer* 27 (2),
128–44.

British Columbia (1932). Cultus Lake Park Act, SBC, 1932, c.63.

– (1939). Cultus Lake Park Act Amendment Act, SBC, 1939, c.9.

– (1961). Cultus Lake Park Development Plan. Department of Municipal
Affairs.

– (1967, 1968). Statistics Relating to Regional and Municipal Governments
in British Columbia. Ministry of Municipal Affairs.

– (1979a). Municipal Act – 1979, RSBC, c. 290.

– (1979b). Condominium Act, RSBC, 1979, c.61.

– (1980). Cultus Lake Park Act Amendment Act, RSBC, 1980, c.61.

– (1982). A Guide to the Relationship between Agricultural Land Reserves and Local Government Plans and By-laws. Ministry of Municipal Affairs and Provincial Agricultural Land Commission.

– (1988a). Frosst Creek Flood Mitigation Study. Ministry of Environment, Water Management Branch.

– (1988b). Consolidated Regulations of British Columbia.

– (1990a). Visitor Satisfaction Survey – Cultus Lake Provincial Park. Ministry of Lands and Parks.

– (1990b). Annual Report – British Columbia Assessment Authority. Ministry of Municipal Affairs.

Broom, L., and P. Selznick (1968). *Sociology: A Text with Adapted Readings*. 4th ed. New York: Harper and Row.

Brown, H.M. (1984). *Lanark Legacy: Nineteenth-Century Glimpses of an Ontario County*. Perth, Ont.: Corporation of the County of Lanark.

Brown, R.H. (1979). "Bureaucratic Bathos, or How to be a Government Consultant Without Really Trying." *Administration and Society* 10 (4), 477–92.

Brunet, Y. (1980). "L'Exode urbain, essai de classification de la population exurbaine des cantons de l'Est." *Canadian Geographer* 24 (4), 385–405.

Bryant, C.R., L.H. Russwurm, and A.G. McLellan (1982). *The City's Countryside: Land and Its Management in the Rural-Urban Fringe*. London and New York: Longman Group Limited.

Bunce, M. (1994). *The Countryside Ideal: Anglo-American Images of Landscape*. London and New York: Routledge.

Butler, R.W. (1984). "The Impact of Informal Recreation on Rural Canada." In *The Pressures of Change in Rural Canada*, ed. M.F. Bunce and M.J. Troughton. Toronto: Atkinson College, York University, Geographical Monograph no. 14. 216–40.

Buttimer, A. (1971). *Society and Milieu in the French Geographic Tradition*. Chicago: Rand McNally and Company, for The Association of American Geographers.

Canada. Environment Canada, Canadian Parks Service. (1988). 1986 Rideau Canal Boater Survey. Prepared by Market Facts of Canada Ltd. Ottawa.

– (1989). 1987 Rideau Canal Land-Based User Survey. Prepared by Market Facts of Canada Ltd. Ottawa.

– (1990a). Rideau Canal Management Planning – Issues Papers – Partnerships. Ottawa.

– (1990b). Rideau Canal Management Planning – Issues Papers – Recreation and Tourism. Ottawa.

– (1990c). Rideau Canal Management Planning – Issues Papers – Shoreline Land Use. Ottawa.

– (1990d). Rideau Canal Management Planning – Issues Papers – Historical Environment. Ottawa.

– (1992). Draft – Rideau Canal Management Plan. Ottawa.

Canada Mortgage and Housing Corporation. (1984, 1986, 1991). *Canadian Housing Statistics*. Ottawa: Statistical Services Division, CMHC.

– (1992). British Columbia Housing Data Special Tabulation. Vancouver: Pacific Region Office, CMHC.

Cater, J., and T. Jones (1989). *Social Geography: An Introduction to Contemporary Issues*. London: Edward Arnold.

Clarke, S.E., and A. Kirby (1990). In Search of the Corpse: The Mysterious Case of Local Politics. *Urban Affairs Quarterly* 25 (3), 389–412.

Cloke, P.J. (1985). Whither Rural Studies? *Journal of Rural Studies* 1 (1), 1–9.

– (1989). "Rural Geography and Political Economy." In *New Models in Geography: The Political-Economy Perspective*. Vol. 1, ed. R. Peet and N. Thrift. London: Unwin Hyman Ltd. 164–97.

Cloke, P., and M. Goodwin (1992). "Conceptualizing Countryside Change: From Post-Fordism to Rural Structured Coherence." *Transactions of the Institute of British Geographers*, n.s. 17, 321–36.

– (1993). "Regulation, Green Politics and the Rural." In *The Greening of Rural Policy: International Perspectives*, ed. S. Harper. London and New York: Belhaven. 27–41.

Cloke, P., and J. Little (1990). *The Rural State? Limits to Planning in Rural Society*. Oxford: Clarendon Press.

Clout, H.D. (1974). "The Growth of Second-Home Ownership: An Example of Seasonal Suburbanization." In *Suburban Growth: Geographical Processes at the Edge of the Western City*, ed. J.H. Johnson. London: John Wiley and Sons. 101–27.

– (1977). "Résidences Secondaires in France." In *Second Homes: Curse or Blessing*, ed. J.T. Coppock. Oxford: Pergamon Press. 47–62.

Cohen, Y.S., and A. Shinar (1985). *Neighbourhoods and Friendship Networks: A Study of Three Residential Neighborhoods in Jerusalem*. Chicago: University of Chicago, Department of Geography Research Paper no. 215.

Columbia Valley Ratepayers Association (1979). June Newsletter.

– (1991). January Newsletter.

Commission on Planning and Development Reform on Ontario (1992). *New Planning News*. Toronto.

Coppack, P.M. (1988). "The Evolution and Modelling of the Urban Field," 5–27, and "The Role of Amenity," 41–55. In Coppack, Russwurm, and Bryant, eds., *Essays on Canadian Urban Process and Form III: The Urban Field*, q.v.

– (1991). Book review of *Conflict and Change in the Countryside*. *Canadian Geographer* 35 (4), 434–5.

Coppack, P.M., L.H. Russwurm, and C.R. Bryant, eds. (1988). *Essays on Canadian Urban Process and Form iii: The Urban Field*. Waterloo, Ont.: University of Waterloo, Department of Geography Publication Series no. 30.

Coppock, J.T. ed. (1977a). *Second Homes: Curse or Blessing*. Oxford: Pergamon Press.

– (1977b). "Second Homes in Perspective." In Coppock, ed., *Second Homes*, 1–16.

– (1977c). "Social Implications of Second Homes in Mid-and North Wales." In *Second Homes*, 147–154.

– (1977d). "Issues and Conflicts." In *Second Homes*, 195–216.

CORTS Advisory Committee (1982). *CORTS: Canada-Ontario Rideau, Trent-Severn Policies*. Ottawa: Canada and Ontario.

Cox, K.R. (1973). *Conflict, Power and Politics in the City: A Geographic View*. New York: McGraw-Hill Inc.

– (1984). "Social Change, Turf Politics, and Concepts of Turf Politics." In *Public Service Provision and Urban Development*, ed. A. Kirby, P. Knox, and S. Pinch. London: Croom Helm. 283–315.

– (1988). "Urban Social Movements and Neighborhood Conflicts: Mobilization and Structuration." *Urban Geography* 8 (4), 416–28.

Cox, K.R., and J.J. McCarthy (1982). "Neighbourhood Activism as a Politics of Turf: A Critical Analysis." In *Conflict, Politics and the Urban Scene*, ed. K.R. Cox and R.J. Johnston. London: Longman Group Limited. 196–219.

Craven, P., and B. Wellman (1973). *The Network City*. Toronto: University of Toronto, Centre for Urban and Community Studies and Department of Sociology, Research Paper no. 59.

Cross, A.W. (1992). *The Summer House: A Tradition of Leisure*. Toronto: Harper Collins.

Crysdale, S., and C. Beattie (1973). *Sociology Canada: An Introductory Text*. Toronto: Butterworth.

Cultus Lake Park Board (1963). Development Plan: Cultus Lake Park. Prepared by Joseph B. Ward and Associates (International) Ltd. Chilliwack, BC.

– (1986). Local Government Options, Cultus Lake, B.C. Prepared by Stevenson Kellogg Ernst and Whinney. Chilliwack, BC.

Dahl, R.A. (1968). "Who Governs?" In *The Search for Community Power*, ed. W.D. Hawley and F.M. Wirt. Englewood Cliffs, NJ: Prentice-Hall. 93–114.

Dahms, F.A. (1980a). "The Evolving Spatial Organization of Small Settlements in the Countryside – An Ontario Example." *Tijdschrift voor Economische en Sociale Geografie* 5, 295–306.

– (1980b). "Small Town and Village Ontario." *Ontario Geography* 16, 19–32.

– (1984). "'Demetropolitanization' or the 'Urbanization' of the Countryside? The Changing Functions of Small Rural Settlements in Ontario." *Ontario Geography* 24, 35–61.

– (1988). *The Heart of the Country*. Toronto: Deneau.

Dahms, F.A., and C. Hoover (1979). "The Evolution of Settlement Functions in the Southeastern Parry Sound District: 1971–1976." *Canadian Geographer* 23 (4), 352–60.

Darroch, K.A. (1992). "An Assessment of the Otty Lake Association and a Recommendation for Future Provincial Policy on Lake Planning." MA, School of Urban and Regional Planning, Queen's University, Kingston, Ontario.

Davies, S., and M. Yeates (1991). "Exurbanization as a Component of Migration: A Case Study in Oxford County, Ontario." *Canadian Geographer* 35 (2), 177–86.

Dilley, R.S. (1985). "Local Government, Public Expectations and Planning Policy in a Rural Recreational Area." Paper presented at International Conference on Management of Rural Resources: Problems and Policies, Guelph, Ontario.

Dykeman, F.W., ed. (1988). *Integrated Rural Planning and Development*. Sackville, NB: Rural and Small Town Research and Studies Programme, Mount Allison University.

Everitt, J.C. (1976). "Community and Propinquity in a City." *Annals of the Association of American Geographers* 66 (1), 104–16.

Everitt, J., and A. Gill (1993). "The Social Geography of Small Towns." In *The Changing Social Geography of Canadian Cities*, ed. L.S. Bourne and D.F. Ley. Montreal and Kingston: McGill-Queen's University Press. 252–64.

Federated Women's Institutes of Ontario (1972). *Ontario Women's Institute Story.*

Federation of Ontario Cottagers' Associations (FOCA) (1991). Executive Directors Report. Subject: Proposed Market Value Re-Assessment. Toronto.

Feitelson, E. (1991). "The Potential of Mail Surveys in Geography: Some Empirical Evidence." *Professional Geographer* 43 (2), 190–205.

Fesenmaier, D.R., M.F. Goodchild and S. Morrison (1979). "The Spatial Structure of the Rural-Urban Fringe: A Multivariate Approach." *Canadian Geographer* 23 (3), 255–65.

Fischer, C.S. (1982). *To Dwell among Friends: Personal Networks in Town and City.* Chicago: University of Chicago Press.

Fitchen, J.M. (1991). *Endangered Spaces, Enduring Places: Change, Identity, and Survival in Rural America.* Boulder, Colo.: Westview Press.

Flynn, C.B., C.F. Longino, Jr., R.F. Wiseman, and J.C. Biggar (1985). "The Redistribution of America's Older Population: Major National Migration Patterns for Three Census Decades, 1960–1980." *Gerontologist* 25 (3), 292–6.

FOCA (1991). Executive Director's Report – Subject: Proposed Market Value Re-assessment. Scarborough, Ont.: FOCA.

Forsythe, D.E. (1980). "Urban Incomers and Rural Change: The Impact of Migrants from the City on Life in an Orkney Community." *Sociologia Ruralis* 20, 287–307.

Fredrickson, G.M. (1980). "Comparative History." In *The Past before Us: Contemporary Historical Writing in the United States*, ed. M. Kammen. Ithaca, NY: Cornell University Press. 457–73.

Friedmann, J. (1956). "The Concept of a Planning Region." *Land Economics* 32 (1), 1–13.

– (1978). "The Urban Field as Human Habitat." In *Systems of Cities: Readings on Structure, Growth, and Policy*, ed. L.S. Bourne and J.W. Simmons. New York: Oxford University Press. 42–52.

Friedmann, J., and J. Miller (1965). "The Urban Field." *Journal of the American Institute of Planners* 31, 312–20.

Fuguitt, G.V. (1963). "The City and the Countryside." *Rural Sociology* 28 (3), 246–61.

Fuller, T., ed. (1985). *Farming and the Rural Community in Ontario*. Toronto: Foundation for Rural Living.

Gans, H.J. (1962). *The Urban Villagers*. New York: Free Press of Glencoe.

Gardavsky, V. (1977). "Second Homes in Czechoslovakia." In *Second Homes: Curse or Blessing*, ed. J.T. Coppock. Oxford: Pergamon Press. 63–74.

Gayler, H. (1990). "The Demise of the Niagara Fruit Belt: The Niagara Case in the 1980s and Beyond." *Urban Geography* 11, 373–93.

– (1991). "The Demise of the Niagara Fruit Belt: Policy Planning and Development Options in the 1990s." In *Rural and Urban Fringe Studies in Canada*, ed. K.B. Beesley. Toronto: Atkinson College, York University, Geographical Monographs no. 21. 283–313.

Geipel, R. (1992). "Territoriality at the Microscale." In *Person, Place and Thing: Interpretive and Empirical Essays in Cultural Geography*, ed. S.T. Wong. Baton Rouge, La: Department of Geography and Anthropology, Louisiana State University. 79–97.

Giddens, A. (1977). *Studies in Social and Political Theory*. London: Hutchinson.

Gilg, A. (1985). *An Introduction to Rural Geography*. London: Edward Arnold Ltd.

Gill, A., and P. Clark (1992). "Second-Home Development in the Resort Municipality of Whistler," British Columbia. In *British Columbia: Geographical Essays in Honour of A. MacPherson*, ed. P.M. Koroscil, Burnaby, BC: Department of Geography, Simon Fraser University. 281–94.

Gill, A.M., and G. Smith (1985). "Residents' Evaluative Structures of Northern Manitoba Mining Communities." *Canadian Geographer* 29 (1), 17–29.

Gober, P., K.E. McHugh, and D. Leclerc (1993). "Job-Rich but Housing-Poor: The Dilemma of a Western Amenity Town." *Professional Geographer* 45 (1), 12–20.

Godin, C., C. Boudreau, and M. LeBlanc (1988). *Étude sur la villégiature dans le district d'aménagement Beaubassin*. Cap-Pelé, NB: Beaubassin Planning Commission.

Golant, S.M. (1992). *Housing America's Elderly: Many Possibilities / Few Choices*. Newbury Park, Calif.: SAGE Publications.

Gordon, C. (1989). *At the Cottage: a Fearless Look at Canada's Summer Obsession*. Toronto: McClelland and Stewart.

Grew, R. (1980). "The Case for Comparing Histories." *American Historical Review* 85 (4), 763–78.

Hale, S.M. (1990). *Controversies in Sociology: A Canadian Introduction*. Toronto: Copp Clark Pitman.

Halfacree, K.H. (1993). "Locality and Social Representation: Space, Discourse, and Alternative Definitions of the Rural." *Journal of Rural Studies* 9 (1), 23–37.

Hallman, B.R. (1990). "Migration, Commuting and Economic Development in Toronto's Outer Urban Field: The Southern Georgian Bay Region." MA, Department of Geography, University of Guelph, Guelph, Ontario.

Halseth, G. (1989). "The Conversion of Summer Homes to Permanent Residences and its Impact on Local Government Provision of Services." MA, Department of Geography, Queen's University, Kingston, Ontario.

– (1992). "Cottage Property Ownership: Interpreting Spatial Patterns in an Eastern Ontario Case Study." *Ontario Geography* 38, 32–42.

– (1993). "Communities within Communities: Changing 'Residential' Areas at Cultus Lake, British Columbia." *Journal of Rural Studies* 9 (2), 175–88.

– (1996). "'Community' and Landuse Planning Debate: An example from Rural British Columbia." *Environment and Planning A* 28, 1279–98.

Halseth, G., and M.W. Rosenberg (1990). "Conversion of Recreational Residences: A Case Study of Its Measurement and Management." *Canadian Journal of Regional Science* 13 (1), 99–115.

– (1995). "Cottagers in an Urban Field." *Professional Geographer* 47 (2), 148–59.

Hamilton, S.W., D. Capozza, and R. Helsley (1986). *Government Involvement in Residential Renovation: A Rationale Review and Study in Intervention Impacts*. Ottawa: Canada Mortgage and Housing Corporation.

Harper, S. (1987). "A Humanistic Approach to the Study of Rural Populations." *Journal of Rural Studies* 3 (4), 309–19.

Hart, J.F. (1984). "Population Change in the Upper Lake States." *Annals of the Association of American Geographers* 74 (2), 221–43.

Hartshorne, R. (1939). *The Nature of Geography: A Critical Survey of Current Thought in the Light of the Past*. Lancaster, Pa.: Association of American Geographers.

– (1959). *Perspective on the Nature of Geography*. Washington, DC: Association of American Geographers.

Haskins, D. (1985). *"My Own Four Walls": Heritage Buildings in Bastard and South Burgess Township*. Council of Bastard and South Burgess Township.

Hasson, S., and E. Razin (1990). "What Is Hidden behind a Municipal Boundary Conflict?" *Political Geography Quarterly* 9 (3), 267–83.

Hawley, W.D., and F.M. Wirt, eds. (1968a). *The Search for Community Power*. Englewood Cliffs, NJ: Prentice-Hall.

– (1968b). "Community Power: The Pluralist Perspective." In Hawley and Wirt, eds., *The Search for Community Power*, 89–92.

Hayes, C.R. (1976). *The Dispersed City: The Case of Piedmont, North Carolina*. Chicago: University of Chicago, Department of Geography Research Paper no. 173.

Helleiner, F.M. (1980). "Recreation and Leisure-time Patterns." *Ontario Geography* 16, 47–55.

– (1982). "A history of recreation on the Trent-Severn Waterway." In *Recreational Land Use: Perspectives on Its Evolution in Canada*, ed. G. Wall and J.S. Marsh. Ottawa: Carleton University Press. 190–200.

– (1983). "Loon Lake: The Evolution and Decline of a Cottage Community in Northwestern Ontario." *Recreation Research Review* 10, 34–44.

Helleiner, F.M., and L. McGrath (1988). "Incipient Urban Centres in the Recreational Hinterland of Toronto: A New Variation of the Rural-Urban Fringe Model." Paper read at the annual meetings of the Canadian Association of Geographers, Halifax.

Hillery, G.A., Jr. (1955). "Definitions of Community: Areas of Agreement." *Rural Sociology* 20, 111–23.

– (1972). "Selected Issues in Community Theory." *Rural Sociology* 37 (4), 534–52.

Hinch T.D. (1970a). *Cottaging in the Toronto Urban Field: A Probe of Structure and Behaviour*. Toronto: University of Toronto Centre for Urban and Community Studies Research Paper no.29.

– (1970b). *A Probe of Living Areas in the Periphery of the Toronto Urban Field*. Toronto: University of Toronto Centre for Urban and Community Studies, Research Paper no.30.

– (1990). "A Spatial Analysis of Tourist Accommodation in Ontario: 1974 to 1988." *Journal of Applied Recreation Research* 15 (4), 239–64.

Hodge, G.D., and M.A. Qadeer (1983). *Towns and Villages in Canada: The Importance of Being Unimportant*. Toronto: Butterworth.

Hunter, F. (1953). *Community Power Structures*. Chapel Hill: University of North Carolina Press.

Jaakson, R. (1986). "Second-Home Domestic Tourism." *Annals of Tourism Research* 13 (3), 367–391.

Jordan, J.W. (1980). "The Summer People and the Natives: Some Effects of Tourism in a Vermont Vacation Village." *Annals of Tourism Research* 7 (1), 34–55.

Joseph, A., P. Keddie, and B. Smit (1988). "Unravelling the Population Turnaround in Rural Canada." *Canadian Geographer* 32 (1), 17–30.

Joseph, A., and B. Smit (1985). "Rural Residential Development and Municipal Service Provision: A Canadian Case Study." *Journal of Rural Studies* 1 (4), 321–37.

Keddie, P.D., and A.E. Joseph (1991). "Reclassification and Rural-Versus-Urban Population Change in Canada, 1976–1981: A Tale of Two Definitions." *Canadian Geographer* 35 (4), 412–20.

Kennedy, J.R. (1984). *South Elmsley in the Making 1783–1983*. Lombardy, Ont.: Township of South Elmsley.

Keogh, B. (1982). "L'Impact social du tourisme: le cas de Shédiac, Nouveau-Brunswick." *Canadian Geographer* 26 (4), 318–31.

Knight, R. (1977). *Stump Ranch Chronicles – and Other Narratives*. Vancouver: New Star Books.

Krueger, R. (1978). "Urbanization of the Niagara Fruit Belt." *Canadian Geographer* 22 (3), 174–94.

– (1980). "The Geographer and Rural Southern Ontario." *Ontario Geography* 16, 7–18.

Lamb, R. (1975). *Metropolitan Impacts on Rural America*. Chicago: University of Chicago Department of Geography Research Paper no. 162.

Lampi, K. "Cottage Country from the Other Side of the Fence." *Globe and Mail*, 16 Sept. 1992, A26.

Leckie, G.J. (1989). "Continuity and Change in the Farm Community: Brooke Township, Ontario, 1965–86." *Canadian Geographer* 33 (1), 32–46.

Lee, S.-A. (1982). "The Value of the Local Area." In *Valued Environments*, ed. J.R. Gold and J. Burgess. London: George Allen and Unwin. 161–71.

Leggett, R. (1985). *Rideau Waterway.* 2nd ed. Toronto: University of Toronto Press.

Lehr, J.C., M. Schultz, and H.J. Selwood (1983). "An Investment in Health: Children's Summer Camps in the Winnipeg Region." *Recreation Research Review* 10 (3), 51–6.

Lehr, J.C., J. Selwood, and E. Badiuk (1991). "Ethnicity, Religion, and Class as Elements in the Evolution of Lake Winnipeg Resorts." *Canadian Geographer* 35 46–58.

Lehr, J.C., H.J. Selwood, and R. Goatcher (1984). "Wilderness Suburbias: Winnipeggers and Their Vacation Homes." *Association of North Dakota Geographers Bulletin*, 34, 17–23.

Leung, H.L. (1990). "'Big Brother' and Small Town Planning." *Municipal World*, Nov., 14–18.

Lewis, G.J. (1979). *Rural Communities: Problems in Modern Geography.* London: David and Charles.

Longino, C.F. Jr., and J.C. Biggar (1981). "The Impact of Retirement Migration on the South." *Gerontologist* 21 (3), 283–90.

Low, W.J. (1979). "Interorganizational Relations in Local Land-Use Planning." MA, School of Community and Regional Planning, University of British Columbia, Vancouver, BC.

McClenahan, B.A. (1946). "The Communality: The Urban Substitute for the Traditional Community." *Sociology and Social Research* 30, 264–74.

McCombs, A., and W. Chittenden (1990). *The Fraser Valley Challenge*. Abbotsford, BC: Treeline Publishing.

McDowell, L. (1992). "Valid Games? A Response to Erica Schoenberger." *Professional Geographer* 44 (2), 212–15.

Mackenzie, F. (1992). "'The worse it got, the more we laughed': A Discourse of Resistance among Farmers of Eastern Ontario." *Environment and Planning D: Society and Space* 10, 691–713.

Magnusson, W. (1983). "Introduction: The Development of Canadian Urban Government. In *City Politics in Canada*, ed. W. Magnusson and A. Sancton. Toronto: University of Toronto Press. 3–57.

Marsden, T., J. Murdoch, P. Lowe, R. Munton, and A. Flynn (1993). *Constructing the Countryside*. London: University College of London Press.

Marsh, J., and G. Wall (1982). "Themes in the Investigation of the Evolution of Outdoor Recreation." In *Recreational Land Use: Perspectives on Its Evolution in Canada*, ed. G. Wall and J. Marsh. Ottawa: Carleton University Press. 1–11.

Massey, D. (1984). "Introduction: Geography Matters." In *Geography Matters! A Reader*, ed. D. Massey and J. Allen. Cambridge: Cambridge University Press. 1–11.

Matthews, L. (1983). "Cultus Lake Park." Speech to Chilliwack Rotary Club, 3 Sept. 1983. Chilliwack, BC: Chilliwack Museum and Historical Society Archives.

Meyer, J.W., and E.K. Cromley (1989). "Caregiving Environments and Elderly Residential Mobility." *Professional Geographer* 41 (4), 440–50.

Meyer, J.W., and A. Speare, Jr. (1985). "Distinctively Elderly Mobility: Types and Determinants." *Economic Geography* 61 (1), 79–88.

Mikesell, M.W. (1960). "Comparative Studies in Frontier History." *Annals of the Association of American Geographers* 50 (1), 62–74.

Moore, E.G. (1991). "Research Agendas and Statistics Canada Products: Geographical Perspectives on Micro-Data Files." *Operational Geographer* 8 (4), 48–52.

Newby, H. (1987). *Country Life: A Social History of Rural England*. London: Weidenfeld and Nicolson.

Oakley, A. (1981). Interviewing Women: A Contradiction in Terms. In *Doing Feminist Research*, ed. H. Roberts. London: Routledge and Kegan Paul. 30–61.

Ontario (1978). Discussion Paper on Seasonal Residential Conversions. Ministry of Housing, Local Planning Policy Branch.

– (1990). *Accommodations*. Ministry of Tourism and Recreation.

– (1990). *Camping*. Ministry of Tourism and Recreation.

Oppong, J.R., and R.G. Ironside (1987). "Growth Centre Policy and the Quality of Life." *Canadian Journal of Regional Science* 10, 281–99.

Orbell, J.M., and T. Uno (1972). "A Theory of Neighbourhood Problem Solving: Political Action vs. Residential Mobility." *American Political Science Review* 66(2), 471–89.

Osborne, B.S. (1988). "The Hinterland." In *New Directions for the Study of Ontario's Past*. Papers of the Bicentennial Conference on the History of Ontario, McMaster University 5–8 Sept. 1984, ed. D. and R. Gagan. Hamilton, Ont.: McMaster University. 267–83.

Osborne, B., and D. Swainson (1985). *The Rideau Navigation, 1832–1972: Its Operation, Maintenance, and Management*. Ottawa: Parks Canada, © A.D. Revill Associates.

Pahl, R.E. (1965). *Urbs in Rure: The Metropolitan Fringe in Hertfordshire*. London: London School of Economics and Political Science, Geographical Papers no. 2.

Parenteau, R. (1981). "Is Canada Going Back To The Land?" In *The Rural-Urban Fringe: Canadian Perspectives*, ed. K.B. Beesley and L.H. Russwurm. Toronto: York University, Atkinson College, Department of Geography, Geographical Monographs no.10. 53–70.

Parson, H.E. (1977). "An Investigation of the Changing Rural Economy of Gatineau County, Quebec." *Canadian Geographer* 21 (1), 22–31.

– (1983). "An Overview of Landscape Assessment and Settlement Policy on the Southern Ontario Section of the Canadian Shield in the 19th Century." *Ontario Geography* 22, 15–27.

Pennier, C., S. Joseph, and A. Mohs. (1984). *How Secure Is Our Future? A Look at Historical and Current Developments within Sto:lo Territory*. Chilliwack, BC: Sto:lo Nation.

Phillips, M. (1993). "Rural Gentrification and the Processes of Class Colonisation." *Journal of Rural Studies* 9, 123–40.

Pierce Colfer, C.J., and A.M. Colfer (1978). "Inside Bushler Bay: Lifeways in Counterpoint." *Rural Sociology* 43 (2), 204–20.

Piven, F.F. (1970). "Whom Does The Advocate Planner Serve?" *Social Policy* 1 (1), 32–5.

Pond, B., and M. Yeates (1994). "Rural/Urban Land Conversion II: Identifying Land in Transition to Urban Use." *Urban Geography* 15, 25–44.

Priddle, G., and R. Kreutzwiser (1977). "Evaluating Cottage Environments in Ontario." In *Second Homes: Curse or Blessing*, ed. J.T. Coppock. Oxford: Pergamon Press. 165–80.

Ragatz, R.L. (1970). "Vacation Homes in the Northeastern United States: Seasonality in Population Distribution." *Annals of the Association of American Geographers* 60 (3), 447–55.

– (1977). "Vacation Homes in Rural Areas: Towards a Model for Predicting Their Distribution and Occupancy Patterns." In *Second Homes: Curse or Blessing*, ed. J.T. Coppock. Oxford: Pergamon Press. 181–94.

Ramsey, B. (1975). *Five Corners: The Story of Chilliwack*. Chilliwack, BC: Chilliwack Historical Society.

Regional District of Fraser-Cheam, British Columbia (1975a). Public Hearing Minutes from 10 November 1975.

– (1975b). Public Hearing Minutes from 1 December 1975.
– (1975c). Minutes of the Regional Board meeting of 16 December 1975.
– (1976a). Minutes of the Regional Board meeting of 22 June 1976.
– (1976b). By-law No. 66, Zoning By-law for Electoral Area "E" of Fraser-Cheam Regional District, 1976.
– (1981). Schedule "A" of By-law 300, Regional District of Fraser-Cheam Official Regional Plan.
– (1983a). Official Settlement Plan for Electoral Area "E," Regional District of Fraser-Cheam.
– (1983b). Official Settlement Plan for Electoral Area "E," Regional District of Fraser-Cheam, Adopting By-law No. 400, 1982.
– (1983c). Public Information Meeting Minutes from 14 December 1983.
– (1985a). Public Hearing Minutes from 12 September 1985.
– (1985b). Minutes of the Regional Board meeting of 25 September 1985.
– (1986). Building By-law No. 280, 1984.
– (1988). *Pre-Feasibility Study for Community Sewage Disposal in Lindell Beach.*
– (1991a). Public Hearing Minutes from 28 January 1991.
– (1991b). Minutes of the Regional Board meeting of 19 February 1991.
– (1992). Public Hearing Minutes from 4 February 1992.
Rideau Valley Conservation Authority (1992a). *Rideau Valley Conservation Strategy.* Manotick, Ont.
– (1992b). *Rideau Lakes Basin Carrying Capacities and Proposed Shoreland Development Policies.* Prepared by Michael Michalski Associates and Anthony Usher Planning Consultant. Manotick, Ont.
Riemersma, J.C (1953). "Introduction to Marc Bloch." In *Enterprise and Secular Change: Readings in Economic History,* ed. F.C. Lane and J.C. Riemersma. Homewood, Ill.: Richard D. Irwin. 489–93.
Robertson, R.W. (1977). "Second-home Decisions: The Australian Context." In *Second Homes: Curse or Blessing,* ed. J.T. Coppock. Oxford: Pergamon Press. 119–38.
Rogers, A.W. (1977). "Second Homes in England and Wales." In *Second Homes: Curse or Blessing,* ed. J.T. Coppock. Oxford: Pergamon Press. 85–102.
Rogers, A., and Woodward, J. (1988). "The Sources of Regional Elderly Population Growth: Migration and Aging-in-Place." *Professional Geographer* 40 (4), 450–59.
Rosenberg, M.W., and G. Halseth (1993). *Recreational Home Conversion in Canada.* Ottawa: Canada Mortgage and Housing Corporation.
Rowles, G. (1978). "Reflections on Experiential Field Work." In *Humanistic Geography: Prospects and Problems,* ed. D. Ley and M.S. Samuels. London: Croom Helm. 173–93.
Royal Trust (1992). *The Cottage: Keeping it in the family … and away from the Taxman.* Toronto: Royal Trust Image Services.

Russwurm, L.H. (1974). *The Urban Fringe in Canada: Problems, Research Needs, Policy Implications*. Discussion Paper B-74-4. Ottawa: Research Branch, Ministry of State for Urban Affairs.

Russwurm, L.H., and C.R. Bryant (1984). "Changing Population Distribution and Rural-Urban Relationships in Canadian Urban Fields, 1941–1976." In *The Pressures of Change in Rural Canada*, ed. M.F. Bunce and M.J. Troughton. Toronto: Atkinson College, York University, Geographical Monographs no. 14. 113–37.

Sanderson, D. (1938). "Criteria of Community Formation." *Rural Sociology* 3 (3), 371–84.

Sanderson, D., and R.A. Polson (1939). *Rural Community Organization*. New York: John Wiley and Sons.

Sauer, C. (1941). "Foreword to Historical Geography." *Annals of the Association of American Geographers* 31 (1), 1–24.

Schoenberger, E. (1991). "The Corporate Interview as a Research Method in Economic Geography." *Professional Geographer* 43 (2), 180–9.

– (1992). "Self-Criticism and Self-Awareness in Research: A Reply to Linda McDowell." *Professional Geographer* 44 (2), 215–18.

Scott, J.W., and R.L. DeLorme (1988). *Historical Atlas of Washington*. Norman, Okla., and London: University of Oklahoma Press.

Selwood, J., G. Curry, and G. Koczberski (1995). "Structure and Change in a Coastal Vacation Village: Peaceful Bay, Western Australia." *Urban Policy and Research* 13 (3), 149–57.

Sewell, W.H. Jr. (1967). "Marc Bloch and the Logic of Comparative History." *History and Theory* 6 (2), 208–18.

Shamas, S. (1992). "How I Spent My Summer Holidays." *Cottage Life*, Sept./Oct., 90.

Simmons, T. (1981). "The Challenge of Rural Perspectives on the Rural-Urban Fringe." In *The Rural-Urban Fringe: Canadian Perspectives*, ed. K.B. Beesley and L.H. Russwurm. Toronto: Atkinson College, York University, Geographical Monographs no.10. 71–86.

Smit, B., A. Joseph, S. Alexander, and G. McIlravey (1984). *Non-Farm Residential Development, Service Provision, Taxes and Policy: The Case of Puslinch Township, Ontario*. Guelph, Ont.: University of Guelph, Department of Geography, Occasional Paper no. 4.

Sosdian, C.P., and L.M. Sharp (1980). "Non-response in Mail Surveys: Access Failure on Respondent Resistance." *Public Opinion Quarterly* 44 (3), 396–402.

Stanley, G.F.G., ed. (1970). *Mapping the Frontier: Charles Wilson's Diary of the Survey of the 49th Parallel, 1858–1862, while Secretary of the British Boundary Commission*. Toronto: Macmillan of Canada.

Statistics Canada (1973 to 1990). *Housing Starts and Completions*. Catalogue 64–022. Ottawa: Minister of Supply and Services.

– (1973 to 1991). *Household Facilities and Equipment*. Catalogue 64–202.
– (1982 to 1985). *Household Facilities by Income and Other Characteristics*. Catalogue 13–567 (occasional).
– (1987 to 1991). *Household Facilities by Income and Other Characteristics*. Catalogue 13–218 (annual).
– (1973). *1971 Census of Canada – Population by Census Subdivisions*. Catalogue 92–702.
– (1979). *1976 Census of Canada – Dwellings and Households Volume 3*. Catalogue 93–802.
– (1982). *1981 Census of Canada – Census Divisions and Subdivisions*. Catalogue E-564.
– (1987). *1986 Census of Canada – Profiles, Ontario, Part 1*. Catalogue 94–111.
– (1992). *1991 Census of Canada – Profile of Census Divisions and Subdivisions in Ontario- Part A*. Catalogue 95–337.
Suttles, G.D. (1968). *The Social Order of the Slum*. Chicago: University of Chicago Press.
Taaffe, E.J., H.L. Gauthier, and T.A. Maraffa (1980). "Extended Commuting and the Intermetropolitan Periphery." *Annals of the Association of American Geographers* 70 (3), 313–29.
Tiebout, C. (1956). "A Pure Theory of Local Expenditures." *Journal of Political Economy* 64, 416–24.
Tilly, C., L. Tilly, and R. Tilly (1975). *The Rebellious Century, 1830–1930*. Cambridge: Harvard University Press.
Tindal, C.R. (1977). *Structural Changes in Local Government: Government for Urban Regions*. Kingston, Ont.: The Institute of Public Administration of Canada.
Tindal, C.R., and S. Nobes Tindal (1990). *Local Government in Canada*. 3rd.ed. Toronto: McGraw-Hill Ryerson.
Township of Bastard and South Burgess (1983). Zoning By-law No. 573. Prepared by J.L. Richards & Associates Ltd. Ottawa.
– (1986). Official Plan of the Township of Bastard and South Burgess (office consolidation). Prepared by J.L. Richards & Associates Ltd. Ottawa.
– (1991). Amendment No. 5 to the Official Plan of the Township of Bastard and South Burgess. Prepared by J.L. Richards & Associates Ltd. Ottawa.
Township of North Crosby (1985). Official Plan for the Township of North Crosby.
– (1988). Zoning By-Law No. 88–13. Prepared by J.L. Richards & Associates Ltd. Ottawa.
– (1992a). Amendment No. 3 to the Official Plan of the Township of North Crosby. Prepared by J.L. Richards & Associates Ltd. Ottawa.
– (1992b). Zoning By-law Amendment – Shoreland Development and Related Issues By-law No. 92–11. Prepared by J.L. Richards & Associates Ltd. Ottawa.

Township of South Crosby (1986). Official Plan for Township of South Crosby. Prepared by J.L. Richards and Associates Ltd. Ottawa.
– (1992). Draft Official Plan for Township of South Crosby. Prepared by J.L. Richards and Associates Ltd. Ottawa.
Township of South Elmsley (1984a). Official Plan for Township of South Elmsley.
– (1984b). Zoning By-law 84–15. Prepared by Larry D. Cotton Associates Ltd. Winchester, Ont.
– (1991). Draft Official Plan of the Township of South Elmsley. Prepared by HMD Consulting Group Ltd. Ottawa.
Triantis, S.G. (1979). "Economic Impact of Tourism and Recreation in Muskoka." In *Recreational Land Use in Southern Ontario*, ed. G. Wall. Waterloo: University of Waterloo, Department of Geography Publication Series no.14. 273–9.
Troughton, M.J. (1981). "The Rural-Urban Fringe: A Challenge to Resource Management." In *The Rural-Urban Fringe: Canadian Perspectives*, ed. K.B. Beesley and L.H. Russwurm. Toronto: Atkinson College, York University, Geographical Monographs no.10. 218–43.
– (1984). "Modelling Change in the Canadian Rural System." In *The Pressures of Change in Rural Canada*, ed. M.F. Bunce and M.J. Troughton. Toronto: Atkinson College, York University, Geographical Monographs no.14. 368–83.
Tye, D. (1994). "Multiple Meanings Called Cavendish: The Interaction of Tourism with Traditional Culture." *Journal of Canadian Studies* 29, 122–34.
Vidich, A.J., and J. Bensman (1968). "Small Town in Mass Society." In *The Search for Community Power*, ed. W.D. Hawley and F.M. Wirt. New Jersey, Prentice-Hall. pp. 65–77.
Walker, G.E. (1976). "Social Perspectives on the Countryside: Reflections in Territorial Form North of Toronto." *Ontario Geography* 10, 54–63.
– (1984). "Networks and Politics in the Fringe." In *The Pressures of Change in Rural Canada*, ed. M.F. Bunce and M.J. Troughton. Toronto: Atkinson College, York University, Geographical Monographs no.14. 202–15.
– (1987). *An Invaded Countryside: Structures of Life on the Toronto Fringe*. Toronto: Atkinson College, York University, Geographical Monographs no.17.
Wall, G. (1977). "Recreational Land Use in Muskoka." *Ontario Geography* 11, 11–28.
– (1989). "Environmental Impacts." In *Outdoor Recreation in Canada*, ed. G. Wall. Toronto: John Wiley and Sons. 199–231.
Webber, M.M. (1963). "Order in Diversity: Community without Propinquity." In *Cities and Space: The Future Use of Urban Land*, ed. L. Wingo, Baltimore: Johns Hopkins Press. 23–54.
Wellman, B. (1987). *The Community Question Re-evaluated*. Toronto: University of Toronto Centre for Urban and Community Studies Research Paper no. 165.

Wells, O.N. (1987). *The Chilliwacks and Their Neighbours.* Vancouver, BC: Talonbooks.

Whatmore, S., P. Lowe, and T. Marsden, eds. (1991). *Rural Enterprise: Shifting Perspectives on Small-Scale Production.* London: David Fulton Publishers.

Wilkinson, K.P. (1986). "In Search of the Community in the Changing Countryside." *Rural Sociology* 51 (1), 1–17.

Wilkinson, P.F., and A.L. Murray (1991). "Centre and Periphery: The Impacts of the Leisure Industry on a Small Town (Collingwood, Ontario)." *Society and Leisure* 14 (1), 235–60.

Windley, P.G. (1983). "Community Services in Small Rural Towns: Patterns of Use by Older Residents." *Gerontologist* 23 (2), 180–4.

Wirth, L. (1964). "Rural-Urban Differences." In *Louis Wirth, On Cities and Social Life: Selected Papers*, ed. A.J. Reiss, Jr. Chicago and London: University of Chicago Press. 221–5.

Wolfe, R.I. (1951). "Summer Cottagers in Ontario." *Economic Geography* 27 (1), 10–32.

– (1952). "Wasaga Beach: The Divorce From the Geographic Environment." *Canadian Geographer* 2, 57–65.

– (1965). "About Cottages and Cottagers." *Landscape* 15 (1), 6–8.

– (1966). "Recreational Travel: The New Migration." *Canadian Geographer* 10 (1), 1–14.

– (1970). "Discussion of Vacation Homes, Environmental Preferences and Spatial Behaviour." *Journal of Leisure Research* 2 (1), 85–7.

– (1977). "Summer Cottages in Ontario: Purpose-built for an Inessential Purpose." In *Second Homes: Curse or Blessing*, ed. J.T. Coppock. Oxford: Pergamon Press. 17–34.

Wolpert, J., A. Mumphrey, and J. Seley (1972). *Metropolitan Neighborhoods: Participation and Conflict Over Change.* Washington, DC: Association of American Geographers, Commission on College Geography Resource Paper no. 16.

Wyckoff, W.K. (1990). "Landscapes of Private Power and Wealth." In *The Making of the American Landscape*, ed. M.P. Conzen. London: Harper Collins Academic. 335–54.

Yeates, M. (1987). "The Extent of Urban Development in the Windsor-Quebec City Axis." *Canadian Geographer* 31 (1), 64–9.

Index